A NARROW STREET

Elliot Paul first went to France during the First World War where he served as a sergeant in the A.E.F. It was at the end of the war that he began the long residence in Paris of which he tells in **A Narrow Street**.

A narrow street, the rue de la Huchette, not more than three hundred yards long, lies in the heart of Paris. There, off and on for eighteen years, Elliot Paul lived as a member of the community, participating in the pleasures and sufferings of his friends and, in the end, witnessing their heartbreaking betrayal. This book is a document which brings back to life a group of French men and women who typify, in all its nobility and degradation, a civilization the world can ill afford to lose.

A NARROW STREET

Elliot Paul

With a Foreword by Sam White

Harrap · London

To
FLORA, MY WIFE

This edition first published in Great Britain 1986
by HARRAP LIMITED
19–23 Ludgate Hill, London EC4M 7PD

First published by Random House, 1942

First published in Great Britain 1947

.Copyright 1942 by Elliot Paul

Foreword by Sam White, copyright © 1986 by Harrap Ltd

All rights reserved. No part of this publication
may be reproduced in any form or by any means
without the prior permission of Harrap Limited

ISBN 0 245-54377-5

Printed and bound in Great Britain
by Mackays of Chatham Ltd

CONTENTS

List of Characters   vii
Foreword   xi

PART ONE

THE POST-WAR TWENTIES

1. A Narrow Street at Dawn — 1
2. A Stairway Down to Antiquity — 7
3. The Women in Black Who Moved in Pairs — 13
4. Of Public Opinion — 19
5. Of Winter, and Minding One's Own Business — 25
6. The News and the Barber's Itch — 29
7. Of Community Entertainment — 38
8. The Maiden's Prayer — 42
9. To the Memory of a Secondhand Accordion — 44
10. Of High and Low Art, and Inflation — 50
11. Of, For and By the People — 53
12. Of Non-essentials — 57
13. The Prevailing State of Grace — 63
14. Of Clothes and How They Make the Man — 67
15. The Shock Felt Round the World — 71
16. Mostly about An Old Profession and Music — 75
17. The Card That Has Slipped from the Deck of the Past — 85
18. Of Western Culture — 93
19. The Central Markets — 101
20. A Bevy of Reds — 109
21. Mene Mene Tekel — 113

PART TWO

THE PRE-WAR THIRTIES

22. Excerpts from a Series of Letters — 117
23. To Be Read on an Island — 129
24. Less Brightness Every Year — 142

CONTENTS

25.	Of Hospitality	147
26.	The Heart to Resolve	153
27.	One Bitter Pill Deserves Another	160
28.	Of Property and Fraternity	168
29.	Of 'Non-Intervention'	175
30.	A Dead Man on the Pavement	182

PART THREE

THE DEATH OF A NATION

31.	Between Relief and Shame	189
32.	Boards Across a Doorway	194
33.	'Unto the Least of These'	199
34.	'Woe to the Weak'	203
35.	'A Time to Sow and a Time to Reap'	208
36.	Of Aid and Comfort to the Poles	211
37.	'A Time of Snow in All Endeavour'	217
38.	A Few Are Chosen	222
39.	Black Rain	226

LIST OF CHARACTERS

HOTEL AND CAFÉ KEEPERS

Hôtel du Caveau
    Julliard, Henri   proprietor
    Marie   his wife
    Berthe   his sister-in-law
    Thérèse   cook
    Georges   *garçon*
    Claude and Philomèle   Julliard's predecessors

Hôtel Normandie
    Sara   proprietress
    Guy   her husband
    Louis   one-armed *garçon*
    Mocha   the dog

Café St. Michel
    M. and Mme. Trévise   proprietors
    Eugénie   drudge

SHOPKEEPERS AND STOREKEEPERS

    Luttenschlager   articles of piety
    Salmon   beef-and-lamb butcher
    Villières   the paint man
    Achille and Geneviève Taitbout   stationery and newspapers
    Noël   taxidermist
    Dorlan   bookbinder
    Mme. Absalom   yarn and thread
    Odette and Jean   dairy
    Colette   their delivery girl
    Monge   horse butcher
    Mariette   bordel
        Mireille
        Consuela
        Daisy
        Armandine
        Mado

LIST OF CHARACTERS

Laniers	laundry
Gillottes	bakery
Lunevilles	drapers
Julien and Mme. Julien	barber, hairdresser
Saint-Aulaire	tailor
Joli	cleaner and dyer
Mme. Durand	flower shop
Dominique	stamps
André and Alice	coal and wine
Gion and Bernice	music shop
Corres, Sr. and Jr.	groceries
Maurice	goldfish

PUBLIC EMPLOYEES

Hortense Berthelot	clerk in prefecture
Frémont	letter carrier
Benoist	policeman
Masson	policeman
Pissy	railway worker
Antoine	his son
The Navet	petty official at prefecture
Jeanne	his wife
Eugène	his son

PROFESSIONAL MEN

Dr. Clouet	physician
Dr. Roux	dentist

PRIVATE EMPLOYEES

The Satyr	chef
Claire	artificial flower maker
Léonard	accordion player
Panaché	floor-walker
Nadia	model

LIST OF CHARACTERS

PRIESTS

Abbé Alphonse Lugan
Father Panarioux
Father Gaston
Father Desmonde

MISCELLANEOUS

Hyacinthe Goujon	
Madame Goujon	her mother
Judge Lenoir	her grandfather
Mary the Greek	
Milka	Communist
Stefan	Communist
Pierre Vautier	Communist
Daniel	*restaurateur*
Elvira and Roberta	Alsatian old maids
M. de Malancourt	*bon vivant*
Mme. Spook (Root)	Englishwoman
L'Hibou	tramp
The Chestnut Man (*L'Oursin*)	

Foreword by
SAM WHITE

Elliot Paul belongs to that pre-war generation of American journalists who were more interested in Europe than they were in their own country. This was understandable enough, for Europe had already been the stage (and was about to become so once again) of a conflict between what were still considered to be the Great Powers, while the United States was as yet at the putative stage of becoming one. These American reporters — many of whom achieved international fame — were of a special breed, who brought to their European reporting the same kind of investigative zeal that had distinguished their coverage of the domestic scene. An outstanding example of the transatlantic journalism of that period was of course John Gunther, whose volume *Inside Europe* was so huge a success, both in his native America and in Europe itself.

Elliot Paul by contrast narrowed his sights not to one country or even one city but to one Paris street, the rue de la Huchette, 'the narrow street' of the title of his book. It was an inspired choice, for the inner life of the rue de la Huchette was as picturesque and intriguing to the eye of a talented reporter as it was in outward appearance to that of a talented painter. (One thinks in this connection of Utrillo's famous painting of part of it, reproduced on the jacket of the first American edition of *The Narrow Street*.) Although it was only 300 yards in length, the rue de la Huchette provided a perfect microcosm of pre-war French life, at both its Parisian and its provincial levels. It was in fact a village street which happened to be located on the periphery of the Latin Quarter, and it is this which gives it its fascinating quality of provincialism thriving in a cosmopolitan world. All this was not really all that surprising, for Paris itself gave the impression in those now seemingly far-off pre-war years of being — unlike the London of that day — a city which resembled more a large-scale market town than a modern metropolis. Its population, far from being largely indigenous, had for the most part first-generation roots in the provinces, and was to a very large extent of peasant stock. As though to underline this, its central food market, Les Halles (or what Zola called 'the belly of Paris') was located almost a stone's throw from the rue de Rivoli and famous hotels like the Meurice and the Ritz, and remained with its famous onion soup a feature of the city's night life until the mid-1950s, when the mounting chaos of the traffic its incoming lorries produced forced the authorities to move it outside the city boundaries. Finally, to clinch the point about the market-town atmosphere of the city it must be remembered that the bulk of the produce flooding into Les Halles in its hey-day came from what were then the outskirts of the city itself. What are now high-rise suburbs lying within a radius of fifteen kilometres from Notre

Dame were then the suppliers of some of the city's choicest delicacies — for example, France's best strawberries and asparagus, to say nothing of virtually its entire vegetable supply.

In short, just at the edge of the so-called 'red belt' consisting of the dismal slums which ringed Paris there was a green belt ready to be savoured and enjoyed by the most deprived proletarian. It was these links with the soil, which for many Parisians involved a direct kinship with the country's peasantry, that made the impact of mass unemployment following the Wall Street crash felt so much less in France than in any other Western industrialized nation. It was this too which lightens the Dickensian gloom of Elliot Paul's description of the social conditions of the Paris of his day. Indeed, speaking of Dickens, the entire book has a distinctive Dickensian quality about it, with its huge cast of characters, its boundless vitality and humour and its often unblushing sentimentality. The characters range from hotel and café proprietors in the street and their clients to the shopkeepers in all their astonishing variety, including those keen competitors the beef and horse butchers and down to the inevitable brothel. It is interesting to note in this connection that horse butchers are a disappearing breed in today's Paris, while brothels are little more than fond memories lingering on in old men's minds of the Paris of their day. Needless to say, the madame who ran the brothel in the rue de la Huchette in Elliot Paul's day — it's called *Le Panier Fleuri* — had a heart of gold.

Otherwise, the book abounds in shocks and surprises. Take this, for example:

> The very poor in Paris naturally, do not keep cats. On the contrary, they frequently stalk them, feed them up in seclusion and eat them. The moderately poor, . . . if they have no children, sometimes permit themselves the extravagance of a pet; but when Minou dies, they do not have her stuffed. Instead, they skin her with a kitchen knife, salt down her hide and sell it for a small sum to a dealer in mittens.

A feature of Paris of the twenties was the ever-present shadow cast by the ubiquitous war widow, typified in Paul's book by Mme Berthelot:

> an inconspicuous middle-aged woman who worked in the enormous prefecture, one of the tens of thousands who, because of widowhood or bereavement in World War I, were allowed, for very small pay, to sit at shabby desks, stand behind grilled windows or splintered counters, and in a sort of perpetual twilight, write words with bent stubpens and violet ink (thick with dust and sometimes dead gnats) on government forms which had been printed in such a way that there was never enough space in which to provide answers to ambiguous questions. One cannot exaggerate the inefficiency of a French public office, especially those to which members of the public were forced, all too often, to present themselves for heckling and abuse.

FOREWORD

Much of the pleasure provided by Paul's book is that it feeds both nostalgia and relief for the changes that have come about in Paris in the relatively short space of the past sixty years. His vivid description of Les Halles provides an occasion for the shedding of a sentimental tear or two. Not so, however, his description of the railway system of his day, which was:

> antiquated, badly directed, under-manned and hazardous. In 1925 there was such an epidemic of railroad accidents that the entire personnel got panicky. Engine drivers ran through signals. Signals were incorrectly manipulated. Rails spread; roadbeds settled; switchmen had nervous breakdowns after they had caused disasters; and one engine driver was so relieved at having successfully brought his train from Nancy into a Paris terminal that he forgot to apply the brakes and crashed through the final bumper.

As for the rue de la Huchette itself, it remains physically much the same as it was in Paul's day, as do the two streets which traverse it, the rue Zacharie and the rue du Chat Qui Pêche, the shortest street in Paris, with only one window and no doors at all. In character, however, the street has altered almost beyond recognition. The two hotels, the Hôtel du Caveau and the Hôtel Normandie, in which so much of the action in Paul's book takes place, have gone, to be replaced with two new ones with an almost wholly Arab clientele. Only the little stationery shop remains. As with the two hotels, so with the street itself — it is now largely Arab in character proliferating in couscous restaurants, oriental grocery shops and Middle Eastern food takeaways.

One aspect of the street, however, remains eternally unchanged. It is described in the magical opening lines of the book:

> At dawn, the sun rising behind the cathedral, Notre Dame de Paris, sent its first feeble rays directly down the rue de la Huchette to be reflected from the windows of the place St. Michel.

Read on from there — a feast awaits you.

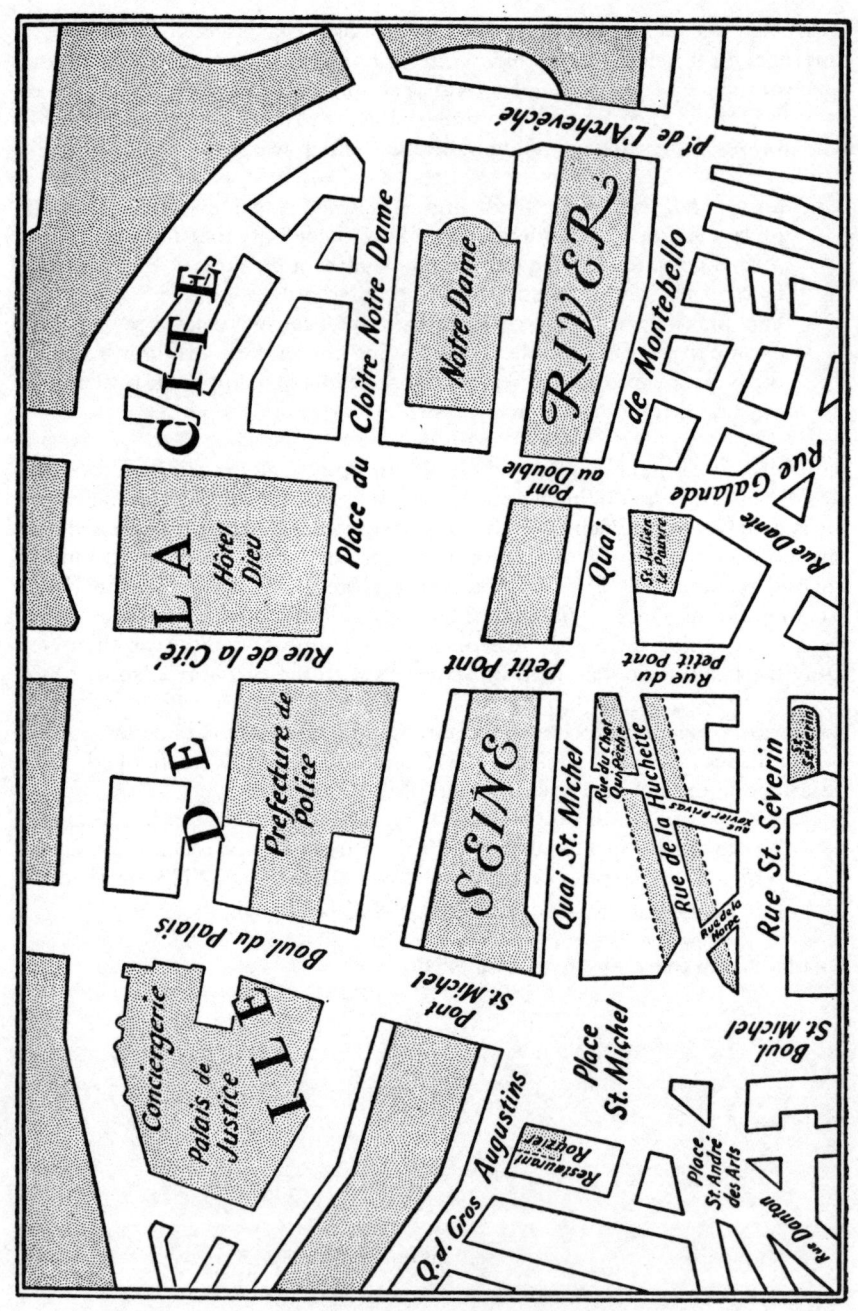

THE QUARTIER

PART ONE

The Post-War Twenties

1

A NARROW STREET AT DAWN

At dawn, the sun rising behind the cathedral, Notre Dame de Paris, sent its first feeble rays directly down the rue de la Huchette to be reflected from the windows of the place St. Michel. A few yards away, running almost parallel to the little street, the south branch of the Seine skirted the Ile de la Cité, and on its yellow-brown waters, in which clouds were mirrored upside down, laden barges drifted, from the north of France or Belgium, bound for Rouen and Le Havre. The Latin quarter and the Cluny lay eastward; across the river stood the grim Conciergerie, the bleak and vast Hôtel Dieu, or city hospital, and the Palais de Justice.

In the place St. Michel, with its dripping fountain and stone dolphins, the Café de la Gare was the first to open, to take care of early customers who arrived by underground train from Versailles and the workers of the neighbourhood who snatched their coffee and *croissants* at the counter before descending into the Métro, near the entrance of which stood a dingy international news stand, with a profusion of provincial and local French papers on sale, as well as the Paris journals. The first comers seldom bought newspapers; they couldn't afford to spend four sous. Across from the Café de la Gare, on the corner nearest the book and music stalls that lined the quai, stood the famous restaurant Rouzier, the corrugated shutters of which were not raised until later in the day.

Midway down the rue de la Huchette, which was about three hundred yards long, the Bureau de Police was always open but never active. All night a sickly blue gas lamp marked its location; by day a cinder-stained tricolour flag drooped from its mast. The Café St. Michel, next door to the Café de la Gare, opened about five a.m. The proprietor had the tobacco concession for the neighbourhood, which brought in many customers and gave the place an air of prosperity. The odour of what the Third Republic called tobacco was purified, somewhat, by the slops and disinfectant used for cleaning the café.

While some of the early risers huddled around the counter to swallow their coffee, often spiked with cheap, watered rum or cognac, and to munch fresh crisp rolls, Eugénie, a pale, brown-eyed scrubwoman not yet forty, was on her knees beside her ill-smelling pail, faithfully scrubbing the back room floor in dimness. She wore drab grey, formless clothes which reeked of Eau de Javel; her breasts sagged; her hands and wrists were raw and red from the caustic; her feet were clad in worn felt slippers. When she was facing away from the crowd, and a little of her white leg showed, some gruff-voiced teamster or bargeman would joke about her *derrière*. One could not quite overlook it. Eugénie would turn her head and fling over her shoulder a gem of reproachful repartee. She slept in a sort of mop closet in the rear of the establishment, with the door bolted tightly, and while it was still dark she slunk over to the church of St. Séverin for an early morning prayer. After meal times she ate of the leavings in the kitchen, when the cook and waiters had been fed. She had not had a day off for thirteen years, not since her mother had died of bronchitis and Eugénie had timorously left a more arduous job to take her deceased parent's place at the Café St. Michel.

Eugénie's chastity, her virginity in fact, was one of the mutual subjects of conversation, a sort of perpetual challenge to the five o'clock customers (male). It also served as a sort of springboard from which sly propositions could be launched toward the less virtuous customers (female). But the sharp-eyed Madame Trévise, the proprietress, who was every inch what the French called a *commerçante*, or business woman, kept this daily ritual within bounds. There was practically nothing the men could or did not say to Eugénie, but none of them was ever permitted by Madame to lay hands on her. The proprietress was not moved by moral considerations; she merely wanted to avoid the inconvenience of having a drudge who periodically became pregnant and had to be fired. So Madame Trévise added to Eugénie's native armour of fear and piety her matronly authority. Once a bashful country boy, much younger than Eugénie, tried to approach her and even went so far to to lie in wait for her in the church at dawn in order to escape the merciless tongues of the café customers. Eugénie ran a high fever and for the only time in her life had to spend two days in bed, so startled was she by the stammered proposition.

I first wandered into the rue de la Huchette in 1923, on a soft summer evening, and entirely by chance. It was possible then to do things without premeditation. An evening lay before me, so I merely dined and strolled. Granite lions and an empty fountain dozed by the ill-matched towers of St. Sulpice; men, women and children sat on the kerbs and doorsteps of the rue des Ciseaux and grumbled as a stray taxi inconvenienced them. The broad leaves of the plane trees along the boulevard St. Germain were still, almost drooping. Activity seemed to have been gently suspended.

Avoiding the Deux Magots, I skirted along the old abbey of St. Germain and in the secluded place Furstemburg, then the hideout of the budding group of Communists to whom no one — least of all Moscow — paid the slightest attention, I paused in front of the old studio of Delacroix where a street lamp revealed a pencil drawing of a panther in the window.

In the place of St. André des Arts I found myself staring with awe into a taxidermist's window. Like all the other citizens of France, the taxidermists of France were individualists. Even French mothballs seemed to have slight differences one from the other. The taxidermist in the place St. André des Arts made a speciality of stuffing pet dogs and cats with which their owners could not bear to part. Monsieur Noël, the tall stuffer of birds and animals, whom I learned to know very well in later days, made them look if not lifelike, decidedly unique. The bourgeois French called parrots 'Coco', cats 'Minou', small dogs 'Frou-frou' and police dogs 'Hanibal', or something corresponding. Monsieur Noël, before undertaking to skin the beasts, would try to divine their character. Since he had a mild class consciousness, the expressions on the faces of his masterpieces reflected something of M. Noël's sardonic philosophy. Noël pointed out to me once, over a bottle of Pouilly, that men and women, like gods, choose pets in their own image. My friend took sly delight in accentuating these resemblances.

On the corner, facing the boulevard St. Michel, was a pharmacy of the second class. That, as pharmacies went in France, was fairly high. A first-class pharmacy was an analytical and quantitative chemist's laboratory plus emergency clinic and dispensary of serums, prophylactics and specifics. The pharmacy in question was closed that evening, but on the front door was a placard explaining that another pharmacy, a couple of blocks distant, was open. According to the law of February 4, 1896 — probably because on February 3rd of that same year some senator's wife had kept him awake with a toothache — pharmacists were obliged to take turns in handling night and holiday trade.

Among some very modern white enamel and red rubber accessories on display in the window in front of me, what caught my eye was a pair of crude mittens made of yellow cat's fur, with the fur outside. Afterwards when I got to know M. Noël well enough, I asked him about those incongruous articles.

'They are in no way exotic,' he said.

The very poor in Paris, naturally, do not keep cats. On the contrary, they frequently stalk them, feed them up in seclusion and eat them. The moderately poor (say, in the £50 to £60 a year brackets), if they have no children, sometimes permit themselves the extravagance of a pet; but when Minou dies, they do not have her stuffed. Instead, they skin her with a kitchen knife, salt down her hide and sell it for a small sum to a dealer in mittens. He, in turn, sells the finished product to drug stores. In winter those Parisians whose houses or rooms have no heating manage to keep warm by rubbing themselves with cat's fur.

Before the days of Police Commissioner Chiappe, there were no lanes studded with brass discs across the boulevards. Pedestrians simply ventured out and crossed in traffic as best they could. Experienced Parisians usually exercised a modicum of caution, but the provincial French had no background that equipped them to deal with the physics of scurrying taxis, lumbering buses and inconoclastic private cars, interspersed with market wagons drawn by stallions, old-fashioned fiacres, rubber-tyred bicycles and improvised delivery carts with three or more wheels.

In 1923, there were thousands of taxis, many of them driven by former cabmen who resented motors and used them with a minimum of mechanical consideration. Between the general public and the taximan a continual feud was carried on, with vehemence and sharp eloquence on both sides.

That first evening I was preceded into the traffic of the boul' Mich' by a dignified Frenchman from Mayenne, who wore an old-fashioned black felt hat and a string tie. A chauffeur jammed on his faulty brakes to avoid hitting the man, and the running board of the taxi barked his shins. Taxi No. 1 was promptly telescoped by another, which in turn was narrowly missed by a bus. If I quote him correctly, the taxi-driver called the incautious pedestrian a 'kind of harlot'. The Frenchman dispassionately reminded the chauffeur that the streets had belonged to the people since the fall of the Bastille. When a cop stepped reluctantly into the picture, glancing disgustedly at the traffic jam, the pedestrian calmly handed him his card. The *agent* read it noncommittally and tucked it into his pocket.

'*Alors, toi*' ('Well! You!') the *agent* said to the chauffeur.

The latter retorted at the top of his voice. It was thanks to his presence of mind, he said, that the 'type' with the string tie and card had not been annihilated and his family left disconsolate.

'Since the days of the Bastille . . .' began the party of the second part.

'That's a long time ago, monsieur,' cackled a drunken old woman from the pavement.

It all ended with the *agent's* escorting me and the professor from Mayenne to the opposite kerb, in front of a reeking public *pissoir*. Then he waved majestically for traffic to proceed. As the taxi sped away, the *agent* noticed that it had no tail light. He blew his whistle furiously, to which the retreating chauffeur paid no attention. Unfortunately, several other dirvers thought the whistle might be meant for them. They looked back, swerved, and one of them clipped the heavy market wagon, so that over the ensuing hubbub, the peasant on the wagon seat bellowed that his assailant was a *cochon* and *voyou*, or a 'pig' and a 'thug'.

I bowed to the professor from Mayenne, who lifted his hat in acknowledgment and then turned toward the *pissoir*, unbuttoning his fly en route. In order to do this the Frenchman had to start about midway between his waist and his chin. In a land of passionate economy, the high trouser top was a baffling extravagance.

My meditations on style were cut short when, after proceeding along a narrow pavement, I heard and saw, respectively, the sharp merry sound of an accordion and the dim silhouette of the most perfect small Gothic church in France, St. Séverin. All I can say is that as I stood there, seeing it outlined against the taller buildings of the street beyond, I breathed more freely.

No ambitious ornament intrudes as one stands before St. Séverin. The carvings of the arch at the entrance are integral parts of the whole; the gargoyles have less literary taint than those of Notre Dame. The little church does not dominate the scene, but rests among secular buildings with modesty and restraint. I was to learn that, while in other localities the Church of Christ had wandered far afield, St. Séverin had remained truly a refuge and consolation of the poor. Its congregation consisted of workmen and their families, and its priests had no bank accounts, were never known to publish books, or to mix in politics. Three of them, I was to learn, played the neatest game of bridge I have yet encountered. At the end of each session they dropped my money into the poor box.

When I emerged from St. Séverin's candlelight and incense, having listened to Father Panarioux playing the Bach B-minor fugue on the adequate little organ, I let myself be drawn across the street by the accordion band and into the Bal St. Séverin.

The waiter was at the bar, receiving from the proprietor a few drinks in glasses the size of thimbles. These he put on his tray and glanced toward me in response to a whispered admonition from his boss. Tray in hand, he guided me a distance of fifteen feet to a bench and table at the far corner of the crowded room, skirting the dancers, each couple of whom seemed to have achieved a sort of plastic unity. Someone had been occupying the table destined for me, as was evidenced by a handbag and an ashtray on the rim of which rested a cigarette butt that had been prudently extinguished with reference to the future. The waiter, still balancing his tray on which the tiny glasses were overflowing in an oily way, picked up the handbag with one hand and tossed it on the bench near another table. Then he said to me '*Voilà, monsieur*,' and with unbelievable daintiness lifted the half-cigarette between thumb and forefinger and deposited it on the empty ashtray nearest the transferred handbag.

The only other occupant of the room who was not dancing, not counting the proprietor and waiter, was a young girl in a flame-coloured dress and nothing whatever underneath. She had large brown eyes with long curved lashes, a rosebud mouth with petulant corners, and bare legs, very shapely, the pallor of which was accentuated by black high-heeled shoes, size three and wide. As our glances crossed, she tilted her gaze toward the low mezzanine balcony where the three-piece orchestra played. The drummer nodded curtly.

When the orchestra struck another tune the male customers rose indolently, blew cigarette smoke from the corners of their mouths, and let it be known with a minimum of ceremony that they chose to dance and with whom. The flame-coloured dress was left partnerless once more; so I stood up, glanced up at the drummer, and made my way to her corner.

'Would you care to dance?' I asked in American French.

'If monsieur wishes,' she replied doubtfully.

I tried holding her circumspectly, but she did not seem at ease that way, and had difficulty in following. So I fitted our bodies together in the prevailing style, as best I could.

'What is your name?' I asked. Up came her long curved eyelashes, and she stared at me in surprise. It was not usual to talk while dancing.

'Suzanne,' she said, and that was the extent of the conversation. She was young, about seventeen I thought, and not muscular like a chambermaid or servant girl. Her high forehead and reddish brown hair suggested Normandy. As we danced I learned that she used unscented Castile soap, that her hands and arms were cool while her torso was supple and warm.

'*Anglais, vous?*' she asked, as if she were speaking to a child, when we were seated again. Marcel, the *garçon*, without prompting, brought my unfinished *dégustation* and placed it in front of me, resting on its saucer marked 2 francs.

It was the 2 francs label that got the first reaction from Suzanne. She raised her eyebrows and looked at my tie.

'*Anglais, ça?*' she asked.

'What will you have?' I asked.

She ordered a cherry, which baffled me until Marcel brought her a neat brown one pickled in brandy. Then I tried to explain that I was not English but American. The task I had undertaken was not so easy as I had thought it would be. Suzanne had seen the sea once and had mistaken it for a continuation of the sky. That America was across the ocean meant nothing to her because she understood but dimly what an ocean was. Americans and Englishmen both spoke English. That was enough for her.

Having started dancing with Suzanne and buying her brandied cherries, it was pleasant to continue. The arrangement seemed to please the drummer and the proprietor, and had the sanction also of Marcel, the *garçon*, who was the real director of the establishment. The Bal St. Séverin was orderly in the extreme. There was no drunkenness, no open quarrels, and if the talk was loud between dances, it was uniformly so. The liquor wasn't bad. Although diluted, it was stimulating. I drank four or five *fines*, and each time Marcel laid another 2 francs saucer on top of my modest stock, Suzanne began to show respect, if not alarm. Suspecting that she might be hungry, I suggested a sandwich. With a quick warning pressure of her cool little hand, which absent-mindedly I seemed to be holding beneath the table, and a fearful glance toward the drummer, she whispered swiftly: 'Not here, monsieur.'

I paid the bill, gave Marcel a generous tip and left the Bal St. Séverin. Once out on the pavement, Suzanne walked fearfully just ahead of me. There was not room for us to move abreast. To our right was St. Séverin. We saw the huge bulk of Notre Dame across the misty river. In the middle ground was the walled churchyard of St. Julien le Pauvre. Moorish music sounded faintly from the Hôtel Rossignol which faced the exit from our street. Algerian and Moroccan rug pedlars convened there, and sometimes smuggled in a nautch dancer who performed by the hour.

'*Les Sidis!*' Suzanne whispered, contemptuously. 'I should not like to sleep with them as Renée does . . . Robert hasn't made me yet.'

Suzanne told me later: 'Germaine is a droll one. She likes to have Robert try to break her arm — not I. I don't like to be hurt.'

Suzanne was steering me at that moment into the rue de la Huchette. I don't know where she is today. It is difficult for me to think of her as thirty-five years old, and torn with suffering. I can only hope she has enough to eat and doesn't understand too much about current events. She led me to the Hôtel du Caveau, and for that I shall eternally thank her.

2
A STAIRWAY DOWN TO ANTIQUITY

The rue de la Huchette, in time and space, had a beginning, a middle and an ending. Centuries ago, when Paris was a walled city on the Ile de la Cité and cows were pastured in what is now the place St. Germain, some of the first Parisians to quit the fortified island area settled along the left bank of the Seine. The rue de la Huchette runs parallel to the river, just a few yards south of the quai. No one seems to be clear about the meaning of its name, least of all its modern inhabitants.

Most of the traffic moved through the little street in an easterly direction, entering from the place St. Michel. This consisted mainly of delivery wagons, makeshift vehicles propelled by pedalling boys, pushcarts or itinerant vendors, knife-grinders, umbrella menders, a herd of milch goats and the neighbourhood pedestrians. The residents could sit in doorways or on kerbstones, stroll up and down the middle of the way, and use the street as a communal front yard, in daylight hours or in the evening, without risk of life or limb from careening taxis. In fact, at dawn and dusk, a pair of bats, never more or less than two, zigzagged back and forth at the level of the second-story windowsills and, when confronted by noise and lights in the *place*, or the rue des Deux Ponts, faltered, wheeled and started back again.

The two larger corner cafés, Café St. Michel and the Brasserie Dalmatienne, belonged to the boulevard St. Michel. They were flanked by staid apartment buildings, four or five stories high, with attic dormers for chambermaids. Hard times, during and after World War I, had caused most of the families to dispense with servants, so the lofty undersized bedrooms, cut in odd irregular shapes by jutting roofs, skylights and rickety tile chimneys, were rented to impecunious tenants who lived alone, except possibly on Saturdays or Sunday nights, and who liked a fairly good address at which to receive their post.

The middle section of the street was cut, but not crossed, by two streets even smaller than the rue de la Huchette — the rue Zacharie and the rue du Chat Qui Pêche, so named because in the early days before the quai was built, a cat used to fish in the cellars when the Seine was high. He must have caught nearly all there were to catch, for although I have seen patient fishermen on Sundays and holidays lining the quai with well-rigged poles and tackle (including a straw fish basket with cover and green leaves inside, a lunch of bread, sausage and cheese, and a bottle of *pinard*, or strong red wine) it was seldom if ever that a *goujon* (or edible minnow) was landed. The rue du Chat Qui Pêche had the distinction of being the narrowest and shortest in the world, with only one window not more than a foot square and no doors at all.

On one corner of the rue du Chat Qui Pêche stood the Bureau de Police, not important enough to rate a police car. It was lucky to have a telephone. The *flics*, or cops, used bicycles or patrolled soundlessly on foot, invariably in pairs.

Not oftener than twice a year a troublesome drunk, crazed with hunger and lack of sleep, would wander into the precinct from the slums to the east. If it proved impossible for the easygoing *agents* to ignore him or chase him into another precinct, he (or she) was mauled and lectured mildly and locked in a damp granite cell, about six by six.

Once, however, in 1926, a small-time burglar tried to break into the grocery store at no. 31. When surprised by the even more astonished *agents*, who unwittingly had popped round the corner, the marauder fired two shots at them, wounding one in the groin. He was kicked to death that night, on the cold stone floor of our little local station, and, with intestines steamingly exposed, was lugged under a cheap stiff blanket to the morgue behind Notre Dame. That ended the unfortunate affair. The Paris police, almost saintly as a rule in their gentleness and understanding, got tough only when their opponents made attempts on their lives.

Le Panier Fleuri, the neighbourhood bordel run by Madame Mariette, was opposite the station house on the corner of the rue Zacharie. The south-east corner was occupied by a laundry which employed three hard-working girls and also served as a *clandestin*. That is to say, men who found it banal to patronize the orthodox establishment could, if they were known to Mme. Lanier, go upstairs with the laundress of their choice. This illegal arrangement increased the income of Mme. Lanier, her non-productive husband, and the girls, and, in the opinion of the easy-going sergeant, did no one any harm. Edouard Lanier, the husband, was a war veteran (Croix de Guerre with two palms), and because he was a '*Gueule cassée*' (a soldier whose face had been disfigured), he was treated with indulgence.

The eastern end of the rue de la Huchette revolved around the Hôtel du Caveau. It was there Suzanne led me in search of a meal.

There I found Paris — and France.

When we entered the Caveau, by means of the door leading directly into the bar and restaurant, a dark-haired Greek woman, somewhat dishevelled, was leaning on a marble-topped table stained with Dubonnet, and staring into space. Behind the bar stood a *garçon*, with collarless white bosom shirt, the brass stud of which had stained his Adam's apple, and a slate-coloured apron that hung down to his knees. His twinkling blue eyes rested shrewdly on Suzanne, then noted my American felt hat and four-in-hand tie. His moustaches were sandy and red with a spread from tip to tip of at least six inches. A glance at Georges could not fail to bring forth a merry smile. I soon learned that he was chronically cheerful — except about twice a month. Quite regularly each fortnight, after he had drunk Homerically, he tried to cut his throat, at which he was extremely clumsy. He always woke up the next morning and was shyly ashamed.

Georges was not a native Frenchman, but a Serb who had deserted from the Austrian army and miraculously made his way to Paris. In 1917, he was picked up by the French authorities, who inducted him without further ceremony into the French army, where he proved to have a wonderful way with horses. After the war he had found a job in the Cirque d'Hiver. The Fratellini Brothers, princes of all clowns, were then the artistic directors. Georges cared for the semi-trained horses of the equestrian acts. He could do more with the troublesome beasts than their trainers, but one evening he found the Fratellinis' performance so excruciatingly funny that he forgot all else and stood, pail in hand, watching Albert, Paul and François go through their barber-shop act. A long-legged roan with a Dutch disposition observed that Georges was off guard and kicked him half-way across the ring. When Georges got out of the charity hospital, three months later, the Fratellinis were on tour in another country. So he loafed about for eighteen months and then became *garçon* in the Hôtel du Caveau.

Suzanne did not choose a table in the small dining-room, but led the way into an empty back-room, opened a small narrow door, and started descending a spiral stone stairway that smelled of antiquity. Below was a cool stone cellar with Roman and Byzantine arches. In Paris one soon learned that relics of all the centuries were shuffled together, if not scrambled. In the same block one would find Roman, Gothic, rococo, fake Greek, Byzantine, modern plaster shacks and bourgeois inadvertencies.

Suzanne found a light switch and turned it. The arches and pillars cast perfect shadows across a clean gravel floor of river pebbles.

'*Par ici, monsieur,*' she said. She then led the way to another stone stairway, slightly wider than the first. This we descended hand in hand. Enough light leaked from above to reveal another arched hallway with a gravelled narrow corridor ahead. The place appeared less likely to produce a sandwich than any I had seen in my life.

In the narrow corridor, my guide found another light switch, and I saw at my immediate left what unquestionably had been a mediaeval dungeon cell in which wine was stored. That such a mediaeval cellar could belong to the dingy bar and dining-room upstairs was hard to believe, but it proved to be a fact.

Facing us at the end of the corridor, beyond the dungeon wine cellar, was a massive studded-oak door spiked with large iron drift pins in impressive design. Suzanne lifted the heavy latch. As the heavy door swung outward, I saw that a light was burning inside, flickering like a taper. The least I expected when I looked into that sealed stone chamber was a Black Mass or hooded conspirators adjusting a torture rack. Instead, the two occupants of the subterranean vault turned out to be a fat middle-aged French woman and a medium-sized Turk, the latter in waiter's garb. In entering without knocking Suzanne and I had startled them, and both had half-risen, the woman fearfully, the Turk guiltily, although between them was a huge magnificent oak table made of three-inch planks and seasoned by the centuries.

'Hello, mister,' said the Turk, in acquired American.

Suzanne looked at him, then at me.

'*Anglais, lui?*' she asked. I had begun to expect it of her. The buxom woman, in drab grey dress and wearing an old-fashioned crocheted shawl, sat down. She looked nervous and perpetually afraid. The Turk smiled reassuringly. He had identified the origin of hat and tie.

'Sit down,' he said, indicating the heavy oak benches that ran the length of the table on both sides. Suzanne thanked him with perfunctory politeness and sat next to the woman. I sat beside Suzanne. All three of us faced the Turk, who resumed his place and leaned comfortably on his elbows.

'Good place,' he said, with a nod and gesture which included the raftered ceiling, the massive stone walls, the oak door, the ponderous table, the wavering taper in a wrought-iron holder and the gravel floor. 'One could make a lot of money here.'

As he made the last remark, he glanced meaningfully at the pale plump woman, who drew her shawl tighter and shivered.

'You're cold,' I said to madame. 'Would you join us in a drink?'

'Me, I'm hungry,' said Suzanne.

The Turk excused himself and departed.

'Do you live here?' I asked madame, and when slowly it dawned on her that I had spoken a kind of French and that she had understood it, she rested her startled gaze on me and murmured, softly: '*Oui, monsieur.*' It turned out that she owned the place, in so far as a married woman in France could own annyything. It had been her dowry — stone dungeons, ancient arches and all.

When the Turk returned, with four glasses, a bottle containing *Marc de Bourgogne*, a small carafe of red wine, a steaming generous portion of *ragoût* and a large chunk of bread for Suzanne, I learned that he had worked in Athens, Genoa, Barcelona, Ceuta, London, France, and America.

'Where in America?'

'Boston, Mass.,' he said. 'Do you know Coco?'

I did know Coco. We reminded each other what a fine man Coco was. He ran the Ararat on Kneeland Street.

While the Turk and I chatted in American, the two women, aged forty-two and seventeen respectively, looked on with polite relief, the former sipping dutifully at the fiery liqueur and the latter doing justice without mercy to the excellent lamb stew. It was easier for them not to understand American than to understand Turkish or American French with effort. The *marc* was undiluted — stupendous, in fact. As soon as my glass was empty the Turk filled it from the bottle near at hand. Meanwhile he talked and drank sparingly but with relish. It seemed that Madame's name was Philomèle, at each mention of which she looked startled and tried to smile. Her husband, the Turk told me, was no good. He was trying to steal the hotel away from Philomèle, but the property could not be sold or divided without her consent. The husband had tried beating her, but her skin was white and thin and bruised very easily, and she had cried all the time for a while. This caused the customers to complain.

Philomèle, by that time, had divined that we were talking about her and grew so restive that the Turk assured her that I was an educated man and could be trusted. That caused her to relax a little.

Suzanne had eaten the stew, a huge dish of string beans cooked with bacon in North country style, about four hundred calories of French fried potatoes, a salad of chicory with oil and vinegar, a large loaf of bread, and was starting in on a soft slab of Brie. She ate so heartily that my own appetite was aroused. I ordered a double portion of the cheese and, curious to know whether that wine-cellar was as good as it appeared to be from outside the grill, was escorted there by Madame Philomèle, who opened the mediaeval padlock with a hefty key she kept on a ring slung from her waist. While I was reading labels, observing dust on bottles and expressing my sincere admiration, we heard heavy footsteps on the gravel and Philomèle in a panic extinguished the light, clutched my arm, and began to tremble and silently to pray.

The head of her husband, whose face and unkempt hair seemed to fit the Turk's unflattering description of him lurched past the grilled Judas window. The man was very drunk, had an ugly look, and muttered threats as he proceeded toward the council chamber. When he entered he saw, not his cringing wife and the imaginary lover he had always sworn to catch *in flagrante delicto*, but his swarthy waiter and a strange girl in a flame-coloured gown. She was on his side of the bench, so he made a grab for her. Suzanne made no resistance, but in her woman's way tried to pacify him and make him feel at home. The Turk, always the diplomat, did nothing to discourage this budding relationship, but tactfully faded from the scene leaving the bottle of *marc* about half full.

Meanwhile Philomèle and I had tiptoed away from the danger zone. When her head appeared through an iron trapdoor behind the bar, the friendly Georges smiled with such sincere relief and pleasure that wrinkles appeared on his forehead and his luxurious moustache wagged up and then down. An instant later, when my head followed Madame's felt-slippered feet, Georges not only smiled but beamed, and his knowing blue eyes rested not on my necktie, but looked straight into mine with mischievous congratulations. He had expected Madame Philomèle to be fearful and bruised.

Madame, without stopping to say farewell to me, moved swiftly toward the hallway. I was sure she did not intend me to follow.

'Have a drink,' I said to Georges, whose beatific smile rewarded me. Under its spell I could no find no reason for leaving that eventful small hotel. In fact, I had my meagre effects transferred the next day from the St. Sulpice quarter and was a guest at the Hôtel du Caveau, if 'guest' is not too distant and formal a term, off and on for eighteen years.

That first evening I was not in the mood for drinking alone, so I paused tentatively by the small table where the Greek woman with the luminous dark eyes was still staring into space. Slowly my American necktie found its way into her clouded consciousness. Mary drew from somewhere inside her waist a dog-eared American passport of a model no longer in vogue, together with some old snapshots and a sheaf of official papers, letters and several certificates from the Paris Mont-de-Piété, or municipal pawnshop. She had the illusion that she remembered her English, but after a few brief exchanges we both lapsed into such French as we could command. Hers was the more unacademical, since she persisted in using the letter 'G' for 'H' (which does not exist in the Greek alphabet) so that words like 'hospital' came out 'gospital', a harmless switch to which I rapidly grew accustomed.

When Mary first had come to the hotel almost any of the denizens would listen to her story, but for a long time preceding my first appearance there she had not had a chance to unburden her troubled mind. She accepted another Dubonnet and quite pitifully smiled.

Mary's misfortunes and hardships had worked havoc with her wardrobe and had weakened her resistance to Dubonnet. It had not destroyed the almost celestial beauty of her face, which would have served as a model for any painter in need of an olive-skinned Madonna, nor had it ruined her mature and memorable figure. As best I could gather, Mary had been brought up in Athens in comparatively easy circumstances. After an exchange of photos she has been sent for by a naturalized Greek fruit-dealer of Detroit to be his bride. In Detroit he had welcomed her gallantly and she had been a dutiful and faithful wife. The fruit business flourished, and two sons were born. Then an Irish girl in an hotel barber's shop had attracted the husband's attention, and Mary had been sent back to Europe for a visit to her folks, via Le Havre and Paris. Her husband had escorted her as far as New York, seen her aboard with tenderness, had given her her passage as far as Paris and assured her that additional funds for her journey to Greece (and return to America) would be waiting for her in a Paris bank. The two children had remained with him.

When the funds failed to materialize, the disinterestedness of the French officials in Mary's case was equalled only by that of the employees of the American Consulate in Paris. In some ingenious manner symbolized but not officially described by the legal papers she carried, Mary found herself divorced, and learned that her two children belonged to the father, who had married the Irish manicure girl. Mary had subsisted in Paris, while haunting government offices until she was forbidden entrance and threatened with arrest, by pawning her jewellery, now symbolized by the out-of-date pawntickets to which she tenaciously clung. Her parents in Athens, unable to rescue her, had died and were now represented by some tear-stained letters, indicating that the distant ex-husband had led them to believe that Mary had wantonly deserted him after misbehaving with ice-men, letter-carriers and casual passers-by.

That Mary had suffered intensely and was in a grave international plight (having no work card or even a prostitute's yellow licence) was all too apparent. Also it was plain that she looked at me, as an American of heart and education, to do something about it. I was feeling inadequate and useless in the extreme when an incident on the pavement, quite clearly visible through the hotel windows, attracted my eye, as well as the amused attention of Georges, the *garçon*.

An angry well-dressed Frenchman about fifty years of age, who looked out of place on the rue de la Huchette, was pummelling with his folded umbrella a young man who bore him a strong family resemblance. The recipient of the informal 'correction' was taller than his father, equally well-dressed (in the French manner) and, although offering no physical resistance, was unyielding to the point that he broke away from the grasp of his indignant parent and entered our hotel. His father did not follow.

The young man (whose name was Pierre Vautier) had a sensitive, not quite effeminate face, and an erect military bearing. It turned out that, in defiance of his father, he had, some time before, left the Army School of St. Cyr, to which only young men of high family and church influence had access, in order to enter the employ of an art gallery on the nearby rue de Seine. It was a small gallery that specialized in ultra-modern paintings of the neo-Cubistic school, the sight or mention of which had, on many occasions, nearly proved disastrous to the father's brittle arteries. Vautier the Elder's aversion to the gallery and its wares had been heightened by the indisputable fact that practically all of the other employees, the owner, most of the artists whose work was on display, and four-fifths of the customers were homosexual.

3

THE WOMEN IN BLACK WHO MOVED IN PAIRS

Hortense Berthelot, when I first met her, was an inconspicuous middle-aged woman who worked in the enormous prefecture, one of the tens of thousands who, because of widowhood or bereavement in World War I, were allowed, for very small pay, to sit at shabby desks, stand behind grilled windows or splintered counters, and in a sort of perpetual twilight, write words with bent stubpens and violet ink (thick with dust and sometimes dead gnats) on government forms which had been printed in such a way that there was never enough space in which to provide answers to ambiguous questions. One cannot exaggerate the inefficiency of a French public office, especially those to which members of the public were forced, all too often, to present themselves for heckling and abuse.

Methods of clerical work in twentieth-century France would not have been tolerated in America in the earliest Colonial days, and surely not before that by the Indians.

It was easy to pass by Madame Berthelot without noticing her. In her long years of public service, she had practised being inconspicuous. Her eyes were soft and brown, her face lined and appealing. She spoke, infrequently, in a low-pitched voice that placed her instantly as a lady of quality who had lost none of it in descending the ladder of fortune. One did not notice at first that she must have been a wistfully beautiful girl in her twenties. Her shoulders were narrow, her hands were eloquent, but thin. Her clothes were colourless, out of date in style, and never had been coquettishly chosen.

Only her gloves and shoes had style and distinction. She bought her gloves, she told me, in the Magasin du Louvre, where she knew a woman who had worked with her in the World War. This friend was able to sequester from the large department-store stock 'seconds' which had no detectable imperfections.

'Ah! You worked in the war?' I asked. I was surprised, having assumed from her manner that she had been sheltered until after that epoch.

'The last two years,' she said without bitterness.

We were lunching together in the Hôtel du Caveau, the day after my arrival. Already I had a strong desire to know everyone in the quarter. Our conversation was interrupted in the salad course (of celery root Lyonnaise) by the sullen entry into the bar and restaurant of the pimp, Robert, of the Bal St. Séverin.

Georges, the *garçon*, was serving drinks to a couple of officials and an oyster vendor from the Café de la Gare. Robert's small eyes were rimmed with red from anger and apple-jack, his face was pastier than it had looked by lamplight, his pinch-back coat was tighter, his purple scarf of a more poisonous shade, his cap at a more aggressive angle. The pimp, reptilian at best, was at his worst in the light of noonday. Georges, who knew what was the matter and was smiling behnd his pale-blue eyes, looked as non-committal and innocent behind the bar as a porcelain bust on an upright piano.

'What will you have?' Georges asked.

'*Il est méchant, le numéro*' (He's a bad one, that fellow), whispered Madame Berthelot.

At that time I did not know with what exactness Hortense spoke French, and did not realize that for her to call a man a '*numéro*' was equivalent to what three women who peddle fish in Marseilles would have meant after screaming all the words in the *argot*. A '*numéro*', in Mme. Berthelot's exquisite vocabulary, was one degree lower than a '*type*', but less severe than '*individu*' or 'individual.' A '*type*' implies that the person to whom the word is applied is of little consequence. A '*numéro*' may be a chap who is dangerous and anti-social, or a droll fellow or Merry Andrew who can be counted on for harmless fun. But a woman with the regard Mme. Berthelot had for the spoken word would not apply the epithet '*individu*' to anyone less villainous than Landru.

The wide gulf between French slang and Academic French was not as confusing as it might have been, owing to the fact that a Frenchman ordinarily stuck to one system of expression or the other. Some baffling French *argot* resulted from nouns made up of pure sounds and having no linguistic roots whatever. Other stumbling-blocks to the French of the streets involved the use of the names of certain objects to indicate other objects which had names of their own. For instance, a cookstove was called a 'piano' and a *bidet*, a 'violin.'

In the year 1923, the 'immortals,' or members of the French Academy, had progressed as far as the letter 'm' in their revision of the official French dictionary, and, at the moment the pimp, Robert, was leaning vindictively on the bar at No. 5 rue de la Huchette, the savants a few blocks west were arguing as to whether the word 'mimosa' was masculine or feminine. In the former event, it would be called '*le* mimosa', and in the latter '*la* mimosa'. Madame Berthelot was of the last-named faction. '*La* mimosa' to her delicate ear sounded more euphonious than '*le* mimosa'. Pierre Loti, Hortense said, used '*la* mimosa'. That clinched it for me.

With his mind on Suzanne in a sadistic way, Robert, *le mecque* or 'mackerel,' ignored Georges' question. 'What will you have?' and simply snarled:

'Where is that girl?'

Had I not noticed Claude, the proprietor, lurching upstairs the night before, with Suzanne in tow, or rather one step ahead, I should have believed Georges' profession of ignorance myself. Georges liked to be believed, and almost always I humoured him, making it easy for him to tell me about the minor misfortunes that forced him to ask for the loan of a couple of francs (2½d.) now and then. Robert, evil eyes gleaming, started for the stairway leading to the rooms upstairs, in one of which, no doubt, was sprawled the drunken *patron* and Suzanne. Madame Philomèle, it developed, had not had access to her conjugal bedroom that night but had been obliged to weep in another and smaller chamber.

Before Robert had reached the doorway, Georges, with twice the distance to travel, was suddenly in front of him, still smiling, moustaches waving up, then down. With the utmost precision he took hold of Robert's pointed nose, which he twisted, clockwise, about forty degrees. He was still smiling.

Robert, as he backed through the door to the pavement, uttered threats to both Georges and Suzanne. I have never seen a Serb less worried.

The bloodless incident put Mme. Berthelot in a sunny humour. She was always gentle and accommodating, but seldom looked otherwise than sad. As the salad course progressed and cheese was forthcoming (a Port Salut that increased my respect for the fat cook who did the daily marketing), Hortense told me about her World War job with her friend who now sold gloves in the Magasin du Louvre.

It seemed that the families of Frenchmen who died in the service of their country (when they had one) had in past years been notified by post, telegraph or telephone. This had proved to be uneconomical. Little or nothing was accomplished, in homes, shops, cafés or factories, within an hour or more of the moment when the postman was due to heave into sight at the corner of a street. Every woman, also every old man and young child, had dear ones at some front (1914–1918), and the more nervous and less resistant among them frequently fainted or had fits of hysteria while watching the snail-like progress of the postman from door to door. There were, in those days, certain grey-blue postcards that meant someone had been wounded or missing, and some black-rimmed white ones that spelled stark death. The women at the far end of streets would, if they saw that the postman's pouch contained no black-rimmed messages, wave and sometimes cheer with an edge of fear diminishing in their voices, and up and down the street the watchers would relax. Very often no such reassurance was forthcoming, and everyone had to wait, breath caught, nerves throbbing, until someone had let out a shriek, or turned wordlessly away or dropped in her tracks and the postman wiped a tear from his eye with the back of his hand before continuing.

So the *Gouvernement français*, which had its soft as well as inept moments, in late 1916 hired tactful well-bred women, who had friends in high office and needed a job, to break the news in person to the nearest relatives in case a soldier was killed in action. These harbingers of sorrow were carefully chosen, and the qualifications were severe. They must present a dignified appearance, and neither be attractive enough to take men's thoughts away from grief nor ugly enough to scare the stricken children. They must have a smattering of practical nursing, in case the recipients of their tidings collapsed, and must be reasonably agile in cases of *folie furieuse*, or fits of grief-inspired madness. These women dressed in heavy mourning, spoke softly and always went forth in pairs.

Thus, trudging from house to house, making a quota of six calls a day, Hortense Berthelot had spent the last two years of the war, after her husband, a captain in the artillery, had been killed by a truck he had tried to crank while still in gear, in the heroic defence of Verdun. When she was no longer needed in the 'archives' department which supervised the 'women in black', she, being a second cousin by marriage of a petty official called 'The Navet' (turnip), was given a job, at lower wages (about £5 10*s*. a month), in the passport department of the prefecture. There she had worked five years without once losing her head when those about her were fairly bouncing theirs from wall to wall and blaming it on the nearest foreigner who chanced to have asked for something he was forced by law to have and could seldom obtain.

In order to reach her room at our hotel, Hortense had to walk up four steep and narrow flights of stairs, but she had moved there from the second floor in order to be out of hearing each night late, when Claude settled accounts with Philomèle. Mme. Berthelot got little exercise, having neither time nor means nor energy, and if she was awakened between one and three each morning by sounds or thuds, entreaties, sobs and curses, it made her eyes ache the next day after hours of squinting in the dingy misplaced prefectorial light and trying to make out the illegible scrawls of all nations. The first two years in the passport department, Madame Berthelot had had the toughest job: that of interviewing foreigners the first time. But The Navet, after culling evidence of a particular rare pastime to which one of his chiefs was addicted, got Hortense transferred to the desk where renewals of permission to stay in France were sometimes granted, after months or years of delay, with a rubber stamp.

The fundamental cause of Mme. Bethelot's promotion (without increase of pay) was a unique establishment on the Ile St. Louis, namely, the only house of ill-fame in the world whose 'girls' were all more than seventy years old. There were men all over Europe who doted on the grandmotherly type. The Navet's immediate chief, a third secretary of a cabinet minister, was one of the regulars at the aforementioned semi-public institution. How The Navet found out about this, Mme. Berthelot did not say, but she willingly admitted that she owed her advancement to his confidential information.

About one o'clock, just before Mme. Berthelot had to rise, shake hands, put on her gloves and walk, hurriedly but with dignity, across the bridge and along the avenue de la Justice to the prefecture, the door from the hotel stairway was pushed gently open and Mary, the badly hyphenated Greek, stepped in. She was followed by young Pierre Vautier, the St. Cyr alumnus, who was adjusting his necktie in a touchingly self-satisfied way. Mary was wearing, not the seamy and shiny blue serge skirt of her heyday in Detroit, but a new one, more in style, which her hands touched fondly.

The evening before, when I had seen at a glance that, in mysterious ways known only to God, the abandoned Greek wife and disinherited French prodigal had some affinity, I had withdrawn from Mary's table to the bar, to further my acquaintance with Georges.

Pierre, it seemed, had slept with his mother from the time of his birth up to his entry, at the age of nineteen, into the exclusive army school of St. Cyr. In order to give the lie to the premature and bitter accusation of homosexuality his father had showered on him, between strokes of the umbrella, the lad had made up his mind to take a mistress, publicly. Having seen Mary so forlorn and unattached, he had acted without delay. They made a touching couple, because Mary, unselfish in the extreme, was able to put aside her own troubles (set forth in numerous documents retained) and turned her ready sympathy to the handsome young boy. So when the Turk brought their lunch from the kitchen, Mary inspected carefully the two portions of *bœuf Bordelaise*, decided that the one that had been placed in front of her was the more attractive and nourishing and deftly exchanged plates with Pierre, who smiled fondly and made no objection.

Both Mary and Pierre were absolutely broke, having bought the new skirt, but The Navet, who entered the hotel bar at least twice a day in order to set the folks right about national affairs, had whispered to Madame Philomèle that Vautier, *père*, notwithstanding his impetuous nature, would never let the family name be tainted with small debts. Thus the lovers enjoyed credit and had no pressing need of cash. On my way to the kitchen, where I intended to compliment the fat drunken cook on the quality of the menu she had prepared, I paused briefly to give the pair my blessing, which was disguised by the conventional *'bonjour' 'bon appétit' 'Comment allez-vous, madame et monsieur'* and *'à tout à l'heure.'* Pierre politely asked me to sit down, to which I replied that I would do so a little later. Such rituals as these were spoken with warmth in inverse proportion to the likelihood of their fulfilment. The celebrated *politesse française* had nuances and ramifications equal to any and all occasions, and enabled one, if used with skill, to keep just the right distance and leave things unsaid which could be implied, while employing euphonious sound effects that did much to enhance the charm of everyday intercourse.

The cook, Thérèse, was a '*numéro*' in all senses of the word. Armed with a butcher's knife and fortified with three litres of strong red wine (her daily consumption was about five), she could be as dangerous as a truckload of scoundrels like Robert. On the other hand, when rubbed the right way, she could be infinitely more amusing than the Deputies in the Chamber and fifty times more loyal. Luckily, I was admitted at once into her small circle of friends and confidants.

This vigorous woman, who weighed about 250 pounds, was harder than nails, and had to splice with rope the largest apron strings she could buy in a bazaar, had endeared herself to the wags of the quarter by having served The Navet stuffed cat (*chat farci*) just after he had tried to tell her how '*œufs au vin*' or 'eggs in wine' were prepared on Sunday mornings in the Haute Marne, Thérèse's native province. That The Navet was from the Midi and had never seen the Haute Marne (up near the Vosges mountains) did not deter him. The Navet was like that. He had not been told about the cat he had eaten until a week later, his informant being the oyster and chestnut vendor from the Loire and the Café de la Gare, the provocation being that The Navet had insisted that the oyster man, who loved to sing and had a lusty natural voice, had garbled the words of one of the marvellous songs of the fertile Loire region. Between the oyster man and The Navet a feud had long smouldered. When it finally broke out, The Navet spend hours in his office, and with his underlings searched books of laws and old ordinances in order to find a statute that could be invoked against the oyster man's way of gaining his livelihood. The oyster man, less vengeful, held up his end by roaring louder than The Navet could talk and expressing political and social opinions that would often destroy The Navet's appetite and inflame him into abusing his deaf wife, Jeanne, and their son, Eugène.

It is related by Rabelais how Panurge, in calling on Herr Trippa, the fortune-teller, for information concerning the future, stumbled over Herr Trippa's wife and a page on the narrow stone stairway. Panurge, the reader will remember, had some doubts about the ability of the fortune-teller who professed to know the secrets of the future and was the only man in the neighbourhood unaware that he was being cuckolded at least thrice daily. In an analogous way, the inhabitants of the rue de la Huchette distrusted the pronouncements of the voluble Navet and relished with glee the local intrigue between his sweet and patient wife, Jeanne, and a champion of social reform from Dijon.

Even to a greater extent than Georges, Thérèse, the cook, was responsible for the solvency of the hotel under the management of the ineffectual Philomèle. And if anyone did not know about Thérèse's triumph over The Navet, or thought she had gone too far, he or she approved *in toto* the cook's contempt for Claude, the *patron*, her refusal to take orders from him or even to allow him to enter the kitchen, and her physical defence, on one occasion, of Philomèle when the latter was being kicked below the belt of a Saturday night. Thérèse's code was 'an eye for an eye', and the result of her interference was salutary in the extreme, for when Claude had appealed to the police sergeant on the corner, three days later when he was able to walk that far, the officer had told him that he had caused enough trouble in the precinct already and then threatened to lock him in either the cell or the toilet of the station (there was little choice between them) if he opened his *margoulette* (trap) again.

I must make it clear that mingling in affairs between husband and wife was not the custom in Republican France. My friend, and fellow labourer in the vineyard of various arts, Wolfe Kaufman, learned an early lesson in that respect in his first month in Paris. Traversing the place St. Sulpice he saw a motorman in heated conversation with a woman conductor. When the motorman kicked the dame resoundingly in the buttock, Wolfe, mild by nature and fresh from America, automatically became Sir Galahad. Instead of taking a sock at Wolfe, the motorman assumed an expression of injured innocence and dignity and began enumerating in a pained dispassionate way the long list of provocations the woman, his lawful wife, had given him before, patient law-abiding man that he was, he had yielded to an irresistible and justifiable impulse. The gathering crowd, always judicious as well as curious in Paris, in this instance including two policemen and one official from the near-by *mairie*, nodded in approval as point after point was made by the first speaker, the motorman. At the conclusion of the opening argument, the onlookers turned to Wolfe to hear his rebuttal. All he could do was to look around for the woman and try to decide whether or not to kick her himself. Having decided against any physical demonstration, he did the handsome thing and apologized, inviting the motorman and the most promising members of the crowd to join him in a drink at a near-by bar. Thus the incident, which at first had threatened Franco-American amity (just then very much talked about, since Poincaré wanted Harding's support against England for his seizure of the Ruhr), ended up by cementing the traditional friendship personified by Lafayette.

4
OF PUBLIC OPINION

One of the coloured touches among the shop windows of the rue de la Huchette was the yarn shop of Madame 'Absalom'. Ranged in coverless pasteboard boxes, her wares ran the gamut of commercial dyes, from the most vibrant orange through vermilions, carmines, emerald, turquoise, ultramarine and gamboge to the assortment of sickly pale pinks and watery blues that mothers buy for infants. The crotchety old woman, who had been left the shop by an aunt she had detested, scorned knitting as a waste of time and disliked needlework to the point that she would not mend her cotton stockings. No one called her anything but Absalom, except a few other old women who tottered from the suburbs, now and then, to quarrel with her on minor matters, exchange kisses on leathery cheeks and depart. To them she was Lucie.

Madame Absalom was thus nicknamed because of her hair, which was salt-and-pepper grey and wiry, and which, when it was not tied up with a black corset of string in a knot on the back of her head, reached down to her prominent collar bones. She had been married once, about twenty-five years before (she married late) to a pharmacist of the second class (not the one on the boulevard St. Michel near by) and when I first knew her she was scanning avidly the local newspapers from Clermont-Ferrand in gleeful anticipation of the demise of her 'ex', as she called him spitefully, who had become a fairly important man in Clermont and was suffering from rheumatism, combined with a tic that spasmodically distorted the left side of his face. I never saw the 'ex' himself, but Madame Absalom was a good mimic.

She was always reading newspapers and drying her bristling hair in a patch of sun that slashed one side of her little shop. Her views about French politicians and the prospect of a reformation of the German national character which might bring about a harmonious and peaceful Europe seemed to me, in the middle 1920s, to be pessimistic in the extreme.

Madame Absalom insisted each day, after reading all the Paris papers, that nothing could be done to improve matters or prevent them from getting worse. The French politicians were scoundrels with their hands in the till; the employers blood-suckers; the employees, ruffians; the peasants, thick-headed fools who were 'good for nothing but work.' Germany could pay. And if Germans starved, what of it? Plenty of Frenchmen had been gassed and shot on their account. France was bankrupt and couldn't pay America. So what was the use of talking about it, and wasting money sending 'commissions' for a joy-ride?

As Madame Absalom orated amidst her multi-hued wools and small cabinets of cotton threads on spools, there appeared twice weekly from an apartment in No. 32 (the building in which The Navet also lived) a dainty girl of six, most carefully dressed, well-mannered and self-possessed, and pushing in a small rattan carriage a doll which looked like her. Her name was Hyacinthe Goujon, and her large round eyes glanced at me appraisingly before she extended her hand and smiled. First she had bowed to Madame Absalom with the courtesy due her in the capacity of hostess and the condescension her status as tradeswoman justified. I, being a foreigner, did not come into any category little Hyacinthe had learned to recognize. The fact that I did not work in the afternoon indicated that I was not a business or professional man. My clothes seemed to her inelegant, my French more so.

'It would be disturbing to marry a foreigner,' Hyacinthe remarked to Madame Absalom after I had gone. 'One wouldn't know how to behave in his country, and he wouldn't be at home in France.'

The old woman replied that it was better than marrying a second-class pharmacist.

Hyacinthe, aged six, had a tiny box of face powder and a small stick of rouge, chose her own perfume, had quite astonishing ideas about her clothes and those of other 'women', and told me, without a flicker of her violet-blue eyes or a vulgar inflection of her well-trained voice, that she remained with Madame Absalom on Tuesday and Friday afternoons because her mother, Madame Goujon, entertained her 'lover' on those days.

'He's married, but distinguished,' Hyacinthe said. Around Hyacinthe's neck hung an ornate cross. Its duplicate, slightly smaller, was around the doll's neck. The forms of religious observance were important to the child, but she would not have thought of entering St. Séverin, which was for the *canaille* or rabble. Instead, she was taken by her mother, also devout, to the Madeleine by bus. Hyacinthe would have preferred a *voiture* or taxi but understood that, on a small income, one must be careful and not wasteful, in common with some of the best names in France.

'Fewer people who matter attend vespers,' she told me, on returning from church one Sunday evening, when from the pont St. Michel one could see reflections of the sunset, between historic bridges, in dove colours shot with carnation and ripples of molten gold, all the way from the Jardin des Plantes with its roaring beasts at feeding-time, past the pont du Louvre, the pont du Carrousel, the pont Royal, to the Trocadéro overlooking the Champs de Mars, where little Hyacinthe loved to go, pay her small fee for a metal chair, and sit along the bridle path to see the handsome army officers ride by on mettled and well-bred horses.

Hyacinthe, of course, would not have been permitted to sit in a park alone, had Madame Goujon known about it. But the cousin (male) to whom the little girl was entrusted had a passion for a card game called *belotte* and knew some cronies in the Gros Cailloux quarter. So he took a chance that nothing would happen to Hyacinthe, and nothing did. Defective as it was, this arrangement was better than those of families who sent their young children to the Luxembourg Gardens with servant girls. In that quarter, an enterprising public dance hall had installed a check-room into which children were herded for small fees paid by the nurse girls, who danced with pinch-backed and scarved young men all afternoon, then collected their babies and returned home.

Little Hyacinthe never noticed the grooms along the bridle path. The man she could love, if the families could agree and his parents would accept her on account of her looks and distinction, without a large dowry, was a captain, tall, a good horseman, soft-spoken but accustomed to being obeyed, with dark-blue eyes, a good forehead, slender shoulders, and a black moustache. Hyacinthe, very tactfully, had bribed the old woman who rented the chairs in the park, to find out the officer's name, and the sound of it had thrilled the little girl, and confirmed her sure instincts. It was Costa de la Montaigne who, when the time arrived, would again use the title of Count his fathers had possessed.

Madame Goujon, the mother of this precocious girl, had one lodger who rented a small room off the hallway, next to the salon in her apartment. In the rear of this she had installed what she and the neighbourhood plumbers believed to be a bathroom, the only one with running hot water in the rue de la Huchette. The tub was enormous and had been smeared with boat paint a shade of grey that suggested wet clay. It stood on four legs like the feet of the fabulous fire bird. These legs were equal in length, but the floorboards were uneven, so that the tub, when one stepped in it, rocked from side to side like a cradle. The gas-heater had been purchased second-hand by Madame Goujon at the Flea Market.

The tenant of this room and bath was a floor-walker from the Samaritaine, the only building in Paris ever ugly enough to be razed on æsthetic grounds by the public authorities. Monsieur Panaché was a pale severe man about twenty-eight years old, fussy and disagreeable, thoroughly hated by the girls who worked under him, and tolerated by his superiors because he able to drive his inferiors with relentless meanness. Once when Hyacinthe caught him using one of the Goujon towels to rub dust from his shoes she made him pay and told him that if he wished to do that sort of thing he should move three doors down the street, to the Hôtel Normandie. Panaché detested Madame Goujon from the top of her authentic bosom to her thick ankles and bunioned feet. Madame blushed easily when annoyed, not that she was ever embarrassed. The floor-walker kept the blood surging up to Madame Goujon's face with his daily remarks about the bathroom for which he paid an extra fifty francs a month. Panaché had been goaded to this extravagance because the superintendent at the Samaritaine had complained that he stank.

The day it was installed, Panaché had filled the tub. When he got in, the water flooded the floor and seeped through to The Navet's ceiling below, which brought an argument that was historic in the street, having been overheard by Marie, Madame Goujon's deaf *bonne à tout faire*, or maid servant. The result was a cash settlement amounting to 8s. 8d. which Madame Goujon got back by scrimping on the daily lunches she served a lawyer-clerk from the Palais de Justice who could not digest restaurant food. Then Panaché insisted that the gas heater was dangerous and refused to light it himself. Madame Goujon tried to demonstrate that it was not, and the resulting explosion burned off her eyebrows and some of her frizzled hair, which made the floor-walker so happy that he failed tht same afternoon to discharge a new girl at the store who dropped a French fountain pen on the floor while showing it to a customer.

In World War I, Anne Goujon had served as a voluntary nurse in a base hospital, up to the day when, turning the pages of a surgical text-book for a young intern in the act of performing an emergency operation he had never seen or attempted, she had turned two pages instead of one, so that the patient, a private of infantry (Croix de Guerre with one palm) had been given the first half of one operation and the second or final phase of another. That he lived was a tribute to the hardihood of the good French stock in the Ain.

Anne's father, 'the Judge' and the doting grandfather of little Hyacinthe, used to taxi to the rue de la Huchette from the avenue de la Bourdonnais. He was seventy years old, wore a pointed white beard and spoke as if he were St. Francis addressing the birds: that is to say, very softly and kindly, but not expecting much in the way of rebuttal from the congregation. Honoré René Martin Lenoir was the way he was described on his birth record, 'Lenoir' was the way he signed his name — not even deigning to prefix himself, and also in protest against the official separation of the Church and State, when the now buxom Anne was about twelve years old. Nevertheless, she seldom referred to him, except to his face, as 'papa' but always called him proudly 'the Judge'.

When the Judge came to the rue de la Huchette his taxi, entering from the place St. Michel, veered over to the wrong side of the street, since he always chose either Tuesday or Thursday and these days were among those the municipality of Paris had set aside for parking on the left-hand side of the street. In order to give even breaks to shopkeepers and cafés on both sides of the city streets, the municipal government had decreed that on Monday, Wednesday, Friday and Sunday, one should park on the right-hand side, and on Tuesday, Thursday and Saturday, the left. This was one of the few things the police were strict about. A friend of mine was stopped by the same cop on the same bridge six nights running, at about the same hour, and advised to turn on his headlights, but had he once parked on the left on Monday he would have been hauled before the local superintendent of police, and official documents would have started to accumulate. In those carefree years, only two other local ordinances were enforced according to the letter. A prostitute was not permitted to stand under a street lamp, and sisters were not allowed to work in the same lupanar.

Often The Navet would leave his office early and slyly on the chance of encountering the Judge. When the Judge entered the dimness of the hallway, being watched with furtive pride by the sharp-eyed concierge, The Navet would step out from some dark corner, would raise his black bowler hat and say obsequiously:

'*Bonjour, monsieur le juge!*'

If the Judge were thrown off his reverie by this, paused to exchange a few polite and guarded remarks, or on rare days extended his hand, and if only a few of the passers-by witnessed this mark of The Navet's distinction, the latter would consider his risky exit from his post of duty well hazarded. The Navet would have liked to have a few persons think that the Judge called at that address to see him. He never offered the Judge his arm while ascending the steep stairway because he had done so once, seven years before, when the Judge was only sixty-four, and the old man seemed to have resented the inference that he was infirm.

This was the extent of the association between The Navet and the Judge, but around the prefecture and in the bar of the Hôtel du Caveau, The Navet spoke of his old friend Judge Lenoir, and quoted the old boy in frequent instances when he wished to publicize an idea of his own.

The Judge, when he achieved the landing of the third floor, paused as many minutes as were necessary before pushing his daughter's bell, in order that she might remark, after kissing him on each cheek perfunctorily, that he 'supported' those dreadful stairs much better than she did. The Judge seldom heard this distinctly, because he made it a custom to totter out to the diminutive kitchen in order to offer a cordial greeting to the humble Marie, whose morning had been made hideous on his account. Madame Goujon was an exacting employer, at best. When she was expecting her father but was not quite sure (the Judge would have no traffic with telephones, or even *pneumatiques*) she kept old Marie hopping and '*Parfaitement, madame*-ing' like a character doll with a concealed spring. Marie was hired by the hour, at a rate of pay that for most of us would barely sustain life for that length of time if we remained in bed. She was seventy-two years old, but neither Madame Goujon nor the Judge seemed to be aware of it.

The Judge was not worried about Germany in those days, and even less about England and the United States, where, according to *L'Action Française*, one ate for breakfast something about the size of a small pumpkin that was coloured like a melon but had a smoother skin. Some radical that year (they called them anarchists, not communists, then) had taken a pot-shot at Léon Daudet, the Royalist leader whose youth organization, the Croix de Feu, was given to rioting. From this, Judge Lenoir concluded that Paris was honeycombed with dangerous characters who were coddled by the godless Republic.

Marie, the Goujon servant, was deaf, but very respectful. Her life had been so blameless that she had never confessed oftener than once a year, even when adolescent. That did not deter Madame Goujon, a cautious person if ever there was one, from keeping the butter, sugar, wine, etc., under lock and key while old Marie was on duty. When those articles were needed for cooking, Marie had to find Madame and ask her for the keys to the cupboard. The only time Marie ever considered quitting Madame Goujon was once when the latter left four sous (a quarter of a farthing) on a dresser quite by accident. The old servant assumed that her mistress was suspecting her of theft and had set a trap for her. On that one occasion, Madame Goujon actually put her arm round the old woman's shoulder and blushed to the roots of her hair. Marie, deeply touched, had wept and begged Madame's pardon, and for a day or two was not scolded because she was continually, in trying to serve meals hot, raising blisters on her fingers, which might be infected from the dishwater, in which case Madame Goujon might have to pay for medical treatment.

After lunching with his daughter, whom he treated as if she were about fourteen, Judge Lenoir would allow her to help him take off his coat and shoes and would doze for an hour and a quarter. Then he would say good-bye and descend the stairway. When the concierge saw his spats at the head of the first flight she would hasten to the kerb to wake the dozing chauffeur, or, if he was already awake and was reading the *Paris-Midi*, she would merely announce that the Judge was on his way. The chauffeur would mutter under his breath a five-letter word frequently paired with *alors*, fold his newspaper, belch, pry himself out of his seat at the wheel, touch his cap as His Honour hove into view and open the door for him. In return he would be courteously given an address in the rue Cadet where lived the Judge's mistress, an ample type named Victoria, who played small parts at the Odéon.

The Odéon, the second national theatre of France, was in a bad way after World War I. There were no funds, even for the first national theatre, the Comédie Française, which went to pot artistically and remained a travesty of its former self until reorganized about 1938. The draughts at the Odéon were traditional, and had not been over-publicized. The French clung to the superstition that air in motion, however balmy, was detrimental to the human constitution. Let a French man or woman feel what he or she called '*un courant d'air*' and something had to be done about it. A French physician in attendance at the American Hospital at Neuilly once paused in the act of delivering a child to complain about a '*courant d'air*' in the operating room, and nearly lost both mother and child while windows and screens were being adjusted to ensure him against catching cold.

The Judge's income amounted to about two hundred pounds a year. Of course, the day set aside for making calls was one of his more active days. Between times, often for a week at a time, he would merely read the *Action Française*, write a chapter of his memoirs, which no one had ever read, and drink one *apéritif* in a Royalist café in the near-by place de L'École Militaire.

It was not until 1925, the year he had his first stroke, that Judge Lenoir came, feet first, to the rue de la Huchette to live with his daughter, Anne. This made it necessary for the latter to relinquish Monsieur Panaché and deprive herself of the room rent for the first two months when the Judge was so ill that she could not tactfully suggest that he make up the financial loss to her from his personal funds.

That the judge made a fair recovery may or may not have been due to old Marie's devotion and her habit of dumping into the kitchen sink various medicines the doctor had prescribed, and substituting other things she had stewed up herself, according to formulæ long honoured in the Aube.

5

OF WINTER, AND MINDING ONE'S OWN BUSINESS

One of the toasts offered by Americans to their French friends was:
'*Vive la France: et les pommes de terre frites!*'
This phrase was spoken in jest, but had an undercurrent of seriousness, too. A French chef or housewife habitually created minor miracles with that humble Irish vegetable introduced into the country by the great gastronomist, Parmentier — the tones of golden brown, the exact degree of crispiness on the outside with the inside left mealy and delicate! It involved

the deft touch, the incomparable flair, applied to a basic supply and filling a utilitarian need with artistic overtones.

The French reply was even more sincere and heartfelt.

'Vive l'Amérique et le chauffage central!'

Winter in Paris did not occur in hotels like the Ritz, or even in the Plaza-Athénée, the Georges V, or that buyer's happy hunting-ground, the Continental. There the daily rates charged American guests would have kept a French family almost indefinitely. In order to attract such guests, hotels had to be heated with mountains of coal and cubic yards of steam. This expensive heating made protestive grunts, groans, whines, whimpers, knocks, thuds and unauthorized drips and bubbles. Its radiators were likely to be off when the indicator said 'on' and vice versa. But it warded off, in part, the dampness of the rainy season, and although the electric lights were invariably placed haphazardly, sometimes in the middle of a ceiling, they dispelled the gloom.

In New York, for instance, the best hotels are not designed to please an exotic race of millionaires from a legendary continent across the ocean, with foreign ways only partially conceivable, manners that are strange (therefore rude) and voices that rise above and cut through the din of native voices like unoiled brakes jammed on. The worst period of our depression, as bad as it seemed, would have appeared to the average European as a sort of heyday of prosperity.

The heating arrangements in the rue de la Huchette were typical of Paris and of France. To all intents and purposes there were none. One of the two hotels, the Hôtel Normandie, advertised *'Confort Moderne'*, including central heating and electric light. That was as far as comfort was supposed to go. The toilets, concealed by curved doors (concave) at the bend of each narrow stairway, were of the type known as Turkish: they consisted of an enamelled metal crater in the floor with a circular hole four inches in diameter in the not-exact centre. Two foot-rests were ineptly placed near the front corners, usually of some material that offered little friction to the damp soles of one's shoes. In the rear corner, on the left-hand side, to make it harder for right-handers to grab them, hung a rusty chain. From this the knob had disappeared, leaving a jagged edge or two on which fingers were easily cut. Somewhere on the damp, soggy wall was a nail from which had fallen an out-of-date copy of a Paris newspaper that used particularly vile ink that smeared. More than half the time there was no newspaper at all.

The trick was, after one had been black-jacked by nature into using one of these conveniences, to get oneself thoroughly buttoned up and in order, to open the curved door, stand as far outside the *cabinet* as one could, and still reach the chain, give it a quick tug and then retreat in fairly good order down the stairs. The resulting flood or angry cascade swept over the entire floor of the *cabinet*, about two inches deep, sparing only the area most in need of cleansing. The real job of cleaning was done by a one-armed *garçon* who had distinguished himself on the Somme and who joined the chestnut and oyster man in singing of the Loire on happy evenings.

In contrast with the Hôtel du Caveau, the residents and personnel of the Hôtel Normandie did not seem like one weirdly assorted family. The Gentile *patron* did not beat his wife, a sad-faced Jewish woman from the Temple quarter, but he let her do practically all the work that the one-armed *garçon*, Louis, did not volunteer to do, when his own huge share had been accomplished. There were plenty of anti-Semites in the rue de la Huchette, the most insidious of whom was The Navet and the most vociferous the pimp, Robert. Louis, the Normandie's *garçon*, was not out of this faction. He had found that Madame Sara, as he called his *patronne*, was one of the gentlest and most patient women alive, and as years rolled by and I got to know her better, I agreed with him unreservedly. There might have been some time, late at night or early in the morning, when Sara was not tending her small zinc bar, or trying to make her cash and the figures in her notebook balance, or showing a room to some prospective client, or making out a bill for some departing guest. When anyone passed her window, at No. 18, she glanced up as the shadow crossed the pane of glass. Her face spelled resignation. In the infrequent cases when the passer-by nodded, she smiled dutifully in return, then sighed and resumed her work.

Sara had been born in the rue de l'Hospitalier St. Gervais, upstairs over a kosher butcher-shop, but World War I had transplanted her to a munitions factory, where her face and hands were stained yellow (and still were not exactly pale). Her protective colouring did not prevent Guy, now her husband, from seducing her rather forcibly, on a sort of wager with fellow munitions makers, none of whom had ever slept with Jewesses and had culled some bizarre notions as to what it would be like. Sara became pregnant, and it developed that an uncle of hers had influence, through a small private bank, with the director of the munitions factory. Guy was hauled up, put on the carpet, and when he learned that the uncle was willing to make a rather generous cash settlement, considered that he had the last laugh on his fellow workers who had been teasing him about his predicament. Guy, having done the handsome thing in the Mairie of the Fourth Arrondissement, considered that his life's work was done, and so, apparently, did Sara, for she never rebuked him. In fact, when he woke as late as nine in the morning, she prepared his breakfast with care and sent Louis upstairs to his room with it, knowing that the sight of her so early in the day had the effect of irritating her taciturn husband.

The respectable apartment building at No. 32, where Madame Goujon and The Navet were the prize tenants, had no central heating whatsoever. In the winter months, one shivered as God had evidently intended. Or, in extreme cases, when company was expected, maybe on Sunday evenings or to cheer the *réveillon* on Christmas and New Year's Eve, the tenants bought kindling wood in little bundles about the size and shape of a bunch of asparagus. These neat little sticks had been dipped in resin at one end, and were bound with haywire. The main fuel was usually soft coal dust, pressed into briquettes the shape of huge black tear drops and just about as ignitable. Wood suitable for use in the small marble fireplaces was on sale, both hard and soft, by the kilogram, and was so expensive that the sight of it burning was a calamity in miniature. So pans of hot coals and ashes from the kitchen were nearly always substituted. Also cat's-fur mittens had their use for rubbing chilled members and limbs. Small charcoal braziers were much in vogue.

This brings us to André and his blue-eyed young wife with honey-coloured hair, who was named Alice and called by her huge husband from the Auvergne, *mon cœur*. This was taken up by the lower-class clients who came in to buy wine and could not afford wood and coal. It was traditional in France that a *marchand du charbon* (or coal dealer) should also handle wine in bulk. The speciality of André's coal and wood store was Mâcon, a most satisfactory wine from the Rhône valley, on the edge of the Burgundy district.

André, the coal man, whose hands, arms and face were always black, almost like those of an old-time minstrel, was the largest and best-natured man in the rue de la Huchette, and because he served also the rue de la Harpe (former residence of Madame de Staël) and several large buildings in the place St. Michel and along the boulevard, he laboured prodigiously in winter. In some of the buildings there were what the French mistook for elevators, some of which would sometimes carry passengers down as well as up and were therefore labelled '*Ascenseur et descenseur*.' But coal men, carrying on their powerful backs and shoulders one hundred kilos (more than two hundred pounds) of coal briquettes or firewood were not allowed to use the passenger elevators, reserved for middle-class tenants and white-collar visitors. Neither were they permitted to use the service elevators in the rear, if there were any, because the service elevators were even more dangerous than the others, so it was said, and were not designed for heavy loads. Besides, if the elevators should drop with a coal man and his wares, the owners of the building could be held responsible.

So André carried the fuel up the steep narrow stairways that caused normal men to puff and blow when merely carrying themselves and their clothes four or five flights. He made enough money in the winter to be able each summer to send his wife, or 'heart', back to her mamma in the country (on the coast of Brittany) with their blue-eyed boy, aged nine, and named also André, who was destined to be twenty-five years old in 1939, and therefore needed plenty of fresh sea air.

Once André broke the skin of his thumb on a rusty nail, and the thumb swelled, then the hand and arm. Doggedly, with Auvergnat stubbornness, wearing linseed poultices bound on by blue-eyed Alice, at whose frown he trembled, this mountain of a man, leaning far to one side to maintain an awkward new balance, lugged up endless flights of stairs, ears roaring and pounding, sweat streaking the coal dust on his brow, tons of coal and wood and gallons of Mâcon wine, counting hours like days and minutes like hours and stairs like stations of the cross, and tossed and muttered with fever in the night, to such a point that Alice appealed in dispair to the chestnut vendor to reason with André and persuade him to go to the city hospital, or at least call a ten-franc doctor.

Spring came early that year, and when the coal trade petered out, André, getting back the use of his hand which was stiff as a board, went fishing from the bridge near the bookstalls, and watched the barges go by, with gay-coloured cheap clothing hung to dry on fluttering clothes-lines, and geraniums in cabin windows, dogs and children on the decks. Some were loaded with cement, and André dimly imagined lugging cement-laden barges up the stone stairs of the quai and the battlements of the Conciergerie, whose history he did not know, and over the chipped gargoyles of the Tour St. Jacques, and brushed from his now non-coal-stained temple a clean yellow bee, and dip went his bright red float, but it was a false alarm. There was no tiny fish, but only gleaming wet line and dangling of hook and lead sinker. There André sighed and fished with no success but indescribable pleasure, with that nightmare of winter dissolving behind him and summer coming on, when he would miss his 'heart' and the boy, but decipher their letters, word for word, by the light of a candle in his bedroom.

What André remembers, at the time of this writing, in a convict gang somewhere in Germany, building roads, he being so well preserved that no Storm Trooper would ever believe he was nearly sixty years old — how much of his 'heart', of bees in spring or narrow stairs or septicæmia is mingled with the dim murder in his simple candid mind, I cannot say, or whom he blames, or whom he should blame, or how it will all end.

Men who carry heavy loads, and on Sunday get time and a half or double pay, remember André, and please give him a hand! It is very much your own and strictly personal affair, and if you don't lend a shoulder, no one will.

6

THE NEWS AND THE BARBER'S ITCH

The news was vital to the life of the rue de la Huchette, where each inhabitant, like other Parisians, chose the newspaper which confirmed his prejudices and fixed ideas.

The larger of the local distribution centres was the international newsstand in front of the Café de la Gare in the place St. Michel. This vendor served the tube patrons, the customers of the three large cafés, and the respectable apartment houses near the boulevard. At the eastern end, however, next door to the Hôtel du Caveau, was the tiny stationery shop of Achille and Geneviève Taitbour, a small squint-eyed couple who shuffled around wearily, maintaining a perpetual relationship in their movements, like figures on a stage. Their daily routine involved getting up at five in the morning to receive a bundle of newspapers brought by a lad on a bicycle. On the infrequent occasions when the delivery boy did not show up, or was late, they pottered and muttered collectively, like a mechanical toy running down.

Monsieur Achille, as he was called, could make a surprising number of mistakes as he ambled from door to door each morning with copies of the *Petit Journal*, *L'Intransigeant*, *Le Journal*, *Le Temps*, *Le Matin*, *L'Action Française* or *L'Œuvre*. The two daily copies of *L'Humanité* (the Socialist organ) he handled gingerly, as if he half expected them to burst into sulphurous flame.

In spite of the fact that his tiny shop was distant from No. 22, Achille delivered *L'Action Française* to The Navet and Madame Goujon each day, timing his call so that the concierge could take up The Navet's paper in time for his breakfast at 8.20 o'clock. Once Achille inadvertently left *L'Œuvre*, a mildly liberal sheet containing the mildly anti-clerical column of Georges de la Fouchardière. By an unfortunate set of coincidences, neither the concierge nor the watchful wife, Jeanne, spotted the substitution in time. As a result, The Navet outdid himself, giving the tremulous old couple such a frightful half-hour that they remembered it with a shudder for several days. The Navet wormed out of the old folks the information that two of their customers bought *L'Humanité* and ended up by jotting down a check-list covering the entire street. He liked to give the impression that he was connected with the secret police.

The three daily copies of *L'Œuvre* went to Monsieur Noël, the taxidermist, Madame Mariette, of *Le Panier Fleuri*, and Madame Absalom. The two *Humanités* were delivered to the oyster man and Madame Absalom respectively. Madame Absalom's only extravagance was to subscribe to practically all the papers and, like an editor on a holiday, gloatingly to compare their errors and discrepancies. The Navet, of course, did not bother his superiors with his private black list, but he forbade his wife, Jeanne, to buy wool or thread from '*cette vieille crotte*'. Thereafter, Jeanne, who had never cared particularly where she bought her sewing supplies, took pleasure in patronizing Madame Absalom, who never knew the cause of her slight boom in trade.

An avid reader of the papers was Henri Julliard, who in 1924 purchased the Hôtel du Caveau from the taciturn Claude and his wife, Philomèle. Monsieur Henri, as he was affectionately called, was an understanding man of well-considered judgment. That he was able to combine a sweet forgiving nature with the ability to run a restaurant and hotel is an indication of his scope and versatility. It was due also, in a measure to his short, stout wife, Marie, who made the harsh decisions about credit, etc., and carried them out during the hours when Monsieur Henri was getting his hard-earned sleep.

It came about thus that the Julliards bought the Hôtel du Caveau. The former *patron*, Claude, disappeared one morning, along with the girl, Suzanne, for whom he had bought a more adequate wardrobe. They were last heard of in Chambéry, where Claude had placed Suzanne in a local bordel while he busied himself by smuggling absinthe from Switzerland. Philomèle took up with the well-meaning Turk, who treated her with impersonal kindness.

Monsieur Henri was a Savoyard with moustaches a little like those of the *garçon*, Georges, but grey instead of red and only half as bushy. He had dark-brown eyes that twinkled, angular knees and elbows that were tireless and capable, and a wealth of human kindness. His partner, the first year, was his brother Jacques, who wanted also to be a good fellow but was too awkward and shy, and who had a slim wife, Berthe, whose character was much like Henri's. Many who knew the brothers and their wives said it was a pity that Henri had not married Berthe, and Jacques had not paired with Marie. In that, they all were very wrong. Henri and Berthe in combination would have given their shirts away. And the cranky old Marie, a caricature beside her distinguished husband, loved Henri with a devotion that was the stronger because of her apparent distaste for the rest of humankind.

It was with Monsieur Henri that I discussed the news events in those days and patiently, from his stock of sound information, he improved my grasp of French affairs. There was much to talk over during Poincaré's regime. France broke with England concerning the Ruhr, moved in, and filled the Paris papers with news about German civilian atrocities, in order to justify its own brutality. Unable to collect reparations, on account of German poverty and 'passive resistance' which became spasmodically impassive, Poincaré declared an embargo on iron and steel into Germany. The German police in the large industrial city of Essen were demobilized, and no police at all were substituted. Respectable inhabitants did not dare leave their homes after dark. Baron Krupp von Bohlen was arrested and sentenced to fifteen years by a French court martial. American troops were withdrawn from Coblenz, to the despair of the German population, and French troops took over, with resulting bloodshed and wholesale hatred.

The death of President Harding got a scant few lines on the inside pages of most of the French newspapers, and many European editors confused Calvin Coolidge, of whom they never had heard, with Professor Archibald Coolidge of Harvard, who had travelled in Europe, spoke several languages, and was hailed as a possible saviour, until the illusion was dispelled.

Each Monday morning, Poincaré's Sunday 'sermons' were printed in full, their import being always that the Treaty of Versailles must be carried out to the letter, at the point of the bayonet if necessary. None of the papers, Catholic, Communist or otherwise, informed their subscribers that the American war debt which the new President Coolidge wished to collect was not money loaned to the French for carrying on the war while it was in progress, but had to do with a payment for American supplies left in France after the Armistice by agreement with the French Government. The United States was derided as a Shylock, exacting its pound of flesh from ruined France, who could not get the reparations money due from Germany because England would not help put the screws on the Boche.

Monsieur Henri saw through a great deal of the camouflage under which various interests, each with a newspaper or two at its disposal, were operating for selfish ends. He believed that France would have to work out her own salvation by making it possible for French men and women to share more equally in the national income, and all civic rights and prerogatives.

His social outlook was broader and less provincial than that of most Frenchmen, but undoubtedly he thought of France as the important and civilized part of an otherwise exotic world. Of a planet without France he could never conceive.

While Jacques Julliard lived, Monsieur Henri took the early morning shift from six until after lunch was served, slept a while in the afternoon, supervised the dinner and about nine o'clock turned over the bar to Jacques again. But after Jacques died suddenly, leaving Berthe a slim widow who looked like an elder sister of La Gioconda in the Louvre, Henri was on duty before breakfast and again from dinner time until after two in the morning. In the mid-morning and mid-afternoon the two women, one homely as a toad in grey, the other mature and lovely in black, carried on.

Green vegetables, meat, poultry, fish, etc., were purchased by Monsieur Henri in Les Halles, or central markets, with skill and discrimination. Some of his staple groceries he bought at the local *épicerie*, or grocery, at No. 27, called 'L'Épicerie Danton' and owned by Jean-Baptiste Emile Denis Emmanuel Corre and his wife, Gabrielle, who looked like a porcelain doll. Mme. Corre had style without *chic*, and a kind of beauty without savour that remained constant throughout the years.

It must not be assumed from the name 'Danton' on M. Corre's neat grocery store that the proprietor admired the revolutionary hero who came to revolutionary grief on the guillotine. M. Corre was stolid Breton, where Catholicism was still in a mediæval stage more like that of Spain than the rest of France. He read *Le Matin* because his wife, a business woman, thought that it was better to have a newspaper less offensive to freethinkers than *L'Action Française*.

In Paris, an *épicerie* did not have green vegetables displayed near the front of the store, and a meat counter in the rear, with glass cases for fish and a large icebox filled with eggs, milk and butter. Meat was sold in the butcher's shop, which was marked with red and white awnings, striped vertically, and matching the curtains on the bloodstained cart that drove up with reeking carcasses, un-iced, four mornings a week. And the butcher's shop was not authorized to sell pork, sausage or horse meat — only beef and lamb. Not even poultry was displayed there, but could be purchased in the *laiterie*, or dairy shop. The pork store handled delicatessen, with sausages from Lyons and Genoa, *rillettes* and *patés*, head cheese, pink sausage dotted with green pistachio, the French equivalent of polony, salami and superb concoctions made of rabbit meat, truffles, etc. A golden horse above the green and white awning at No. 15, near the rue Zacharie, was the emblem of the horse-butcher, M. Monge, who sold only horse meat, and very good horse meat, too.

It was one of the many superstitions in France that horse hamburg, cooked in thin bouillon, was good for invalids and convalescents. Anyway, horse meat was cheaper than beef and was used in low-priced restaurants in dishes that were not specifically labelled 'beef' on the menu. The menu, in those places, consisted of a blackboard or a slate on which the bill of fare was chalked. For a first course, these small establishments (which always served the prescribed number of courses, an appetizer, soup, fish, meat, salad, cheese, dessert) frequently resorted to what was known as Belgian *paté*, half horse meat, half rabbit; that is so say, one horse to one rabbit.

The horse butcher in the rue de la Huchette, No. 15, also had a sideline of mending hunting horns, so that when one passed his awninged and curtained doorway with the golden horse's head aloft, one frequently heard their flourishes or plaintive moans. This same M. Monge also played an obsolete type of horn, like Hoffman's famous *chapeaux chinois*, in an amateur orchestra connected with the Society for the Preservation of Ancient Music. He was of middle height, broad and fat, with a couple of extra necks and chins, so that, when he walked or sat with the gaunt taxidermist, M. Noël, they looked like a caricature by Willette.

The butter-and-egg store was almost across the street from L'Épicerie Danton, at No. 24, and was operated by Odette, a worthy woman with a long triangular face, sloe-brown eyes, large feet and bony wrists. She wore green-black clothes and looked pious and demure. Actually she was an infidel and a socialist. Her meek little husband, Jean, had a small voice and a straggly moustache. Once he had run fifth in a six-sided contest for deputyship in his native town in the valley of the Chevreuse. The milk sold at specified hours by M. and Mme. Odette was brought in large dented cans from a wholesale dealer in Les Halles, who received the cans by cart from the country about twenty miles away. To American eyes it was bluish and watery in appearance and tasted even paler than its faint sickly odour. To regular customers in the rue, this was delivered in converted wine or brandy bottles which had been washed in non-running not-cold water and not thoroughly rinsed.

The deliverer was a milk-smelling, well-rounded girl of sixteen who wore cloth slippers and no stockings, and most certainly no brassière, and whose firm behind was playfully slapped or pinched by every *garçon* in the quarter at least twice a day. Her name was Colette and she shared with the drudge, Eugénie, at the Café St. Michel, a local reputation for chastity. Colette would discuss what was uppermost in the minds of men with frankness and disarming wit. She was saving her money, a few pennies at a time, to take a course in nursing, because nurses wore stout strong shoes she could never afford and worked in an atmosphere of chemical odours that bore no resemblance to the smell of milk or cheese. She admired the trim determined Madame Mariette, who kept order in the bordel a few doors away.

Colette was not hesitant in telling the men and boys who tweaked her buttocks as she sped up or down the dark stairs that if only she were the 'type' she would sell what the good God gave her, and not give it to the likes of them for nothing.

The eggs on sale *chez* Odette often bore unmistakable evidence of having been near hens. In some dairy shops in more expensive residential quarters, the eggs were white and were carefully scrubbed. Madame Odette and her customers believed that a dealer who scrubbed eggs must have an ulterior purpose, and that, once scrubbed, a fresh egg and a stale one looked altogether too much alike.

One had to choose between doing without milk worthy of the name and suffering the disapproval of thrifty servants and neighbours by dealing with the Necessary Luxuries Company. In rare cases the French could forgive such extravagance in the interest of an ailing male child. But for healthy adults to pay ten times the price of store milk and use it unboiled was tactless in the extreme.

In the last decade, a few of the high-priced cafés and restaurants achieved ice cream that might have passed at a country fair in the American dust belt. Up to that time, except at Rumpelmayer's and a few pastry or confectioner's shops intended for the *haut monde*, the ice cream was like snow over which something melancholy had been spilled.

The vegetable supply of the rue de la Huchette was displayed on barrows in the rue Zacharie, which had a small ancient square. Cabbages, cauliflowers, onions, carrots, parsnips, turnips, potatoes, lettuce, romaine, *chicorée* and other salad leaves, tomatoes and peppers, and other products of the soil, made up in sightliness and freshness for the unattractive meat and dairy products whose prices were unreasonably high. Vegetables were so cheap and plentiful and diverse that it was scarcely worthwhile for a vendor to cheat a customer. Nevertheless they tried it, in a half-hearted way.

The barrow men and women bought their goods at five in the morning in the marvellous central markets and sold them in the forenoon in the little side streets. Most of the green stuff had been picked the afternoon before and hauled in lorries, neatly loaded, to Les Halles, in the night.

It will be readily understood that by the time the vegetable dealers, the milk store, the beef and lamb butcher, the pork and delicatessen man, the horse butcher and a few other specialists got through, there was little left but dried beans, peas, canned goods, spices, and preserves for the grocer, M. Corre, to sell. As I mentioned, his speciality was dried beans, which he handled and arranged with loving care, squinting at them as they lay in thousands in the shallow wooden boxes. These he had labelled painstakingly, so that a yellow-eyed pea bean seldom got into the bin intended for small kidney beans, and the mauve Indian bean, shaped like an elongated pearl, was seldom found with the *flageolets* or *soissons*. It was seldom M. Corre had a call for the giant *favas*, four times the size of the large old-fashioned lima beans, but he kept them in stock just the same, and was repaid two or three times a year when some wondering Spaniard or Catalan would enter, saying he was sent by so-and-so, whom M. Corre had forgotten.

'*Mais, oui,*' M. Corre would say with pride, when asked if he had *favas*.

Of course, the Épicerie Danton had limas, normal-sized and 'baby', Canterbury, scarlet runners, pintos, tropical turtle beans, snapping beans, chick peas, shell beans marbled with onyx, blue beans veined with gold, as well as cracked corn (red, orange and white), rice from the best fields of Annam, wild rice from Valencia, whole wheat, potato flour to relieve barber's itch, and two American articles. The first American item was maize meal, which was said to be used by Americans for frying fish and veal cutlets. From time to time, M. Corre let a little of this slip over his stubby fingers which afterwards he sniffed knowingly. No one had bought maize meal for cooking during the years of his proprietorship of the Épicerie Danton, but Monsieur the Horse Butcher (M. Corre was not good at names, not even his neighbours' and clients') had once tried it for barber's itch, there being no potato meal available.

Barber's itch, quite prevalent in Paris, was not always contracted in a barber's shop, but often in a public bath or sometimes in a church. With barber's itch, one itches all over, as a sort of background or accompaniment to the principal and truly diabolical he-itch that crawls over and around one's shoulders, back and torso. It is caused by a microscopic creature which has little else to do. The poor, when afflicted with this horror, went to the hospital of St. Louis, where the skin specialists had worked out a cure. The patient stood naked in a sulphurous shower bath (containing other mysterious ingredients) and then allowed himself or herself to dry while reading back numbers of *The Catholic World* or *La Vie Parisienne*. Finally the victim put on clean and different underwear and clothes (except shoes which do not carry the bug) and went home feeling like Lazarus in reverse. The contaminated underwear and clothes should have been burned, but not one in a hundred clients of the free clinic at St. Louis could afford that, even if they itched perpetually. Therefore, the beneficent doctor in charge asked the engineers who ran the heater to rig up a steam sterilizer that would kill the bacteria of the itch without destroying the garments. As so often happened in latter-day France, one branch of science could not keep pace with another. The sterilizer, while it killed the itch bugs and whatever else moved around, shrunk cheap coats, trousers, shirts and underwear and blended the inexpensive dyes into a dismal neutral tone.

The middle-class sufferers, too proud to mingle with the lowly in the Clinique St. Louis, called on a local ten-franc doctor, who advised the patient to sprinkle potato meal on his bed sheets and roll when the itch got unbearable.

I don't know by what clairvoyance Madame Absalom found out whenever anyone on the rue de la Huchette got the barber's itch. She, herself, being in league with the evil spirits which produced such minor torments, was immune. But the moment one of her neighbours showed the first furtive symptom, Madame Absalom was alert and gleeful.

'Won't he look pretty, that one, flopping around in meal like a frog? He's got hair all over, of that I'm sure. *Pas?* It's worse for a *type* like that.' And the old girl would chuckle off and on throughout the days ensuing. One of her best 'cases' was M. Panaché, the floor-walker from the Samaritaine, who got the itch and tried to blame it on Mary the Greek. M. Panaché, after losing his room and bath with Madame Goujon at No. 32, moved into the renovated Hôtel du Caveau under Monsieur Henri Julliard's new management. The chestnut vendor loathed Panaché at sight because the floor-walker pandered to The Navet.

The chestnut vendor, to keep M. Panaché in a perpetual hell of suspicion and rage, whispered to him that Monsieur Henri, who would not have cheated a fly, rented Panaché's room now and then for twenty-minute periods to street-walkers who did not draw the colour line. Monsieur Henri merely laughed, thinking Panaché was joking, when the outraged floorwalker confronted him. But once a suspicion entered Panaché's mind, it festered there. He contrived to enter at unexpected hours, which was difficult because he didn't dare leave the store. He sniffed, got down on his knees to look at the dust, left toothpicks leaning against the door, listened behind panels before entering the hallway, tried to pump Georges, who understood what was up and was purposely non-committal. At last, Panaché got the itch and Madame Absalom, that time, didn't wait for customers to come in order to spread the good tidings. Swiftly she made the rounds, up and down the street. Whenever Panaché appeared, heads popped into windows and out of doors. Madame Absalom went to Panaché's department at the Samaritaine and cackled the story to one of the salesgirls. The latter informed the chief, who summoned Panaché to the dreaded *bureau* and, at a markedly safe distance, had a heart-to-heart talk with him. For the safety of the Samaritaine, the chief said, he should fire Panaché, but since that would ruin the latter's career, he would give him three days off, without pay, to be deducted from the annual week's vacation-without-pay, in order that he might go to the Clinique St. Louis for treatment. Panaché, before being admitted to the store again, would have to present a medical certificate that he had no tick or contagious disease of any kind whatsoever, he was told.

'Now we'll find out if that *salaud* has the pox or not — the doctor'll soak him twenty-five francs for the certificate, even if he hasn't. That's what they did to *mon ex* in Clermont when he asked for insurance, the old cod-fish,' Madame Absalom said.

Panaché proceeded, more dead than alive, from the store across the Seine to the place St. Michel, where from the bars of the Café de la Gare and the Café St. Michel sly and malicious eyes were glued on him and followed his course. Along the rue de la Huchette, shopkeepers spoke to him politely, but too politely. Ordinarily they almost ignored him. In every inflection of their voices and expression on their faces he detected an awareness and a relish of his predicament. When he entered the Hôtel du Caveau, Mary the Greek was sitting in the chair he used habitually.

Panaché did not speak directly to Mary. He grew livid, clenched his fists, wheeled and addressed Monsieur Henri: 'That foreign girl of the gutters has communicated to me a foul disease for which she, or you, will have to pay,' Panaché said.

Monsieur Henri merely smiled and stroked his grey moustaches.

'You exaggerate, monsieur,' he said, not entirely without a warning undertone. Panaché, in his rage, missed the warning.

'That girl is sitting in *my* chair,' said Panaché.

'The chairs belong to everybody,' said Monsieur Henri.

The chestnut vendor, who had overheard, stopped laughing long enough to start singing the Marseillaise.

Mary, only half understanding that the row was in some way connected with her, rose and turned her expressive eyes on Monsieur Henri.

'Does *Monsieur* want this chair?' she asked, and accommodatingly extended it towards M. Panaché.

Georges the *garçon* stepped in with a towel and playfully dusted off the chair seat, pretending to catch a few small hopping things with his free hand. Madame Marie's small terrier called 'Maggie' started scratching herself furiously, rolling over and biting her side. That set off Panaché, whose white-hot rage had stirred up the itch bugs. Buffeted by roars and squeals of tearful laughter, Panaché retreated up the stairs and that night appeared, naked, in the disconsolate line of patients in the Clinique St. Louis. Twelve hours later he was pronounced cured, but when he asked for a certificate to that effect, the overworked clerks of the hospital were annoyed. It had taken less than two hours for Panaché to become the most unpopular patient of the year. He got as far as the third assistant to the head doctor before he was ordered to leave the premises.

The doorman at the Samaritaine was equally adamant. He had had instructions not to admit Panaché without a clean bill of health. No certificate, no admittance. Panaché demanded to see his chief.

'You'll have to call at his home. No doubt he has one,' the doorman said.

Late that evening, when there was no one else at the bar, Panaché told his troubles to The Navet, who had been attending a Rightist meeting and had stopped for a nightcap on his way home, hoping at last to surprise Jeanne with a lover. He had cunningly told Jeanne that he would not be home that night at all. The Navet got so little of the respect he craved, in the rue de la Huchette, that he liked it from the abject Panaché. So he told Panaché that he would get the necessary certificate from one of the prefectorial doctors (strictly in confidence, of course), not for the full price of insurance certificates, namely twenty-five francs, but for only twenty francs. Panaché wrote out his full name, age, and whatever else The Navet wanted to know, and the next day The Navet brought back, very secretly, the certificate. It set forth that Gaston Panaché (whom the doctor had never seen) was free from contagious or infectious disease and in good physical condition.

'I might have known,' said Madame Absalom, when she learned that Panaché was back at work. 'He's too mean to get the clap. Or, more likely, the certificate was *truqué* (faked).'

7
OF COMMUNITY ENTERTAINMENT

The apartment on the fourth floor of No. 32, above that of Madame Goujon, was rented by a jolly *bon vivant* of uncertain age named Monsieur de Malancourt, whose frequent arrivals at all hours by taxicab were the more conspicuous after Judge Lenoir had taken to his bed. Monsieur de Malancourt had a more elaborate domicile in one of the expensive Right Bank hotels, a château with moat in the Chevreuse, and was the nominal head of a private bank from which he drew as much money as he could spend and for which he gave no accounting. He was thought by his friends and employees to be eccentric because he had no sense of responsibility, no fear of the hereafter, no alarm about the state of France, and enjoyed himself hugely from day to day, having the rarest of blessings among Frenchmen: a robust constitution.

Monsieur de Malancourt might never have seen the rue de la Huchette, which would have been too bad for it and for him, had he not been persuaded by an American millionaire who gave out trophies for automobile races to drop in at a fashion show at Maggy Rouff's one afternoon. As the two gay old boys stepped into the salon, a Polish model, Nadia Visnovska, was standing, hands on hips, in front of a triple mirror, naked as a goddess and many times as beautiful. She had ivory skin and blue-black hair, a body that could be young and strong without muscles or bulges, tapering hands and feet and a rich mezzo voice that made her Polish-French electric.

'The chief cutter tells me she's a virgin,' the American philanthropist whispered to Monsieur de Malancourt.

From that time onward de Malancourt had something to occupy his imaginative mind. He followed Nadia, discreetly, to the rue de la Huchette, where she turned in at No. 32. It would have been too crude to bribe the concierge, and he did not want to risk embarrassing the girl, and perhaps be the cause of having her deported, by inquiring from the Ministry of Justice about the details of her domicile. So he visited a flower shop in the place Vendôme, where for years he had been a generous customer, and arranged for a boy to deliver, just before Nadia was due to reach No. 32 each evening, not a vulgar display of flowers, but carefully chosen small and exquisite bouquets, with pale forget-me-nots, rosebuds or lilies-of-the-valley.

Nadia, in the course of her work, had been approached by all kinds of males, from American buyers to Lesbian actresses. Being fastidious and independent, and as non-mercenary as only a Slave can be, she had held herself aloof to such a point that the virginity legend which had reached the ears of de Malancourt was fairly current in the dress-making trade. She was naturally affectionate and companionable and was touched by the lavish delicacy of Monsieur de Malancourt's approach. When she saw him, after the most complicated arrangements for a rendezvous at La Poire Blanche, a tea-room in the boulevard St. Germain, she liked him wholeheartedly and thoroughly. She had loved once or twice, with all her heart and Slavic passion, but in each instance the recipient of this amorous flood had been a poor man, and proud, and both parties had known that the affair must eventually come to an end. Monsieur de Malancourt was not only handsome, vigorous, tender, cultured and essentially fine, but apparently had all the money in the world. Nevertheless, Nadia insisted on continuing her work, which in turn inflamed the old roué's respect and tormented him with jealous thoughts of her peeling off her clothes in the presence of all and sundry in the couturier's establishment.

To make things more cosy, de Malancourt rented the apartment below Nadia's attic room and fitted it up for her in a style that staggered the concierge.

So imagine the excitement in the rue de la Huchette the afternoon its residents saw in all the newspapers the genial smiling countenance of their neighbour, Monsieur de Malancourt. The accompanying story dealt with the kind of racy occurrence that periodically stirred Paris and awakened in its population a feeling of kinship and unity, transcending class lines.

The bare facts were these: Monsieur de Malancourt, who disliked to do anything banal, had — in this instance we cannot say 'sat' for a photographer, because de Malancourt had instructed the astonished camera artist to take an art photo of his plump and symmetrical backsides, without drapery. After selecting the best from a dozen proofs or so, de Malancourt had had expensive prints made and mounted, had autographed them and sent them by mail and messenger to his intimate friends and some other persons to whom he wished to convey his regards in a subtle and accurate manner. One pompous gentleman of the latter group, who fancied himself an art expert, received his copy enclosed with an oil painting signed Watteau which he had tried to sell to Monsieur de Malancourt. Incidentally, false Watteaux were plentiful in Europe at that time, to such an extent that even the Louvre, manned by France's most renowned experts, had bought two fakes allegedly from the brush of that master.

Monsieur Latour Latour, the art expert who received Monsieur de Malancourt's token, interpreted it as an implication that the returned Watteau was not genuine, and was highly insulted. His dignity and reputation had suffered irreparable damage, M. Latour Latour contended. Had he been ten years younger, he would have challenged de Malancourt to a duel in the Bois at dawn. As it was, he sent by Negro messenger a letter to de Malancourt, demanding an apology. By some chance, the letter got into the hands of a gossip writer for *Figaro*, and all Paris started chuckling behind Latour Latour's learned back.

There was a lively exchange of correspondence before the story appeared in the popular press, but when Latour Latour entered suit for libel against de Malancourt, the affair became public property. That is, it was considered public property elsewhere than in the rue de la Huchette. There it was local and private property, giving each inhabitant a sense of distinction and participation in the life of the *haut monde*. When Mademoiselle Nadia (no one ever attempted her Polish last name) appeared on the pavement, way was made for her as if she were a queen. The arrival of Monsieur de Malancourt's taxi, after he had attended a session of the trial (which lasted ten days, to the increasing delight of judges, lawyers, journalists, spectators and the Parisians of all walks of life), was watched from doorways and windows with awe and approbation. Monsieur de Malancourt, enjoying the approval of his neighbours, bowed, smiled and lifted his hat courteously when he descended from the cab. His words and phrases, gems of wit and humour, were on everyone's lips, and Nadia's employer, the already famous *couturier*, did such an estate-agent's business that he (don't be deceived by the 'Maggy') turned clients away daily, considering that more dignified for a house of his reputation than building an annex or hiring a hall.

Monsieur de Malancourt, disdaining the aid of counsel, defended himself, and his defence was worthy of the grand French tradition, exemplified by Rabelais and Voltaire. A picture of one's backside, he argued, was more intimate and personal than a photograph of one's face. To sent it to a friend or acquaintance, therefore, was not an insult, but a mark of affection and esteem. Furthermore, it was a token more permanent and honest than the conventional photograph, since one's bottom changes less rapidly and radically than one's face, the latter being exposed to wind and weather as well as the ravages of time. The human face, Monsieur de Malancourt remarked, is like that of a fish and has been much overrated as an art object, being painted by artists from time immemorial principally out of regard to the model's convenience when posing for hours at a time. No such consideration was necessary, he pointed out, now that the camera could be adjusted quickly and even the longest exposures required only a few seconds.

Before the first day of the trial was over, the jury could no longer keep up a pretence of neutrality. Monsieur Latour Latour's rage was more comical the higher it mounted. He had with him a battery of the stuffiest lawyers in the Paris bar, and that is saying a lot. The judge and his two assistants entered into the spirit of the thing and permitted a wide range of discussion. Always the gentleman, de Malancourt publicly offered *not* to raise the question of the genuineness of the Watteau he had failed to purchase. Latour Latour, vibrant with outraged dignity, demanded that the painting be brought into court and expertized. It was, and three out of the five experts agreed that it was not by Watteau. It developed that Latour Latour had exchanged it with another expert for a Corot, which he insisted be returned to him. Four out of five experts declared the Corot was a forgery, too.

Each succeeding triumph scored by de Malancourt was enjoyed in the rue de la Huchette as its very own. Madame Absalom hobbled from shop to shop with glee. Monsieur Noël, the taxidermist, and his stout pal, the horse butcher and horn player, talked art with Monsieur Henri at the Caveau bar until far into the night, with Mary the Greek, Madame Berthelot, Pierre Vautier, the cook, Thérèse and Georges, the *Garçon*, hanging on their words and drinking happily the while. The Navet insisted that he had known about the fake Watteau bought by the Louvre before the deal was made and would have warned the director had the latter not in his youth been a Dreyfus supporter and therefore a Jew-lover and a traitor.

The chestnut vendor suggested that Monsieur Panaché follow the example of de Malancourt, and even carry it further than mere photography. He recommended, in fact, that the floor-walker cut a hole in the seat of his pants and make a practice of walking on his hands, in order to improve his appearance and present a more amiable exterior.

In times of excitement and general good feeling in our little street, human fellowship and tolerance blossomed and penetrated dim corners with a wholesome fragrance. A drink with a friend became a symbol reaching back into time and forward into the future. A nod or conventional greeting was accompanied by a warmer smile. Enmities, if not forgotten, were temporarily laid aside. One of the most important elements in national or community life is public entertainment, not the formal kind that is presented, like canned food, for sale at a price, but piquant incidents the people make their own and in which they have the illusion, at least, of being participants.

In the rue de la Huchette, while the *procès de Malancourt* was under way, Madame Mariette of *Le Panier Fleuri* used to leave her joint in charge of the big good-natured, middle-aged 'girl' named Armandine and steal a half-hour just after midnight in our little bar, listening to the talk, joining in half-wistfully at times, and always with ready wit. Mariette was beloved in all the quarter, and a few years before had caused almost as much of a stir in Paris as had Monsieur de Malancourt's trial. She was short and *petite*, but womanly and not doll-like. She was neatly shaped, with rosy cheeks and frank grey-blue eyes with lashes not too long or too short. Her voice was rich in timbre and well modulated, her wrists and ankles small but not fragile. In repose her face was sad but instantly grew animated and responsive when one spoke to her.

Madame Mariette had saved her money quite a few years in order to attract a respectable and worthy husband, who would share her dream of a home in the country with plants and domestic animals, after her years in the bordel were over. She had never worked as a prostitute in the brothels she had directed; the clients called her 'Madame' and respected her person as well as her acumen. So when the time came for Mariette to marry the railroad conductor of her choice, there was a difference of opinion among the priests of St. Séverin as to whether, technically, she could be married in white, the emblem of purity. Mariette, when she heard about this, solved the problem herself. She had a bridal gown made by one of the best *couturiers* in Paris and instructed him to use every colour of the spectrum. The resulting creation, for use only in the church, became fasionable for a time. Mariette also had a white bridal gown made for the wedding breakfast in the upstairs salon of the Café St. Michel. As soon as the church ceremony was over, she changed from the rainbow creation into the white one and all the neighbours attended the breakfast and drank champagne, including Father Panarioux and Father Desmonde, who feasted at a special table set for them in a little alcove.

8
THE MAIDEN'S PRAYER

Not long after I arrived in the rue de la Huchette the newspapers announced the deaths of several important foreign leaders, all of whose passing aroused more comment, pro and con, than did that of our handsome Harding. The first of these was Lenin, known to nobody on our street as Vladimir Ilyich, except a couple of exiled Serbian students (male and female) who shared a room at the Hôtel du Caveau. The female, Milka (or Amélie to the French) was grief-stricken and disturbed and tried to explain in halting French what the world had lost. Being overheard by Panaché, who told The Navet, she was visited by the police the next day, held forty-eight hours for questioning, and narrowly escaped being shipped back to Yugoslavia for torture and execution.

Notwithstanding that Lenin's political and social significance was little understood in the rue de la Huchette, nearly everyone was fascinated by the tales of his embalming. Tut-Ankh-Amen was excavated and publicized about the same time, and most Parisians thought Vladimir Ilyich would be trimmed up like Tut and were disappointed when news pictures showed him wearing a collar and tie. The treatment of bodies after death was a lively subject in Paris whenever it arose. When the beloved American Ambassador Herrick was embalmed by Bernard Lane, the American mortician and publicity hound, one of the French dailies carried a two-column interview setting forth in detail how Herrick's inner organs were removed and pickled.

The next celebrity on Charon's list that year was Hugo Stinnes, the German multi-millionaire who made his fortune while others in Germany were starving in the streets. Madame Absalom was in favour of sending a French expeditionary force into Germany to appropriate Stinnes' money, and when informed by Monsieur Henri that the said money was scattered all over the world in banks much safer than those of Germany, the old woman accepted the story as another proof of Germany perfidy. The Navet, right for once, insisted that a substantial chunk of the Stinnes loot was in Paris, and would be held there safely for the heirs. The big shots stuck together, he contended, regardless of frontiers.

No one in the street was aware that an Austrian paper-hanger named Schickelgruber, and calling himself Hitler, had been arrested in Munich and thrown into jail. The death of Eleanora Dusé completely overshadowed that little item.

The Matteotti murder had little impact in the rue de la Huchette, there being few Italians in the quarter. Italians and Serbs do not mix, and when they do, the Italian has about as much chance as the rabbit matched against a horse in a Belgian paté.

Woodrow Wilson's death was associated in the minds of the news-conscious group in the rue de la Huchette with what seemed to Monsieur Henri a scrambled policy announced by the new President Coolidge, to the effect that war debts should be collected from France, loans made to Germany, that the United States would never join the League of Nations, which seemed to exist in a half-hearted way, but would support a non-existent or renovated 'world court' in some other city than Geneva. Meanwhile, Vice-President Dawes, according to the Paris press, was formulating a plan whereby France was to get less and less and Germany was to be financed and rehabilitated.

The Navet insisted that Harding's death had been a carefully staged plot so that Dawes and Coolidge might play German's game.

I noticed that in the Caveau bar, where nightly men and women gathered for conversation, the few foreigners like myself who had seen other countries said almost nothing, being so badly handicapped in a free-for-all talk by a few inelastic facts that it would have seemed almost bad taste to inject them into the discussion. My French friends preferred to hear about strange things like grapefruit and tinted toilet paper. These items did nothing to improve the standing of an American as an informant on more serious subjects.

It was no coincidence that the French writer who gave the most enchanting picture of distant Africa had never been nearer that continent than St. Cloud. Parisians loved to dream of distant lands but seldom visited them. M. Corre, the grocer, whose practicality was represented by his assortment of dried beans, had a romantic side to his nature. He would stand by the hour, hands behind his back, head tilted upward, sighing and looking longingly at his spices. Cinnamon would start him dreaming, so would the miracle of ginger, and as for nutmeg . . .

The day I told him that in a small American *département* wooden nutmegs had been manufactured and sold, the pained astonishment of M. Corre was impressive to behold. His onion eyes bulged behind his thick-lensed glasses. He puffed and blew. His chubby hands twitched spasmodically.

'*Sans blague!*' was all he could manage in the way of comment, but after I left the shop, according to Gabrielle, his porcelain madame, he minutely examined every nutmeg in his stock, scratching each one with a pocket knife and dropping it on the hard-wood counter at the cash-desk, in the hope of finding a wooden or 'American' specimen for a souvenir.

The Épicerie Danton carried cassia, cloves, caraway and coriander; mace, cumin, anise, capers; cardamom, chervil, basil, tarragon, savoy, curcuma, fennel and other treasures of Arabia, but on days his business took him near the Madeleine, M. Corre would treat himself to an hour or two with the peerless importers of that quarter. There he would stare and sigh at bean sprouts from China, canned tamales from Mexico, fabulous products in cardboard boxes from America, labelled 'Quaker Oats' and in extreme cases something allegedly shot from guns. M. Corre had come to Paris, not in *sabots* but the same kind of shoes with elastic sides he wore until the end, from a small Breton village called Erqy, which has a tiny beach and crayfish (Zola's liquid fire) and a kind of serpent called 'vipers' no living man had seen but in which all inhabitants believed. He had always wanted to go to Versailles. After thirty-two years of waiting in Paris for the opportunity, he got there thirty minutes before German Panzers caught up with the wagon he had hired.

This fell far short of requiting him for the loss of his son, his stock, his business, his country and the only kind of medicine that would keep his diabetes in control and which was needed in Berlin.

M. and Madame Corre had had other plans for their son, who was one of the few French boys who stood his ground when deserted by his officers near Sedan. They had sent him to Berlin to learn German, to London to learn English and to Rome to learn Italian, hoping that he would not have to sell only beans, canned goods and spices, but would branch out into the importing trade and carry, in a larger store in some other quarter, Chinese bean sprouts, American breakfast foods and a yellow substance like snuff used by Hindus in making curry. The son had married a tall quiet Catholic country girl of good family from somewhere outside Dijon, who is quietly starving and sitting very still in a chair, alone in a room with lace on the cushions, lace antimacassars on the chairs and a hand-painted green velvet cover on the top of an upright piano she now never plays. This young woman, dutiful and obedient from birth, is trying to dull the pangs of hunger and bereavement with a bewildered hope that she has not been misled about the future life, which cannot be far away, and that somewhere beyond the clouds one can hear Gottschalk's 'Last Hope' or the 'Liebestraum' or angels singing *Madame Butterfly* and that her resurrected young husband will not be a *gueule cassée* throughout Eternity.

9

TO THE MEMORY OF A SECONDHAND ACCORDION

One summer in the late 'twenties, when it rained practically every day and the city drooped and dripped under clouds that leaked like French plumbing, a witty street ballad appeared, entitled *'Il n'y a plus de saisons!'* That was true in certain years, but usually the Paris seasons were defined in traditional ways that transcended accidents of weather.

In Spring one would be aware of a fragrance or balm in the air, sharpened by petrol fumes. Suddenly, on the way to lunch, one would see a small irresponsible dog rolling over in a patch of sunshine. New leaves would appear on the plane trees and horse-chestnuts. Turtles, pigeons, hens, canaries and love birds would be placed on the pavements in front of pet shops and feed stores. The first *bateau mouche* (small passenger steamer) would pass under a bridge with a load of shivering passengers. Café terraces would spread in area and show sudden animation. Pale children would emerge from winter hiding with nurses in regional costumes or flat-faced women in pyjamas from Annam. There would be a few seeks' respite before tourists from the United States would show up, and take possession of their smug regions on the Right Bank, centring about the American Express, the Café de la Paix, and the de-luxe shops in the place Vendôme. In the rue de la Huchette there were no trees nor tourists, but just across the rue des Deux Ponts, and clearly visible from the top windows of the Hôtel du Caveau, lay the quiet walled garden of St. Julien le Pauvre — grass and trees, old stone benches and a few, not many, neighbours who liked the quiet shelter. Earlier each day the morning sun would stream through the little street, making dancing miracles of dust batted from rugs held out of the windows. For the beef and lamb butcher, M. Monge, the radical socialist horse butcher, Madame Abaslom and others, the coming of spring would mean a slump in trade, therefore less confinement. The barrow men and women, the milk dealer and the café keepers would get ready for a boom, as did the pimp, Robert, Madame Mariette of *Le Panier Fleuri*, and Madame Lanier in the *clandestin* and laundry.

France at that time was increasingly athletics-conscious. One heard the word 'sport' even in byways like the rue de la Huchette, where the son of M. Corre set out now and then for a game of soccer and the son of M. Henri Julliard (who had been established in a struggling typewriter repair shop) put on a *costume de tennis* and batted soiled balls to his fiancée, who squealed happily and showed more good will than co-ordination. Paris was host to the Olympic Games in 1924 and while German athletes were barred, which was just as well since they were underfed to such a degree as to make competition unsportsmanlike, Austrian and Hungarian athletes were welcomed with self-conscious hospitality.

In sport as in music, individual Frenchmen were likely to be brilliant if undependable performers. Their team work left something to be desired. They were in continual subconscious rebellion against regimentation and, because of this, they fell steadily behind the progress of an age in which concerted effort and mass production were essentials. They did not bet as heavily on horses as the English do, but they took the defeat of their prize horse, Épinard, very much to heart when he was beaten by Wise Counsellor at Belmont Park. Monsieur Henri, of course, could never have been a bad loser, but he thought Épinard must have been the faster horse and had been thrown off form by the long sea voyage. He himself, mackerel fishing off Erqy with M. Corre one holiday week-end, had had a taste of seasickness which made him understand with a shudder what Épinard had to endure for eight days at sea.

The summer in Paris, in quarters like that of St. Michel, where tourists never swarmed, was marked by closed shutters. Most shops were sealed during August. The poorest tradesmen stopped making or losing money, as the case might be, one month out of twelve and went to the country. Sometimes the 'country' was only a half-hour away; again it might be all the way across France. Many small restaurants also closed, and in the rue de la Huchette the two hotels were minus half their guests, the lupanar was understaffed, the morning mass at St. Séverin was sparsely attended, the neighbourhood street walkers were more conspicuous in the evening hours, the laundry was closed, the sound of The Navet's voice and the ring of his pompous footsteps were absent. The taxidermist was in Normandy, the butcher in the Alpes-Maritimes, the beans and spices at Corre's grocery lay dormant in the boxes and on the shelves, the students were away, also most of the professors.

On account of her disabled father, Madame Goujon could not leave her apartment, and little Hyacinthe, who disliked the country because the trees and flowers seemed to distract attention from her dainty costume and precocious remarks, was taken frequently by Madame Absalom, and, after I had gained her mother's confidence, by me, to the children's theatre in the Luxembourg Gardens where La Absalom and I were obliged to sit round the rim of the auditorium so as not to obstruct the view of the small spectators. The children, as a whole, entered into the spirit of the Punch and Judy shows. The puppets behaved as the kids longed to do, being tough, uninhibited, unbreakable and subject only to their own perverse law. The most demure and quiet little boys and girls were enthusiastic when retribution caught up with the villain. But it was Madame Absalom who most enjoyed the show. She whooped and protested shouting warnings and advice when the hero was in danger, and pounded her bony knees, her eyes gleaming, when the cop's resounding stick was whacking Punch's head. Punch, I am sure, she always identified with her 'ex' in Clermont. Little Hyacinthe did not like the show at all. It was not romantic. But the day I took her to a matinée in a variety theatre and Loie Fuller's girls performed their scarf dance, I began to love Hyancinthe whole-heartedly, forgiving freely her snobbishness, her relentless practicality, her selfish outlook on the social world. Her intensity was touching and tremulous. Then and there she resolved to be an actress.

Autumn was signalized by the re-opening of the schools with wan tired children in drab smocks trooping in early and returning late. The French school system imparted considerable standard knowledge to its victims, but it cast a pall over childhood and exacted from frail bodies as much as it placed in submissive or rebellious minds. Discipline was strict, and imposed for the convenience of underpaid teachers without reference to the needs of the child. In the Catholic schools scholarship was subordinated to memorization of the Catechism without understanding it, and if the kids undressed in pitch dark, the duty of the sisters was done.

In the Luxembourg, a short walk from our dingy street, the head gardener made a speciality of late-flowering flowers. The gardens were riotous with rich autumn colours, shrubs with garnet leaves, dahlias, asters, chrysanthemums, exotic foliage and flowers in neat designs, others less symmetrical, in scarlet and vermilion, plum-colour and damask-purple, mahogany, ebony, amethyst and ochre, resplendent in the cooling sun, resistant to the deepening chill of night.

Along the Seine, not far from the Louvre, a colony of giant sagacious crows returned from the suburban grain fields to their town quarters in the ancient trees along the quai. These crows had learned that living in Paris, near the central markets where, at dawn each day, scraps of nearly everything a crow likes and needs were easily obtainable, was easier than rustling in the country, exposed to the farmers' shotguns.

One of the features of a Paris winter was the annual rise of the Seine. This provided a flood of conversation whenever talk lagged anywhere, any time, between December and April.

Much has been written about the dangers of the Arctic cold and the heat of Calcutta, but I have known many husky adventurers who could tolerate any climate without weakening except that of Paris, France. The thermometer seldom fell below freezing-point; there was almost never any snow. Some days it failed to rain, and occasionally the sun came through the clouds. Nevertheless, it was impossible to get warm and to keep warm and even harder to get dry. Dampness was everywhere. Walls were mouldy, pavements soggy, clothing humid. Worse than that, everyone had colds, ranging from simple ones through laryngitis and bronchitis to pneumonia. I could walk with my eyes shut through the rue de la Huchette and identify each cough as I passed.

That these respiratory afflictions were communicable was a modern fact that neither the Church, State nor the population of Paris was willing to take into account. Cooks and waitresses sneezed, snuffled and coughed without stint. So did assistants in shops. Business was complicated by fevers, flushed cheeks, running noses, watery red-rimmed eyes, voices that squeaked and scraped, inflamed tonsils, choked tubes and raw-papered lungs.

When the Seine was high, the cellars in the rue de la Huchette would be flooded, and this tendency of water to seek its level always caught the inhabitants unaware, ruined some vegetables and, occasionally, a few bottles of wine. The newspapers would recount each day how a certain number of families down river had been driven from their homes, and would print a few pictures of them being rescued in rowboats very clumsily manned.

One morning before dawn, when I was crossing the place Notre Dame on my way to the Hôtel du Caveau, I heard angry voices over the parapet and, looking down, I saw a disgruntled cop holding one end of a rope and leaning over the dark angry water. I descended the stone stairs, glanced over the edge and saw that on the other end of the rope was a tramp who had either fallen in, had been pushed or had tried to commit suicide. He invoked some kind of constitutional right not to tell us which. During ten minutes the bum and the cop abused each other. Then I saw dimly a boatman struggling with a top-heavy dory.

'What kind of service is this?' the bum asked. 'When a citizen is in the river, how long does it take to bring up a boat?'

'If you don't shut up, I'll let you drown,' shouted the cop.

'That's the way you *flics* do your duty! Who pays you? The citizens. If you can't hold a rope, while this other lout is learning to row, let go! I didn't ask you to throw it to me anyway!'

River traffic had to stop when the waters of the Seine reached the knees of a granite Zouave on the abutment of the pont d'Alma. All tugs had smokestacks that could be tilted flat when the craft passed under a bridge, but after the flood had reached a certain height, recorded faithfully by the stone Zouave, there was a danger that the entire superstructure might be swept away. During this short season when the flow of goods to Le Havre had to be suspended, a marvellous community came into being around the place de la Bastille. Barges by the dozen were tied up there, side by side, so closely that one could hop from one deck to another. The hardy river men, women, children and dogs renewed acquaintance, rested, drank, danced and frolicked and enjoyed their only respite from months of strenuous toil.

Monsieur Léonard, the mild little Belgian who played the accordion in the Bal St. Séverin and occupied the attic room next to mine on the sixth floor of the hotel, knew many of the barge people, especially his own countrymen, and used to stroll over to the Bastille on winter afternoons carrying his accordion. Now and then he took me with him, and the memory of some of those afternoons still causes coloured shirts to flutter beneath my eyelids, and petticoats and cabin geraniums and kids and terriers and snatches of Javas, one-steps and foxes, legs in cotton stockings, strong wine drunk from mugs and jugs, cheese and fresh bread and all the bits and trifles now swept into the ash heap of history and progress.

It was on a narrow side street on the way to the Bastille quarter that I found the laundry for men with only one shirt.

One winter week-end, Georges, the *garçon*, always depressed by stretches of bad weather, got boiled on Saturday night, and in attempting to cut his throat spilled blood all over my laundry, which was in his room at the time. I found myself with no clean linen and confided my predicament to Monsieur Léonard, the accordion player, who said it would be all right to start out with a soiled shirt — that we would have it washed and ironed on the way. Monsieur Léonard then led me to the *Blanchisserie des Imprévoyants* (Laundry for the Non-foresighted), where conversing or reading, naked from the waist up, on crude benches placed around the wall, about a dozen men were waiting unhurriedly. They ranged in ages from twenty-two or -three to sixty. Some looked wasted, a few depraved, others thoughtful and resentful, one or two philosophic. A cadaverous hairy man was drawing a caricature of another with carpenter's chalk on the wall. A small old man with stained silver beard was murmuring over a volume of Verlaine. Four tramps were playing *belotte* with greasy cards.

As Léonard and I entered, a villainous-looking man in a striped sweater and rakish cap appeared from the steaming kitchen with an immaculate white shirt, washed, starched and ironed, which he handed to the old amateur of Verlaine. The latter wiped a tear from his eye, which glittered like the Ancient Mariner's, accepted the clean shirt and, before he put it on, took four sous from a coin belt of onion skin. These he handed over to the sweater and cap, who started to put them in his pocket, then glanced at the doorway in which was standing a huge belligerent woman. Smiling at the woman the sweater and cap changed his mind. He dropped the coins one by one into the cash box.

The other occupants of the room had gathered around Monsieur Léonard and his accordion. Their desire for music was too insistent to be denied; so Léonard unslung his instrument and played one after another the pieces of his repertoire. He could play a fair accordion part in a small orchestra from a marked piano score, but in a long life of accordion playing he had learned only three pieces by ear.

One of the most depraved of the tramps, with deep dirty lines in his face, a hoarse whisky bass for a voice, scars on his arms and torso, and one ear chewed off, grabbed the suds-slippery madame, who yielded, although she could have tossed her partner all the way across the room. A cop looked in, hesitated, then grinned. He had come to check the 'papers' of the vagrants. Seeing that everyone was enjoying himself, the cop contented himself with asking me for my credentials. I showed him my American passport and he went his way. I went out for liquor and brought back a bottle of cognac and a gallon of red wine.

At seven o'clock that evening, four of the tramps were still standing. The big washerwoman had dragged her tramp somewhere out of sight but not completely out of hearing. So I strolled into the back rooms where the tubs were, washed my own shirt, and after hanging it on a line near the back of the stove to dry, decided to take a nap. I awoke, cold and stiff, to find that it was four o'clock in the morning and that the fire had gone out. The prudent sweater and cap was fast asleep on a bench in the front room. Léonard had tottered as far as a barge and had been laid away by some Belgians he knew, who had taken care not to puncture his accordion.

I became dissatisfied with the well-meant efforts of Monsieur Léonard on the accordion and resolved to take up the instrument myself. So I bought one in the place Clichy.

After struggling with it awhile, to the mild amusement of Georges, the *garçon*, I went back to the place Clichy to enquire about a teacher. I had got farther in a few days than Monsieur Léonard had in several years, but I wanted to play well. To my astonishment, I was given an address in the rue Zacharie, not two hundred yards from my hotel.

The teacher turned out to be a large, dignified, gruff Frenchman, who had a Marseilles accent on which he could have hung his bowler hat. His first admonition was that I should buy a leather apron, like those the blacksmiths wear, to protect my trousers legs. Then he played me an exercise which I repeated by ear at once. He looked annoyed.

'You have little patience,' he said reproachfully, and dug up another and more difficult exercise. By that time I realized that I was dealing with a sensitive man. So I refrained from playing the second exercise too easily and said I would practise it faithfully at home.

The fact of the matter is that Monsieur Trexel taught me little that I wanted to know about the accordion. He had other pupils who were very poor and pathetically anxious to be able to hold down jobs in dance halls, and his instruction tended to make one into a shrill component of a small dance combination. However, there was something big and expansive and musician-like about M. Trexel that inspired me to practise hard and learn for myself. Curious to find out what could be done with two accordions, I arranged the slow movement of the Beethoven violin and piano sonata in E-flat, took him the manuscript, and we played it side by side. Monsieur Trexel was impressed and amazed. He had never heard accordions sound like that before. We played the piece again and again, but when at the end of the lesson I tried to pay him the customary ten francs he looked at me with injured dignity.

We hit on a compromise, finally, which worked well for everyone except my news editor. Twice weekly I went to M. Trexel for a lesson. We played standard and classical selections together. Then we went down to the subcellar of the Hôtel du Caveau, and I spent my ten francs on refreshments. In those days one could get a powerful lot of refreshments for ten francs. At 7.45 he staggered eastward toward the Panthéon and I wandered off westward to the rue Lafayette to the *Chicago Tribune* office where another drunken subeditor, more or less, made no difference at all.

10

OF HIGH AND LOW ART, AND INFLATION

As the Seine went up that year (1925) the franc went down. The middle-class French, accustomed from birth to count the sous, were pained and confused by the amended price tickets. The government machinery creaked and fell farther behind. Farmers refused to produce. Industrial workers grew sullen and put fear into the hearts of their employers, who grudgingly handed out increases of pay that did not correspond to the mounting cost of living. The poor listened more readily to the Marxists; the rich were disquieted by the rumblings of the poor. The French Deputies, reflecting the naïveté of the French voter, assumed that the way to cure inflation was to change prime ministers.

Poincaré gave way to Herriot. Herriot was succeeded by Aristide Briand, an orator with a face that looked like a composite of all the earnest animals in the zoo. His voice ranged from a guttural growl to a baritone legato. For sound effects and pure sob-stuff in the Chamber, no French politician had the edge on Aristide Briand, who was sincerely devoted to the idea that peace was a wonderful thing.

Certain news items of that period were indeed, revealing, although given scant attention at that time. Two clerks of the Bank of France, during Herriot's incumbency, were arrested, tried and jailed for having advised some farmers to sell their holdings in French Government bonds and invest their money elsewhere. This pair of martyrs to the truth did not suffer in vain. Their message was not lost on the men and women of the rue de la Huchette. Madame Corre, who made the important decisions after her plodding husband had spent hours on the ledger, sold the family debentures and put the funds into Dutch securities. The beef-and-lamb butcher sold his bonds (amounting to £65) and stuffed the francs into a pewter pitcher on the mantel-piece, sweating daily when he read about their shrinkage in purchasing power. Monsieur Henri applied every franc he could get to paying off his indebtedness on the Hôtel du Caveau. For this purpose 'inflated' francs were just as good as any. Madame Absalom tried to put the screws on her 'ex' to make him jack up the small sum he had agreed, in writing, to pay her monthly, and her failure to get results kept her hopping like a fish in a pan.

The Navet, fatuously pleased with himself because he was making paper profits by speculating secretly on the exchange, passed on the tip now and then to Monsieur Panaché. Madame Mariette, of *Le Panier Fleuri*, bought Swiss francs on the Q.T. Madame Sara, of the Hôtel Normandie, made pilgrimages weekly to the Ghetto and handed her receipts to her old uncle, who was spurred to shrewder activities by anxiety. The milk shop, run by Odette and the mild little Jean, raised prices as fast as the authorities would permit. In their stationery shop, the aged Taitbouts dozed more fitfully.

The French army completed a sloppy evacuation of the Ruhr and Franco-German negotiations about trade and customs receipts floundered and finally bogged. Kellogg, known to American newspapermen as 'Nervous Nellie,' was promoted from the Court of St. James's to the Secretaryship of State, where he played harmless transatlantic ball with the eloquent Briand.

Having given up the invasion of Germany as a bad job, France joined Spain in a war against Abd-el-Krim, and was aided by some intrepid veterans of the American Lafayette Escadrille. These fliers, like the late son of Mussolini, saw flower-like beauty in bombs bursting below on non-air-minded natives of Africa.

In spite of all the foregoing, life in the rue de la Huchette continued to be charming and abundant. The sun glowed in the east behind the towers of Notre Dame and three inhabitants of our little street, including myself, attended a magnificent performance of the Berlioz Requiem in that majestic cathedral. I refer to Milka, the Communist student, and a lonely man from an attic of No. 8, known in the neighbourhood as 'The Satyr' because of an alleged tendency to self-exposure. His accusers were two sisters from Alsace who jointly ministered to the needs of a retired lieutenant-colonel on the fourth floor of No. 7.

The Requiem, which Berlioz had written for the French Government in the late 1860's and which had been refused by the politicians who had ordered it from the composer, had been played not more than three times: once at Berlioz' own funeral as the first mark of national recognition; again in the spacious chapel at Les Invalides, or the national soldiers' home; and once previously at Notre Dame. The kindly old French musician, Gabriel Pierné, whose gentle little 'serenade' is known to piano pupils everywhere, organized and directed this top-flight musical event. At the head of his male and female chorus and full orchestra supplemented by a military band and several extra trumpeters, old Papa Pierné looked like Santa Claus in mufti.

His benign appearance was the more incongruous because of the breadth and vigour of his interpretation. The horse butcher, Monsieur Monge, was ill with bronchitis at the time, with such a high fever that he was obliged to surrender his priceless ticket to the Satyr. My extra press ticket went to Milka because of her hunger for good music and the slander to which she was subjected on The Navet's account.

I will not say that, while being swept by surges of glorious sound, I did not, with tears in my eyes, subscribe to the notion that France and French genius could never pass away and by no means could be dispensed with. And when later I told my Marseilles accordion teacher that the experience had disabled me from practising the squeeze-box for a week, he nodded, blew his nose, and understood. We consumed twenty francs' worth of refreshments on that lesson day, almost wordlessly, and as I drank all graves were opening at the blast of twenty of the best French trumpeters, plus the Archangel Gabriel, and the resurrection and the life were roaring in my ears.

On another day, I would stroll with Pierre Vautier to the Renoir exhibition in the rue la Boëtie and see deathless French blues and captured sunlight and flesh tones that had eluded the Academy. And again the rumblings of workers and economics and the sinking of the franc and the twitterings of 'Nervous Nellie' went out of earshot, and France was vital and indestructible.

My disinherited friend, Pierre, recently of St. Cyr, was having soul-storms which had little to do with world affairs. He confided in me that Mary the Greek was taking an attitude, lovingly and firmly, that had much in common with that of his unreasonable father. She had visited, on one unfortunate occasion, the art dealer's store in the rue de Seine, to bring him a registered letter. There she had formed the same uncharitable opinion of Pierre's co-workers that Vautier *père* had forcibly expressed. Particularly she had viewed with misgivings the dainty and pink-cheeked middle-aged proprietor who wore corsets and addressed Pierre as 'lovey'. The proprietor took a corresponding aversion to the dark female beauty from the Mediterranean.

Pierre, flushed and earnest, insisted that Monsieur Bertrand, the art dealer, had made no improper advances. Also he confided in me that since Bertrand had mentioned it, he could not deny to himself that Mary exuded a faint gamey odour, unresponsive to soap. Also hips and breasts were essentially non-æsthetic, were they not? Was he unnatural, and lost? Or should he go back to military school and impose a self-discipline that would enable him to stand apart from women, men, boys and whatever else life had to offer?

'If only I were a believer,' he said wistfully, 'but faith is the most disgusting of all delusions. I cannot be a hypocrite, and unluckily I am *not* a fool.'

I could offer no solution. Pierre soon broke with Mary and she drifted back to Dubonnet before our eyes. She could seldom pay her room rent, but Monsieur Henri let her stay in the hotel, in spite of the protests of Marie, his wife.

Georges, the *garçon*, was tender to Mary, not selfishly or with veiled intent. Strange as it may seem, Georges had no difficulty in enjoying more girls than his poverty and humility would seem to permit. When any one of the neighbourhood women got lonesome, which was often, and had no other place to go, Georges would be likely to find her in his cot. Naturally he would accept the situation manfully and philosophically.

In an ideal civilization most of us would have to be radically altered. I believe Georges would remain unchanged, the most wayward follower of Jesus and, perhaps, the most beloved.

11

OF, FOR AND BY THE PEOPLE

Frémont, the letter-carrier, his wife, Mathilde, and their blue-eyed daughter, Yvonne, lived in the cramped concierge's quarters on the ground floor of No. 11, a narrow four-story apartment house between M. Monge's horse-butcher shop and Dorlan's bindery.

Many of the families along the rue de la Huchette were set at odds by occasional quarrels. The Frémonts were always in accord. Monsieur Frémont sometimes on Sundays and holidays laid aside his letter-carrier's uniform for a light grey cotton suit from the Bon Marché. He bought his shirts on the boulevard St. Germain in one of a chain of stores called '100,000 Chemises' and his socks were knitted by his wife, who bought wool from Madame Absalom. His passion was social justice, his weakness strong red wine. Frémont's postman's walk was near the Porte St. Martin. In our quarter he performed odd jobs with a screwdriver, oil can, pair of tweezers, a bit of putty, beeswax, fishline, scraps of tin or zinc, a used paint-brush, and, in extreme instances, a hammer and saw.

He would respond good-naturedly when summoned from his home or the Caveau bar, brush dampness from his forehead after taking off his cap, and then deny any knowledge, technical or practical, of the object or apparatus in need of repair. Readily he would accept a tumbler of red wine, which he relished as an owl loves baby mice, chat a while about the national predicament, amble home for material and tools, and finally get to work.

One of his creditable successes was to glue together the Colonel's bed-pan which had been dropped by one of the Alsatian old maids in No. 7. This he did so neatly that the ex-officer never knew that it had been broken and consequently never deducted the 1907 value of it from Elvira's 1905 rate of pay. In 1926 he repaired a hole which had been punched with a broomstick through an oil painting of Judge Lenoir. About once in three years, he fixed Madame Corre's Singer (pronounced *san jhay*, with the accent on the last syllable), and it was he who set up the Café St. Michel's complicated nickel-plated coffee machine after the man from the dealer's had bungled the job.

A NARROW STREET

Of the men and women in our little street, an inordinate number were directly in the employ of the Republic. In addition to The Navet, Hortense Berthelot, the policeman in the little station, an inspector of gas meters who lived at No. 9, a Gentile inspector of kosher meat at No. 22, the driver of a watering cart, a telephonist, and numerous others, there was Frémont and his friend, Pissy, who checked trains in out of the Gare St. Lazare.

These *fonctionnaires* or government employees were the hardest hit by the fall of the franc. Unlike industrial workers, they could not strike, and neither had they the farmers' facility for producing their own food. Their immediate bosses were small-minded men who had risen through superior meanness. The higher-ups did not know them by name. After twenty years of service (1919 to 1949) Monsieur Frémont drew down, for himself and his family, about four shillings per day. Monsieur Pissy did just about as poorly, but he had a son, and not a daughter, so he was in a better position to 'defend himself' as times got worse and worse.

Looking wistfully at Yvonne, his handsome daughter, Monsieur Frémont said one day:

'What a pity! She's too good-looking to marry a working man.'

By practising the strictest economy and because of his odd jobs, the Frémonts were able to put aside a dowry for Yvonne, from their dollar a day, minus dues to the union. In 1920 this nest-egg amounted to 2,000 francs (£57) and in 1926 to 4,500 francs (£25). Of such mathematics are world disasters made.

Yvonne, as a girl, could not go out without her mother or father, and neither of them had much time, so she met few young men. She learned to embroider and make her own clothes with an aptitude for copying good models but no talent for original design. She got average marks in school, tried to read some of her father's Marxian pamphlets and failed to understand them, and her only small sin was sipping secretly at the family Benedictine. This made her feel warm, excitedly patient and expectantly calm.

Class-conscious and aggressive types like The Navet, the floor-walker Panaché, and the small-souled beef-and-lamb butcher, who believed his francs, concealed in the pitcher, were losing value because of the growth of the trade unions, denounced Frémont as a drunkard and a dangerous radical. Frémont dismissed them as victims of circumstances, blinded by their capitalistic education for which they could not be blamed.

The Navet was afraid of practically everybody, but especially of Madame Mariette, whose grey eyes could be as cold as death on occasions and who had some nugget of information stored away that kept The Navet within bounds.

Men of all sorts strayed into Mariette's establishment. It was equipped with a small schoolroom with school desks and blackboards on the walls for very small women who could make up and act like schoolgirls in their teens. Also it had a small salon where non-commercial motion pctures (for which the costume bill had been the smallest item in the cost of production) were displayed. Also a sound-proof chamber where a creditable flagellation act was staged when prosperous customers felt that way. Old Armandine and a tough young woman named Mireille were on the receiving end of a black snake whip on those gala evenings, and it was said that Mireille really liked it and Old Armandine did not. Madame Mariette's high-class clients were able, in those days of unbalanced budgets and inflation, to buy champagne at fifty francs a bottle (the first round being genuine) and often confided their little secrets to Madame, which for the most part, she guarded with professional discretion.

Under the oppressive Code Napoléon, framed to keep Frenchwomen in subjection, which did not permit them to have bank accounts, or to buy or sell property without their husband's consent if they were married, or their father's if they were not, Madame Mariette was better able to hold her own than many of her more conventional sisters. She had a husband who made few demands and enough state secrets to protect her from petty persecution.

A piquant illustration of the Code Napoléon comes to mind. A woman of my acquaintance received a telegram to the effect that her husband, a captain in the French army, was dying in Algeria. When she applied for permission to go to his deathbed, the police officials ruled that she could not do so without her husband's permission. Since the husband was too far gone to sign the necessary permission, he had to die without her, while she remained in Paris.

France, a nation of 40,000,000 people, maintained a huge standing army, the officers of which were, for the most part, contemptuous of republican ideals. On top of this, the French supported an even larger and less efficient horde of public employees who sapped the public morale and resources. These civil servants were so underpaid that they had no spirit except of resentment, no purchasing power, no prospects of anything but slow defeat.

'After all, in France there is no unemployment,' The Navet said to me, during the period of our American depression. The fact of the matter was that while few Frenchmen were out of work, a large percentage of them were unproductively employed. In the long run that is worse than having them jobless. It costs less to support an idle man than one who is perpetually in the way.

One might have thought that with this huge swarm of public employees drawing pay, however inadequate, the public services in France would have been passable. Nothing could be farther from the truth. In our little street, there were less than half a dozen telephones. The population of the quarter was about 2,500 souls. If one of then wished to speak with some distant person, usually he saved time and trouble by taking a bus, the underground, or even a train. The semi-public phone in the Café St. Michel was out of order about half the time. Madame Trévise, busy woman that she was, liked it better that way. In order for a client to use the phone he had to buy from her a metal disc or *jeton*. This was good for a local call, in case one could (a) decipher the complicated directions as to when to take off the receiver, drop the *jeton*, etc., etc.; (b) attract the attention of an over-worked and semi-hysterical operator who hated foreigners like poison and natives like medicine; (c) obtain the right number, if it hadn't been changed or listed incorrectly; (d) and provided that one's party was at home, and (unlikeliest of all) had a phone.

The unlucky Parisian who was forced to walk, as a last resort, to call long-distance, had to walk to the nearest branch post office and wait in line from thirty minutes to three hours.

The installation in Paris of dial telephones took several years and for a while complicated the already faulty system to such a point that telephoning almost went out of vogue. When it was resumed, the improved apparatus proved recalcitrant to a high degree.

Frenchmen took these things as a matter of course. Parisians who would deny their grandmothers a set of false teeth in order to 'save money' never grasped the idea of 'saving time.' Never in the history of France had the ordinary citizen received good service of any kind. The finest collection of paintings in the world, housed in the Louvre museum, were so placed that daylight never reached them and the artificial lighting was atrocious. The Métro, or tube system, when constructed, had been modern and fine. After World War I it was overcrowded and inadequate.

The railway system was antiquated, badly directed, under-manned and hazardous. In 1925 there was such an epidemic of railroad accidents that the entire personnel got panicky. Engine drivers ran through signals. Signals were incorrectly manipulated. Rails spread; roadbeds settled; switchmen had nervous breakdowns after they had caused disasters; and one engine driver was so relieved at having successfully brought his train from Nancy into a Paris terminal that he forgot to apply the brakes and crashed through the final bumper. Result: 6 dead, 44 injured. When one escaped with life and limb from a railway journey, one had been jolted and blown full of cinders, taken on detours and generally discommoded and delayed to a fantastic degree. In the first class, one was slighted by the poverty-stricken employees, and served sloppily in the dining car, if any. Second class was jammed with bourgeois, third class with peasants and soldiers. Travelling became an ordeal and a hardship, and one was considered eccentric and vulgar if one did not assume it would be like that. Trains were dirty, unheated, irregular and late. Once when employees were goaded into striking for less inhuman conditions, the then prime minister of France (I believe it was Briand, the lover of peace) found some old law under which he could induct them into the army as reservists, and then as soldiers have them shoot themselves for high treason.

The post office was no better. Mails were slow and unreliable; the offices were insanitary and under-manned. Street cleaning was confined to the tourist sections. In the little streets debris was washed from gutters up on the pavements by old-fashioned watercarts that blew like porpoises. Dustbins were systematically overturned and picked over by scavengers about four o'clock in the morning with such an attendant clatter that sleep was interrupted. Then about six o'clock the official collectors thumped and banged.

Gas meters leaked and sometimes exploded; electric lights wavered and ran up disproportionate bills; installations were outmoded and defective; and the whole maudlin process was complicated by trick systems of switches and fuses like an apprentice's nightmare. City water was unfit for drinking. Taxes piled on taxes. Government tobacco was impure, malodorous and unsuitable for smoking. Government matches had a sulphurous stench that brought tears to one's eyes, or came in little boxes labelled 'safety'. The stalk of a safety match was splintered and brittle; the head would not ignite or it glowed without flame, hopped to one's trousers or shirt where it burned a hole, then had to be found and extinguished forcibly on the carpet, which thereafter bore a charred spot for which one had to pay when the inventory was taken, if one rented an apartment.

One can easily imagine how such services could become inadequate and extremely annoying. An American with a nostalgia for the efficiency of his homeland might indeed nourish a feeling of resentment over such minor inconveniences. Here he would search in vain for the well-ordered streets of his own country. Shaded lights and gadgets, modern and infallible, belonged to another world. Telephones and ice-boxes and sound-proof bathrooms were far, far away from the rue de la Huchette.

But it had the finest and bravest and most companionable of men and women! It had two dusk-faring bats and mound upon mound of fresh vegetables that glowed on the barrows, and the haunting cries of itinerant vendors. It had life that streamed like the rays of warming sunshine. It had, above all, men and women of warmth and compassion, and also some of the lowest types extant. It had a scholar who read Plato by the light of a street lamp through his dusty window and an old harlot who knitted for her nieces in the country. Behind the façades of its houses and shops were to be found the treasures and traditions and the fine or ignoble predicaments of living in the present. Love and hunger and hope and kindness and fear and humour and the struggle to survive on the rue de la Huchette, as elsewhere in France and the world, were the components of the drama frequently called human and now and then divine.

12

OF NON-ESSENTIALS

Most of the men and women of the rue de la Huchette were active, if not productive. They sold food and produce, shelter, sex or refreshment, or scribbled in large ledgers. There were some others, equally interesting, who seemed at first glance to be a part of the scenery. The barrows around the corner in the rue Zacharie swarmed with customers and gave rise to lively chatter and hoarse invective. Men strayed in and out of bars, women in and out of stores and shops. Children trooped to and from school, pale and subdued, having been regaled with chocolate and a breakfast egg.

Even the florist at No. 23 had steady customers from larger restaurants and hotels. The shop of Madame Durand was situated within easy walking distance of the fragrant *Marché aux Fleurs*, or central flower market, behind the prefecture. Two mornings a week this market spilled over its boundaries on the quai and flooded the near-by bridges with potted plants and cut flowers, not to mention shrubs and, in season, Christmas trees. Therefore Albertine Durand could undersell other florists who could not have their wares transported so cheaply and easily. Durand did a business quite out of proportion to the size of our street. She got up at five each morning, and dressed without waking her husband, the Gentile inspector of kosher meat, whose hours were from eight to six.

Having selected fresh flowers for her shop, Madame Durand would hire a couple of tramps. These derelicts would borrow a kind of hod with shoulder hooks; the flower merchant would load them down until they looked like floats in a spring parade; and, herded by Madame, they would trudge to the rue de la Huchette. For this service Madame paid five cents per tramp regardless of the cost of living.

La Vie Silencieuse at No. 28 was a goldfish shop and, like its name, was peaceful. Passers-by paused to marvel at the fish and sea plants in glass tanks in the window (the shop was only twelve feet wide) and about as often as the Seine fishermen along the quai caught a minnow a customer would stray in. Of course, the shop was poorly located, from a commercial point of view. In order to find it, one had to know positively where it was and how to get there.

The proprietor, Monsieur Maurice, was never called by any other name. Of all the shopkeepers in the rue de la Huchette, only two allowed themselves the luxury of getting to their places of business as late as nine in the morning. The two late risers were Monsieur Maurice, who appeared as if by magic each morning on a bicycle, and Monsieur Noël, the gaunt taxidermist.

'Man and boy I have been a taxidermist like my father and his father before him,' Monsieur Noël remarked one day. 'In the course of those three generations,' he added, 'no one ever came with an animal or bird to be stuffed, or to buy one already stuffed, before ten o'clock in the morning.'

Monsieur Maurice must have felt the same way about tropical fish, which are purchased during mankind's mellower hours, toward the last of the afternoon, when the fishes of *La Vie Silencieuse* had the sun on them and were shimmering appreciation. He brought his lunch to our street each day, having strapped it under the seat of his bicycle in a rack provided for the purpose. When the suspended activities of the street seemed to indicate that it was lunch-time, Monsieur Maurice moved his one kitchen chair, the only non-piscine furniture in the shop, about twelve feet to the rear, unwrapped his package and started munching a sandwich (French style, with a long split crusty roll) and some nobby little pickles moist with wine vinegar. Then he locked his shop, strolled over to the bookstalls and bought at random a second-hand volume which he would read, from cover to cover, in those exceptional cases when both the front and back cover of the book remained.

Having read the book, he would turn it in next day in part payment for another. In all the years I knew him, he never found one he wished to retain and read a second time. He was a medium-sized man with wavy hair, dressed drably and quietly, responded politely with a warm smile when addressed and had a habit, when greeting a customer, of ungreedily rubbing his hands together. His taste for reading matter was catholic in the extreme. One day he would follow the adventures of some pioneer priest in the wilds of Canada, the next would find him mildly astonished by Mademoiselle de Maupin. In order, he would read with polite attention and quiet relish: a text-book on the care of bees, a volume from Fi to Kl of an obsolete encyclopedia, and *Les Sœurs Marx* (The Marx Sisters) by Louisa May Alcott.

To British readers this requires a word of explanation. 'Little Women' translated directly into French as '*Petites Femmes*' would have a meaning that would have distressed Louisa May, of Concord, Massachusetts. The Frenchman of the streets confused the name 'March' (the family name of Miss Alcott's *Little Women*) with Marx, made famous in France as elsewhere by the inimitable Groucho, Harpo and Chico. So *Little Women* was named *The Marx Sisters* and was believed by many purchasers, who were later disappointed, to have the many qualities which have become synonymous with America's distinguished comedians.

No one knew where Monsieur Maurice went after crossing the place St. Michel at the height of evening traffic on his bicycle. The apéritif clients of the Café St. Michel and the Café de la Gare marvelled at his co-ordination and judgment of distances, for nightly he steered a zigzag course between roaring buses, honking autos, rogue taxis, ambulances and harassed pedestrians without ever so much as nicking a delivery boy or sustaining a minor injury himself. Drinkers paused to watch his hair-raising performance, told their friends about it, and even made bets on his chances. Of this Maurice seemed to be oblivious. He had to get somewhere on his bicycle at precisely that hour. His route, as a crow would have flown, involved crossing the busy *place*. Therefore, he did it.

One morning in 1927, Maurice's shop did not open, although a strange sad-faced boy arrived about noon to feed the fishes and arrange the sea plants in the tanks. The next day Maurice appeared with his bicycle loaded down with bundles and a straw hamper. A barrow with a few other effects followed later. Maurice purchased at the small bazaar or draper's shop at No. 19 several yards of flowered cretonne, choosing a semi-oriental pattern that did not clash with fish. From the *Marchand du couleurs* (paint and dye shop) at No. 4, he bought some picture wire. Meanwhile, because of the black band round his upper left arm and the black ribbon round his bowler hat and the black tie against his clean white shirt front, the neighbours paused and expressed their concolences, not knowing exactly for what. It was not a mother, father, sister or brother who had died. Probably an aunt. Anyway, from that day on, until February, 1939, Maurice slept on a cot in the rear of *La Vie Silencieuse* and within a month he sold his bicycle to one of the apprentices of the bookbinder's shop at No. 9. The apprentice, who lived up-river, across from the Halle aux Vins, did not cross the place St. Michel of an evening, but left the rue de la Huchette by the eastern gate, facing Notre Dame. This lad was so far below Maurice in skill that he was clipped by a siphon wagon, on his third night out, sustaining a broken collar bone.

It was exceptionally hard luck for Maurice that the book or pamphlet he had hit upon that day in 1939, was entitled *The Communist Manifesto* and that his initiation into the poetry of Karl (not Groucho or Louisa) Marx was interrupted by special plain-clothes investigators from the Sûreté Générale who were making a routine check-up. These investigators, who had been able to make little showing in the neighbourhood, since so many inhabitants were already gone, disbelieved Maurice's story as to how he came by the volume, and booked him as a 'red.' His papers were years out of date, since no official of any kind had ever paid him the slightest attention before.

Two doors eastward, on the same side of the street with *La Vie Silencieuse*, was a shop only ten feet wide with a sign reading: *Au Philatelogue* (To Him Who Knows about Used Postage Stamps). The proprietor, Monsieur Dominique, was a grizzly, villainous-appearing old man in felt slippers and in frayed shirtsleeves. He wore glasses that fitted him so badly that he took them off whenever he examined one of his prize stamps or filled small envelopes with assorted specimens and marked in ink the price of the lot, which ran from five to eighty francs. The valuable stamps he kept in a small old-fashioned safe, and these were said to be worth as high as 1,500 francs apiece, having been expertized and labelled in 1907 when the franc was worth tenpence.

It was Monsieur Noël who discovered that Monsieur Dominique was known throughout the stamp-collecting world as an authority, that he contributed articles under a pen-name to several international magazines devoted to that hobby, and that he had been called to London on one occasion to testify in a British court (through an interpreter) and there had exposed a clever forgery.

In mid-summer, when the kind of people who like stuffed cats were away and when all kinds of animals, benefiting from the vitamins in the sunshine, were usually healthy anyway, Noël had lots of spare time. The mortality of pets, he told us, was highest in the months of April, May, and in early June. In that season their fancy lightly turns to thoughts of love, makes them restless and incautious and leads them to their doom.

Mocha, the sleek black dog of the Hôtel Normandie, was not a thoroughbred, but he was the same colour (soot-blue-black) all over. His short healthy coat did not shine or glisten but seemed to absorb the sunlight. He had a noble head, with brown tranquil eyes, a nose neither blunt nor pointed, and a long tail he was careful not to sling around promiscuously. Mocha was a careful dog. He had to be, in a narrow cheap hotel where drinking was done, in order not to be trodden upon. He was never kicked. Frenchmen of the city were extremely considerate of dumb animals, and in the country animals like horses, cows, pigs or oxen were too expensive to be abused and neglected. It always astonished me how well the city-bred French understood their pets, refrained from hurting their feelings, condoned their foibles and treated them like honoured guests. In return, the dogs and cats responded according to their individual temperament. Maggie, the unspeakable terrier beloved by the grouch Madame Marie at the Caveau, took every advantage of her mistress's indulgence. She scratched and chewed furniture, tore rugs and antimacassars, refused baths when she smelled to heaven, splashed in mud when she was clean. But the moment Marie was safely in bed and Monsieur Henri took over, Maggie became circumspect, performed tricks, kept out of the customers' way, did not snap at strangers or beggars, and became a she-angel.

Mocha, of the Normandie, was always the same, rain or shine, day or night, in sickness or in health. He was attached to three persons: Louis, the one-armed garçon, Sara and the worthless Guy. With respect to Guy, I learned that Mocha, who respected him, was right, and that I had been hasty in my judgment.

One evening when a drunken client made some slighting remark about Jews, Guy rose in wrath, strode over to his table and said firmly: 'My wife is a Jew, Monsieur!'

Not content with that, Guy delivered a concise impassioned talk against race prejudice.

Of course, the next evening, Guy complained that Sara had sent him a rumpled napkin, and seemed to blame her because the baker's crescent rolls got smaller as the franc went down.

It was astonishing how Parisians reacted to flowers. One had only to carry an exposed bouquet or even a single rose or chrysanthemum along any Paris pavement, to see passers-by turn their heads and often gasp and exclaim aloud in admiration. Louis Aragon, an imaginative Frenchman if ever there was one, once gave an old beggar woman fifty francs and an orchid, on condition that she would memorize and never forget as long as she lived the name of the woman he loved. I would stake my life on it that the miserable old witch kept her part of the bargain. For the French, so penny wise in the midst of colossal folly, knew the value of gestures. I once saw a most prosaic-looking man in a public bus in Paris brush tears from his eyes as he read an article in *La Semaine Littéraire*. At the next news stand I got off the bus to purchase a copy. The story was an excerpt from a little-known diary of Oscar Wilde, who at the time he was trying to recover from the ordeal of his imprisonment was crossing a Paris bridge and saw a man drowning. Wilde was a strong swimmer and was about to plunge into the Seine when it occurred to him that his act would be interpreted as a theatrical gesture and a bid for public favour. In his pathologically sensitive state that thought held him back and left another burden on his troubled soul.

The barber shop and hairdressing salon in the rue de la Huchette (No. 20) was on the borderline between essentials and luxuries. Our local barber-in-chief was named Julien, who had worked for the famous Riess, near the place St. Germain des Prés, and whose tireless wife, Elaine, had been watched and prodded by Madame Riess, until she knew what surveillance really meant. When one got shaved *chez* Julien, Julien tucked a sheet around one's collar and then lighted a gas jet, over which he warmed about a cupful of water. The lather was about like the meringue on a lemon pie at room temperature, and smelled of various things like bitter almonds. It dried quickly and thoroughly, especially around one's ears. The razor was stropped adequately, and Julien was pretty good with it, but once he had taken off the whiskers his part of the operation was over. One groped one's way to the sink, washed in tap-water and dried oneself with a diminutive stiff towel, which had a way of resisting dampness almost entirely.

Julien's haircuts made one look like a nineteenth-century advertisement for hot chocolate, but they had an artistic touch, just the same. The bore the stamp of their creator.

Like most barbers, Julien had his favourite story, and his was a good one and true. His former employer, the great Riess, had commanded top prices for 'styling' women's hair and had attracted many rich Americans for whom the tariff was special. One of these, an advertising woman, built short and stocky like an embroidered pine tree with head and shoulders, consulted Monsieur Riess and paid her large fee in advance. The master walked around her several times, patted her head, exclaimed, called his wife to witness and then said:

'Madame! You are already perfect! It would be a sacrilege to disarrange one hair.'

Julien used this story as a mental test for his clients. If they looked blank when he had finished, he gave them scant attention thereafter. Those who chuckled wholeheartedly were treated with special solicitude.

Madame Goujon had a routine all her own which she used on any men who strayed into her salon. It was not a funny story, but merely a way of getting the conversation on risqué ground. It seemed that while her husband had still been alive (and that is all she ever said about him) they had been invited to a party at which parlour games were played. The hostess had a leaning toward literature of the Paul Bourget variety and had asked each guest to write a short composition, later to be read to the assembly, on piquant subjects drawn from a decorative spun-glass basket. Madame Goujon had been asked to describe *les frissons* (the thrill that authors frequently describe by the use of asterisks).

'Now how could one do that, Monsieur?' she would ask.

All that I could say was that many great writers had tried it, and almost always had come a cropper.

'Perhaps Proust,' I said, casually.

On the strength of those two words, Madame Goujon, an economical but emotional woman, bought the entire seventeen volumes of *Remembrance of Things Past*.

13
THE PREVAILING STATE OF GRACE

To say that the French had lost their religion or wandered after false gods is inaccurate in the extreme. I have never lived in a country where the Church caused less trouble than in twentieth-century France. The famous 'separation' from the State occurred early in the century and broke the hold of the clergy on general education. The Jesuits did not dominate big business, as they did in Spain, and the priests, when they meddled in politics, did so discreetly, following a time-worn Vatican policy of lying low when years were lean.

Generally speaking, priests were not ignorant or bestial in France. In fact, they were sometimes better informed on worldly affairs than the average run of secular politicians. One of the best of them, the Abbé Alphonse Lugan of St. Germain des Prés, who had travelled the world as a missionary and had written several books in English about American government, offered a daily prayer which struck me as profound.

'Merciful God, make me neither rich nor poor.'

In France there was little Protestant influence. Either one was a Catholic and went through the motions or a freethinker and thought less about heaven or hell than who was prime minister or whether his mistress was to be trusted. The farmers and their wives were mostly churchgoers. Industrial workers were not. The civilian employees of the government were good Catholics or not, according to the zeal of their superiors.

But in the army organized Catholicism was powerful indeed. High officers, if they were not conspicuously Catholic, had to be brilliant, almost phenomenal, to get along. The Catholic officers formed a powerful clique, and private soldiers who wanted leave or favours made it a point to attend mass with more regularity than sincerity.

But even among the most influential supporters of the Church, there was little fanaticism. The year that the Archbishop of Paris sprained his ankle when stepping from his limousine, which he had brought to the church of St. Christophe, the patron saint of vehicles, to be blessed according to the annual custom, no one laughed harder than the bishops and generals.

Cardinal Verdier, who was renowned as a builder of churches in Paris, was visiting one in progress of construction and overheard a mason who had bruised his finger with a stone say: '*Nom de Dieu*.'

'You mustn't say that, my good man,' the Cardinal said. 'When things don't go right, say *merde*, as everybody else does.'

As far as I know, the only things the Parisians were not willing to laugh about were the price of bread and the Tomb of the Unknown Soldier. The night that the eternal flame went out in a most irreverent way and the plumbers couldn't get it lighted again for fourteen hours, there was little irreverent comment. Editors and journalists continued to refer to the flame as 'eternal' and most of them did not mention its hours of non-eternity for fear of stirring up the touchy war veterans.

The most pious inhabitant of the rue de la Huchette was a sad handsome woman of thirty who lived on the fifth floor front of the Hôtel du Caveau. Madame Claire dressed in deep mourning, kept her eyes to the floor and spoke to no one except Monsieur Henri, who treated her with divine consideration. For twelve hours each day Madame Claire made artificial flowers in a large dressmaker's establishment, and the rest of the time she prayed, either in St. Séverin or St. Augustin. She rose early, so as to be alone in the café with Monsieur Henri as she swallowed her coffee and bread. She felt unclean, like a leper, and destined to the sulphurous flames of hell because her husband, to whom she had been utterly faithful, had left her and divorced her in defiance of the Church.

The capacity for suffering of this gentle woman was frightening, if not shocking. She cringed as she put on or took off her clothes. The sharp wicked eyes of men and the remarks they made as she passed stung her like barbs of cat-o'-nine-tails. Her world and the world to come had crashed around her ears, and nothing Father Panarioux could say or do would induce her to relax. Monsieur Henri prevented her from starving herself, feeding her as if she were a sick child, as indeed she was.

'The trouble with Madame Claire,' said the cook, Thérèse, with finality, 'is that she has no sins of her own to weep about.'

'She doesn't know what she wants,' Georges said, as if he knew quite well.

A drunken American reporter who miscounted the stairs blundered into Claire's room one night and did not discover that she had practically swooned until too late. As is often the case, the mysterious ways of Providence turned apparent evil into miraculous good, for after floods of tears and protests, and a three-day bout of incessant praying, the clouds seemed to lift from Claire's troubled soul. Thereafter she went to mass, but not to excess, got a better job and one Easter morning showed up in coloured clothes and said '*bonjour*' to everyone.

The store at No. 1 rue de la Huchette sold crucifixes, prayer books, stained glass windows, altar trappings and other supplies for the faithful and the churches. The proprietor was a mild Alsatian who was meticulous in his religious observances because otherwise he would lose his neighbourhood monopoly. I think Monsieur Luttenschlager was a thwarted sculptor or painter, for he turned out the most amazing assortment of *crèches*, or holy cribs, in the Christmas season. These little mangers, with baby dolls representing Jesus, porcelain Josephs and Marys, wide-eyed cows of papier maché, and shavings for straw, were purchased by pious parents for well-behaved children at Christmastide.

In France the custom of exchanging elaborate Christmas presents was not in vogue. Small tokens such as flowers or decorative cards were sent one's friends on New Year's Day.

Monsieur Luttenschlager could be seen early in December on his knees, in his shirtsleeves, in his window, giving the last artistic touch to his gems

THE PREVAILING STATE OF GRACE

of representative and symbolic art. Had Salvador Dali taken a good look at a Luttenschlager creation he would have spared the world much hooey.

The carpenter next door went to church when some relative died. After years of 'Republicanism', France still had well-defined classes for funerals. One day I happened into St. Séverin just after a second-class funeral and found one of the younger priests matter-of-factly going the rounds and blowing out every other taper. We were good enough bridge companions for me not to mind asking him why.

'We're having a third-class funeral right away,' he said.

The line-up as regards believers and infidels in our street was about as follows:

Hôtel du Caveau (No. 5) Madame Claire . . . all other residents neutral or indifferent; No. 7 contained the very pious and aged Taitbout couple who sold newspapers, and the middle-aged Alsatian old maids and their army colonel (retired). All of these were pious.

The bookbinder, who was alleged to use human skin, was a free-thinker, whenever he had time. Frémont was a socialist infidel; so was Monge. Monsieur and Madame Lanier (of the laundry and *clandestin*) went to mass each Sunday morning and then took a trip on the Seine boats or a bus in the afternoon. Most of the girls of *Le Panier Fleuri* went scuttling to St. Séverin, trembling, whenever bad news arrived.

On the north side of the street, the line-up was about like this:

The beef butcher had been born a Catholic and decided to let it go at that.

The paint dealer (who rented superbly beautiful copper kettles for two francs a day in the preserving season) went to mass about three times a year and sent his son to a parochial school.

The pork butcher, a pal of Luttenschlager's, approved but did not attend, being too tired of a Sunday.

The Satyr's habits were not known to anyone among his neighbours, but he would have been more likely to patronize a black mass than a white one.

Noël, the taxidermist, was a highly intelligent man who had no superstitions whatever, so he insisted

Madame Absalom had ceased to believe in God progressively, as she got better and better acquainted with her slippery 'ex' in Clermont years before.

Odette and Jean, of the dairy, were Socialists, and called religion the 'opium of the people'.

Had one asked Monsieur Corre whether or not he was a Christian, he would have blinked and said, '*Evidemment!*'

Madame Corre was as neatly religious as one of Luttenschlager's porcelain Marys. Dr. Clouet (of whom we shall hear much more) was an infidel who drank but did not take dope in any form. The dentist, on the other hand, was fairly meticulous in his relgious observances, and consequently was given a small rake-off from parish funds for examining the teeth of the pupils in the parochial schools.

Naturally, the spade-bearded military tailor, who looked like Tolstoy, was a churchman *sans rapproche*. Otherwise he would have had to make a speciality of sport or hunting outfits, or evening clothes. Julien, the barber, was a free non-thinker; the stamp collector was a scholar and scoffer; the owner and assistant at the music store confessed now and then; Maurice of *La Vie Silencieuse* had not made up his mind; the publisher at No. 30 was commercially pious, since he handled semi-religious books. The Navet was a pillar of religion. You already know about Judge Lenoir, Madame Goujon and little Hyacinthe.

However backward the Church is in Spain or was in Mexico or is in South America, and notwithstanding the equivocal political manœuvres of the Vatican, the Church in France behaved circumspectly. The French clergy intensely patriotic and comparatively urbane, did not foster or encourage fanaticism. The priests, high and low, deplored it. I have heard many Americans express shocked surprise at the perfunctory and seemingly casual way in which French congregations went through the motions while mass was being sung. They knelt or crossed themselves as if they were thinking about something else, mumbling their responses, strolled in and out during the services and were dealt with sternly by the beadle only when they failed to come through with the requisite small change. A Frenchwoman, with grave pale face and black clothes, veiled and gloved on one hand, would skim the other over the Holy Water font like a sparrow wetting the tip of its wings, in about the same manner and spirit as if she were flicking a speck of dust from her skirt. There was neither the fervent intensity nor the crude brutality of a Spanish church in Paris, and the decorations were not in such atrocious taste at their worst, nor nearly as magnificent as Burgos or Toledo at their best. One of the Chapels at St. Germain des Prés had murals by Delacroix, another by the neglected master of Poussin, a tramp genius who was the real father of French painting. This was mentioned in guide books, but nothing was ever done to light the paintings properly, so they never could be seen.

The general run of French priests was far above the average of the Irish-American clergy in mental capacity and education, psychological understanding, tolerance and everything but warmth. The French priest did not see himself as a higher type of policeman. There was very little scandal involving priests and women of the congregations, and if a clergyman wandered now and then, in plain clothes, into a public establishment like *Le Panier Fleuri*, safely removed in distance from his parish, no one in the world seemed to care a hang. There was no outward evidence that the Church was a burden to the poor. It seemed to derive its money and prestige from the rich. In fact, in no land as in France had Catholicism adapted itself to modern conditions with more grace and fewer incongruities.

Father Lugan told me, with a twinkle in his wise old eyes, that for several days before taking a boat for America he 'practised' wearing trousers so that he would not be continually walking around with his fly unbuttoned, accustomed as he was to robes in France. In whatever costume, he was the same good intelligent man. When German priests came to St. Sulpice, the missionary headquarters, Father Lugan spoke Latin to them and sometimes good-naturedly rebuked them for their lack of fluency in the grand old mother language.

The French people do not, like the suffering Spaniards, carry hatred in their hearts for the clergy. They know their priests are with and behind them, sharing their hardships and their ignominy, contributing to their dignity, but never wanting to betray them and prey upon their misery. They know that Frenchmen in robes, ordained and sanctified, would not persecute or condone or encourage the persecution of their helpless countrymen. Father Lugan's prayer, 'Let me be neither rich nor poor', struck a response from his communicants because, simply, they knew he meant it in all sincerity and humility.

14

OF CLOTHES AND HOW THEY MAKE THE MAN

In the middle 1920s it began to dawn on the people of the rue de la Huchette that France had not won the war — in fact, that nobody had won it. Early in 1926 Painlevé introduced a bill to reorganize the French army from thirty-two to twenty divisions. To this was attached a joker, increasing the term of universal compulsory military service from one year to eighteen months. The mothers of our quarter, particularly Madame Corre, Madame Marie of the Caveau, the baker's wife, and Madame Trévise of the Café St. Michel, grew haggard and tearful. This economy measure was accompanied in the French Senate by a bill to impose an 'income' tax on all foreigners resident in France (and not earning but spending money).

Each day the reactionary French columnists and editors came out more vituperatively against foreigners, particularly Americans. Since I was the only American in the rue de la Huchette (and many of the inhabitants did not know whether I came from North or South America), I was asked all too often to explain these scurrilous items and to make it clear what Coolidge, Dawes, Owen Young, Kellogg, J. P. Morgan, the monkey-trialists of Tennessee, the Ku Klux Klan, Al Capone, the Fundamentalists, Henry Cabot Lodge, *et al.*, were about. In each instance I had to start, not from scratch, but several yards behind the line.

On the Right Bank, floods of American tourists were arriving with each incoming liner, spending dollars that had multiplied in value because of the lop-sided exchange, eating expensive food badly chosen, drinking avidly because of Prohibition at home, purchasing objects of art and carting them away and enriching the owners of the big hotels. This had little effect on the rue de la Huchette, except through the daily papers.

It was at that time that an enterprising American newspaper man temporarily out of journalistic employment organized what were known as 'whoopee' tours of thirty days duration, on which fifty to one hundred thirsty countrymen of mine (without their wives) were treated to a protracted bout of inebriation and debauch unequalled by a Shriners' convention or an annual meeting of the American Legion.

An American Negro, wearing a full-feathered head-dress and a blanket, and representing himself as the Chief of all the American Indians, deposited a wreath on the Tomb of the Unknown Soldier on behalf of our sympathetic red men.

The Mellon-Berenger war-debt pact, giving France sixty-two years in which to pay a small fraction of a fabulous amount, was signed, and the State Department promptly lifted the ban on private loans to France.

Dr. Coué died at the age of sixty-two; Nicholas Murray Butler predicted a Franco-German entente in the near future; eighteen naturalized Americans were conscripted into the French Army; Chamberlain and Mussolini staged a love-feast in Rome; Paul Claudel, a French writer, was sent to Washington as ambassador; our own Ambassador Herrick threw the weight of his amazing popularity into the balance against the rising tide of anti-American feeling that the press was feeding throughout France. Caillaux was publicly exonerated of the charge of traitorous complicity with the enemy, reinstated in political life and petitioned the United States Government to spare the lives of Sacco and Vanzetti. The Nobel Peace prize was divided between Aristide Briand and Dr. Stresemann, whose Locarno peace pact was side-stepped by Calvin Coolidge. Typewritten documents were officially admitted as evidence, and for purposes of record in the French courts.

There was much comment, pro and con, because the American institution known as the 'cocktail hour' was being taken up in tourist hotels on the Right Bank. One afternoon I was urged by my friends at the Caveau bar to mix an American cocktail so that they would be in a better position to judge between the xenophobes who denounced the New World *apéritif* and those milder critics who said it made no difference what Americans drank before the kind of meals they habitually ate.

Deeply aware of my responsibility as an 'unofficial ambassador', I shook up a pint of Gordon's Gin with a quart of dry vermouth, ignoring the observations that the gin was English, according to its label, and the vermouth was a product of France. That the pint of gin cost enough to feed a French family for a week or more was another point I refrained from discussing. When I sprinkled in the Angostura bitters, for which I had been obliged to journey a mile or more, all my friends had to sniff the mysterious little bottle and taste the contents cautiously.

Monsieur Henri was the first to taste the Martini *sec*. He was polite but reserved.

'It's strong,' he said.

The chestnut vendor choked on the olive, which got stuck in his windpipe. Monsieur Noël thought the drink would be better without the vermouth or bitters.

Hastily I explained that this was not the only kind of American cocktail, that most bartenders could make at least twenty different varieties, and I tried, in vain, to translate such names as 'Side-car' and 'Bronx'. The affair wound up with Georges, the *garçon*, drinking what was left of the pitcherful, about fifty per cent, and none of the French men or women were converted to the 'cocktail hour'. They preferred a drink before dinner that did not paralyse the taste, make them suddenly fond of strangers and hostile members of their families, induce them to sleep with their clothes on, and miss buses and trains.

When I cooked oysters in milk my French acquaintances were adamant; they simply would not taste the stew. When I brought a package of Quaker Oats into the hotel, the well-meaning cook Thérèse made a soup, following a recipe she used for soup made of squash or pumpkin, convinced, in spite of what I had told her, that I had something else in mind.

The younger French, some intellectual and others not, made a fetish of everything American and 'modern'. What a French tailor turned out when he tried to imitate the cut of an American 'business' suit was equalled only by the output of a professional French instrumentalist when he attempted *le hot* or American jazz.

The spade-bearded Monsieur Saint-Aulaire, who presided over the two-man tailor shop at no. 21, could not afford a shop on the boulevard. He had never prospered, and had never gone broke. So he acted as if he were tailor by appointment to the Duc de Guise, and although his manners were impeccable, he did not consider it as much of an honour to make a chalk mark on the shoulder of Senator Berenger as on that of the penniless Honoré de Senlis, who played billiards with a duke.

The first time I entered the shop of Monsieur Saint-Aulaire to order a suit, being a devotee of the neighbourhood idea, I did not know all this about the owner and director. And now, years afterwards, I chuckle and gasp whenever I try to guess what Saint-Aulaire must have thought of me, a shabby-uninformed and obscure foreigner (an American to boot), who wanted, not one of Saint-Aulaire's impressive creations for morning or afternoon or evening wear, but a copy of what I took to be a suit that had been made by a fair New York tailor.

'Can you make a suit like that?' I asked, after the required *bonjours* and amenities.

I learned what a pair of eyebrows, fairly bushy, were able to express. Monsieur Saint-Aulaire looked at the garments I had laid on his table, half-covering his illustrated style book, and made a superb effort to control himself. He did, to a certain extent. Picking up the coat (blue serge and shiny) as if it were Exhibit 'A' in a trial for treason, he glanced at it and put it down again.

'Exactly like that?' he asked.

'Exactly,' I said.

'Unfortunately I have no American cloth,' he said, and hoped politely that the incident was closed.

I told him that French cloth would be all right if it didn't shrink, or

English cloth if it were not too expensive. He must have needed money badly, for he called his assistant, who lifted down the bolts of cloth from the shelves. In order to break the ice that was rapidly forming, I said what a shame it was that the Empress Carlotta had died.

'She was 86,' said Monsieur Saint-Aulaire, dispassionately.

My selection was a serge from Lyons which Monsieur said 'naturally' would shrink, but before it was cut. I left my old suit for him to copy, agreeing to return a week from the following Thursday. I left a deposit of 200 francs (the price was to be 450 francs, or about £1 16s.) and then was measured. I had not counted on that. My old suit fitted me, and I assumed in my innocence that a tailor could measure the suit and let me go free.

The eyebrows outdid themselves, and the assistant looked positively alarmed, as if he were to be arrested or fired. He was a meek little man who held rows of pins in his mouth, slouched a bit like Groucho Marx and glanced frequently at his master like a dog who is performing tricks while needing urgently to be taken out to the pavement. The measuring did not take more than an hour, and meanwhile, as a sort of challenge, I tried one subject of conversation after another, in the hope of causing Saint-Aulaire to thaw. The sixth or seventh try hit the jackpot. This superb champion of mind over matter was fond of amateur theatricals, which consisted, in his mind, of Molière, Racine and Shakespeare. He had played Hamlet at a benefit staged by the Duchesse de Rohan, and Shylock according to his own interpretation, which, I learned, was at odds with that of the director of the Odéon.

At this point I took the long chance that won me Saint-Aulaire's friendship.

'One could hardly go wrong, in disagreeing with him,' I said timidly. Even the assistant smiled, and Saint-Aulaire decided that in spite of my sartorial inelegance and atrocious French pronunciation, I was susceptible to cultivation and refinement. From then on, things were better — all except the suit.

'Jews,' said Monsieur Saint-Aulaire, 'have been deprived of everything except their laughter. When they lose their money or property, one does not feel it in his heart. One is provoked into laughter.'

Saint-Aulaire's 'Shylock,' then, was a comic character, and his audience fairly split their sides when his wench of a daughter got fed up with him and consorted with a Christian. As for the ducats — 'Monsieur, there is where the woe becomes lyrical. One assumes when a Jew makes money — he and you both know, monsieur — that someone will take it from him when the time comes, *n'est-ce pas?*'

I got him away from Shylock with some deft cape work, and up north into Denmark. The French version of *Hamlet* most in vogue has been embroidered into rhyme, so that the immortal 'to be or not to be' comes out something like this:

> *'Être, ou ne pas être?'*
> *Dormir, rêver, peut-être?'*

From a third-story window of her 'salon,' Hyacinthe Goujon had her eyes fixed on the tailor's window, since the legendary Count Costa de la Montaigne habitually ordered his uniforms there. Perhaps I should not have, but since little Hyacinthe was so frank with me, I talked to her as if she were a sophisticated adult. Hyacinthe was determined to remain a virgin until such time as she reached the age when Costa de la Montaigne might be given the opportunity to try to seduce her. Where this child got all her knowledge or information I never was able to understand. She told me candidly that when she went to Madame ———'s select school she intended to have an affair with one of the young teachers in order that she might not become too nervous on account of chastity unnaturally prolonged.

When the distinguished but Nazi-minded author of *Journey to the End of the Night* set forth that French schoolboys ten years old sometimes kept themselves in pocket money by blackmailing innocent men they had spotted as homosexuals, many American readers were incredulous. In that instance, the Americans were wrong.

The second Thursday after my first visit to his shop at No. 21, I began to have misgivings about the coat that was in process of creation. The assistant, it seemed, could not cut a coat so that it would fall straight down in the back. The force of long habit was too strong. Monsieur Saint-Aulaire had not taken me at my word when I said my American suit was to be copied. That, from his point of view, would have been an unfriendly act. My new suit had a waistline and hips, not to mention trousers that were too tight in the legs and came up four inches too high. Also the shoulders were padded coyly, there was no watch pocket, and an array of practically indestructible buttons intended for suspenders had replaced the belt straps of the original model.

Either I had to refuse to go through with the deal, lose my 200 francs and be sued for 250 more, or modify my notions about style. I might have been obdurate had I not been reluctant to wound Monsieur Saint-Aulaire's professional pride.

'It's not your *genre*, Monsieur Elliot,' Hyacinthe said thoughtfully. 'But it will make you less conspicuous.'

15

THE SHOCK FELT ROUND THE WORLD

The only occasion on which I felt utterly ashamed and lonely in the rue de la Huchette was the night of August 22, 1927. For in distant Massachusetts that evening, my native State, a 'good mason and a poor fish pedlar' were put to death, after seven years of mental torture, for a crime they had not committed.

What had been confused and distorted on Beacon Hill was perfectly clear to the inhabitants of my little street, and to the workers of Paris generally, namely, that Sacco and Vanzetti were being murdered because they had been 'anarchists' and foreigners and that Judge Thayer and Avan T. Fuller destroyed them for the good of their privileged kind.

Previously it had seemed to me that the slogan of 'Frenchmen first and partisan afterwards' had retained its force, but in little side streets like mine and on the broad boulevard Sebastopol the hand that turned the switch in the Massachusetts prison that night started the preliminary rumblings of a series of quakes that jarred France's hostile inimical classes apart and ended in the death of a nation.

Monsieur Henri Julliard was tending the bar that evening, and grouped silently around it were the oyster vendor, Messrs. Noël and Monge, Frémont, meek little Jean (the dairyman), Madame Mariette (who was too nervous to stay in her bordel that evening), the tough and courageous Mirielle, Georges the *garçon*, and Maurice of *La Vie Silencieuse*. At a near-by table sat Hortense Berthelot, all in black, Madame Berthe Dossot, and the drunken old woman who thought she sang like Yvette Guilbert.

A hush fell over the company when Monsieur Henri, who had gone to the corner to telephone, returned with incredulous sorrow on his face, looked apologetically at me and dropped his eyes.

'They have killed those men?' asked Noël in his deep bass voice, almost a whisper.

Monsieur Henri's head inclined itself a little more. The women gasped.

'That was ignoble,' said Madame Berthe Dossot.

Conspicuously absent from our little street that night were The Navet, Monsieur Panaché, the beef-and-lamb butcher, spade-bearded Monsieur Saint-Aulaire, and all others of the extreme right who had expressed themselves on the case perhaps too freely. Shutters of certain shops were drawn at dusk; pilgrimages to safer quarters where men who worked were not predominant in numbers had started that afternoon. *Le Panier Fleuri* had few high-class customers; the merchants and factory executives who patronized it ordinarily were reluctant to show themselves in public.

'The *canaille* will make this a pretext for a night of thievery and disorder,' The Navet told his son. He added, smugly: 'I have it from someone close to the commissioner that the police will shoot them down. It's time they had a lesson.'

The son promptly went out to join the manifestants in the boulevard Sebastopol. The indignant mob, somehow, with bare hands and Vanzetti's dying words for inspiration, pulled out of their concrete beds some iron street-lamp posts and tossed them through plate-glass windows.

Had I been The Navet's son and other prisoners of various kinds of starvation, I should have had an outlet for my grief and shame. As it was, I was the man from Boston, and wherever I went, to paraphrase the English poet, a bit of Massachusetts went with me.

It was no new thing to the French to have undesirables framed up and executed on one flimsy pretext or another. But, somehow, they had hoped it was different in America, and so, in my innocence, had I. It would have been easier to bear if my friends in the café had not been so considerate.

There was little drunkenness that evening. The drinkers started recklessly and soon found that the stuff did not have its usual kick, and that made them listless and discouraged. I stood at the bar a decent interval, then started for my room, and decided half way up the first flight of stairs that I did not want to be alone, and could think of no one I wanted with me. I returned to the café and sat with Hortense Berthelot, and she consented, concealing her astonishment, to go with me somewhere in a taxi, in which she had not ridden since her pre-war days. We went to a Russian night club in the rue Henri-Martin, where there were rugs on all the walls and a large Balalaika band and a Caucasian who danced with a hoop and sang a song I shall always remember about a tame bear which could not see a woman suffer so he went away into a forest and she was hurt and he wondered why. Mme. Berthelot and I drank near-champagne at high prices, she very sparingly but willing to do her part. At dawn we taxied to the Bois de Boulogne and drove slowly round the lake (tall silent trees and green moss on trunks and a swan on the water), and Mme. Berthelot, whose gloved hand rested on my forearm, said calmly:

'He spoke with exactness, *le pauvre* Vanzetti. "I forgive *some* of these people. . . ."'

In that same season Papa Doumer, one of the most harmless Presidents of the late Third Republic, signed a bill authorizing the construction of six new warships for the French Navy, and Briand, on the other hand, cooked up a treaty with Kellogg and the wary Coolidge 'outlawing' war between France and the United States. The French Chamber voted to 'nationalize' all industry in time of war.

'We are *foutus*,' said Monsieur Henri Julliard. 'When there is so much talk about peace, we are sure to have another war.'

'It will be beyond our means,' the horse butcher said.

'We will have it just the same,' Monsieur Henri said sadly.

Within a week seven billions of francs were earmarked for the construction of what turned out to be the Maginot Line.

All of these events had an impact in the rue de la Huchette but did not hamper its traditional activities. Articles of piety, cabinet-making, public women, paints and dyes, haircuts, yarn, goldfish, soap, felt slippers, used postage stamps, sheet music, flowers, spices, medical and dental treatment, and other local commodities and services were, as always, in demand. The man least affected by world trends and portents was probably Monsieur Dorlan, the bookbinder.

While at work, which seemed to be almost any time between seven a.m. and midnight, Monsieur Dorlan wore a smock soiled with ink, glue and other materials of his exacting trade, also a pair of ill-fitting spectacles which had to be pushed upwards or laid aside when he had to be most careful. Neither he nor his two pale apprentices spoke, except to customers, during working hours. Each was preoccupied with seemingly unrelated tasks. The window was filled with battered worn volumes waiting their turn for parchment or leather bindings. So were all the shelves and corners and a large share of the floor area, and the tiny back room.

My own experience was probably characteristic. Time, for Monsieur Dorlan, did not exist. What mattered was doing his work as well as or better than anyone else in the world. In the course of a year he handled precious books in Hebrew, Sanskrit, Babylonian, Arabic, Latin, Provençal and all the modern languages. He knew only French.

The job I had for him was to bind into two volumes twelve monthly copies of a modern magazine, containing among other baffling items several plates or reproductions of paintings by contemporary experimental artists, which his apprentices were just as likely as not to turn upside down in the hope of making their message more intelligible. I gave the volumes to Monsieur Dorlan one afternoon in February, and we spent several hours together, he questioning and making notes on torn fragments of used envelopes, and I explaining what I wanted done.

We agreed on a price which troubled my conscience, it was so low.

April 1st was the date we set for me to call for the books. On April 15th I glanced through the dusty window and saw by the light of a street lamp that my magazines were stacked just where Dorlan had put them two months previously. Delicacy prevented me from prodding the conscientious old man. When the leaves began to fall that year I was strolling one Sunday along the quai St. Michel and was halted by a man in a black suit and bowler hat (late Empire) surrounded by his sizable middle-class family, consisting of large wife and assorted children ranging in ages from twenty-four to nine. Only when he began speaking did I realize that he was Monsieur Dorlan. It was his wedding anniversary, he said, to explain his absence from his shop. Furthermore, there was a question he wanted to ask me about the periodicals I had left with him. Would I drop in some time within a fortnight or so?

I waited another decent interval, and just before Christmas I called on him (having walked past the shop at least twice daily in the interim) and agreed that the table of contents should be in the front of the book, not in the back, according to English and not French custom.

In March I observed that some of my magazines, enough for Volume One, had left their dusty place in the right-hand corner of the front room.

Soon afterwards I had to make a short visit to America, about a year in duration.

On my return, Monsieur Dorlan sent one of his hardworking boys to the Hôtel du Caveau to inform me that my books were almost finished, and early in the following January I went to claim them, paying fifty francs the volume, which at the prevailing exchange was about eight shillings each.

Just then I was having my daily lunches with Madame Goujon, whose tottering, deaf Marie put up memorable grub. As a contributor to the Goujon budget, I was given wider latitude in escorting Hyacinthe to the Comédie Française, the Grand Guignol, and tea at Rumpelmayer's or the Poire Blanche.

Call it what you like, I was deeply attached to that phenomenal young girl, who could witness with relish a stage performance in which a man's head was chopped off and spouted blood all over the footlights, or an episode in which a mad old hag gouges out the eyes of a young woman in the violent ward, using a knitting needle for the purpose. Hyacinthe also could vibrate like a sensitive viol when the company turned in a moving performance at the Comédie. Without musical training, and reared in the midst of her mother's atrocious taste, she could drink in modern or classical masterpieces and make, right off the bat, more intelligent comments than nine-tenths of the professional Paris critics.

Madame Goujon's newly acquired volumes of Proust did not benefit her, but they transformed Hyacinthe. In turn she devoured Villon, Rimbaud and Baudelaire, rejecting lesser poets with a sureness of instinct.

'You, my friend,' she said to me one afternoon as we looked up and down the Champs Elysées from the terrace of Fouquet's, 'will want to possess me one of these days. We have so much in common. You have looked so deeply into my heart, have had so much patience with my immaturity — such flattering confidence in my latent qualities you discern, and only you, dear Elliot.

'But I foresee that it may be wiser, more stimulating, yes, more satisfactory in the end, if we remain as we are. I swear that no one shall ever be closer. You know that. With us, it is not necessary to say everything. To define is to destroy. After all, you have no lack of mistresses. That is one respect in which I envy you, as a man. I shall understand, and there never will be anyone like Hyacinthe.'

It would have been brutal not to have replied in kind, and in so doing I cribbed my Huysmans. She knew it and overlooked it and lost no respect for me. It was all in the game.

'You tempt me,' I said, 'since I have had a share in creating you. Sin at all times is delightful, but a new sin, involving one's own creation, would be a refinement of incest, requiring theological interpretation . . .'

'Please. Don't be sacrilegious,' she said, earnestly.

16

MOSTLY ABOUT AN OLD PROFESSION AND MUSIC

In some ways the French were the least musical people in the world. Perhaps that statement is too dogmatic, and not just. What I mean is that there was no folk music that was part and fibre of Frenchmen, anywhere, any time, like the Spanish *flamenco*, or American jazz. Tastes were individual and varied; there were cliques and schools and genres. Concerts were cheap in Paris and mediocre. A crystalline, rather brittle school of piano playing, exemplified by Alfred Cortot, was taught by a few high-priced piano teachers to rich and ambitious pupils. On Saturdays and Sundays three or four orchestras like the Pasdeloup organization rendered German classics half-heartedly, Russian pieces in a Gallic style, and neglected the sound French music of the eighteenth and early nineteenth centuries in favour of trite selections familiar to the crowd.

News items leaked through to America how Koussevitsky had cancelled an engagement in Paris because the French musicians would not rehearse (since no one could afford to pay them). I once saw poor Schneevoigt do everything but throw his baton at the Frenchmen under his command, without attracting anything but their superficial attention. The Opéra Comique existed for American tenors and sopranos who wanted clippings about a European success, and practically anyone with a thousand dollars to spend could sing Mimi or Madame *Boot er flee* (with the accent on the last syllable) once. French critics were so corrupt and cynical that for anything ranging from a lunch to a five-pound note, a performer could get a press notice that was not abusive. In the same way, authors could purchase literary praise, painters could get a canvas into the Luxembourg Gallery, etc. There is much just complaint in America about a corrupt press. In Paris individual newspapers were even more venal and unscrupulous, but no one expected them to be any different, and there were so many of them that every group had its say in one or another.

A cross-section of music in the rue de la Huchette is characteristic of the Paris of the Parisians, which had no resemblance, I cannot repeat often enough, to the American Express, the Café de la Paix, the Hôtel Ritz, onion soup at the Escargot, the Dôme, etc., etc. Moving from east to west along the street, the state of musical development, habits and preferences was about as follows:

The beef-and-lamb butcher had no awareness of music at all. He was like old Papa Doumergue, ex-president of the former Republic, who had to have a special secretary at his side on state occasions to nudge him when the Marseillaise was being played, so that he could make the appropriate official gesture.

M. Luttenschlager, the dealer in articles of piety, hummed Alsatian (mostly Germanic) songs of poignant beauty and charm, and kept fairly well on the key, but could not keep time.

The proprietor of the paint and dye shop, Monsieur Villières, was neutral, and the carpenter across the street in No. 3 had no work songs to ease the monotony of saw and plane. The pork butcher strung along with Luttenschlager, specializing in children's songs about the snow, as he handled strings of sausages in a city where winter meant mud, influenza and a drizzling rain.

The Hôtel du Caveau had several assorted musicians among its residents, but most of these were foreign and they seldom got together when sober. Monsieur Léonard, the incompetent accordion player, was a Belgian; Mary the Greek sang the Missouri Waltz without words in her cups; Pierre Vautier went in for 'The Six' French moderns who stemmed from Satie and were friendly with Ravel until his bolero became a public nuisance with the advent of the T.S.F. or radio. Georges the *garçon* hummed circus music; Thérèse, the cook, liked bawdy songs consisting mostly of words and gestures.

The Satyr, like Monsieur Noël, was a devotee of the splendid and neglected French music leading up to Rameau and Couperin. The Taitbouts were tone deaf; the Alsatian old maids never sang because it would have annoyed the ex-colonel. Madame Absalom disliked music because it competed with her gossip. Dorlan, the bookbinder, thought of it in terms of early Catholic notation in old manuscripts. Lanier, war veteran and father of a family, sang 'Madelon' now and then.

Where music meant the most, in a limited way, was in *Le Panier Fleuri*. Mireille, with the indestructible hide and roguish blue eyes, had once been in the chorus at the Casino de Paris, before the days of Josephine Baker (*Baa care*) and did much to relieve the gloom that stole into that parlour of joy so frequently. She would sit on the sagging sofa, beside old Armandine, who also was somewhat of a clown, singing and imitating the chorus girl's come-on tricks. And when rich customers wanted a living-picture show, a grave demure-faced girl, with dark hair wound around her head in a braid like a halo of St. Cecilia, played Chaminade's 'Scarf Dance' on a cheap ornate piano, wearing a bathing suit cut rakishly to expose one breast and cover the scar of her Cæsarean.

Sara, the Jewess at No. 18, when alone in her small café late at night, sang nostalgic laments like 'Eli, Eli'. But her faithful *garçon* and platonic worshipper, the one-armed Louis, loved to sing, as a Spaniard or a Swede or Russian does, and when Monsieur Henri Julliard tried to exploit his mediæval sub-cellars which had been frequented by Robespierre, Louis was given an old French costume and allowed, for a small fee, to sing songs like 'My Wife is Dead' (familiar to American tourists who were taken to the Lapin à Gil [not *Agile*] near Sacré-Cœur).

Nothing much ever came of Monsieur Henri's attempt to make a nightclub of his splendid property, the Caveau, because the place, the songs and the neighbourhood were genuine. Tourists had become so accustomed to a certain amount of flim-flam that they could not be happy without it. This, Monsieur Henri could never grasp or understand. So his subterranean night-club became a neighbourhood hangout which was truly interesting and colourful but not profitable.

Of the man, wife and son who ran the little dry-goods shop at No. 19, where the neighbourhood servants and workers got their felt slippers, aprons, overalls and articles of plain clothing, I have said little because there was little to say. The family name was Luneville, they all were from the north and used the guttural r. They paid decent attention to their stock and customers, had their meals in the back room on time, and all three slept in the cellar. Their conversation was confined to 'yea, yea,' and less frequently, 'nay, nay'. They took no part in protest strikes, did not drink in cafés, read the *Intransigeant* (known as the janitor's newspaper), closed the store in

August to spend the vacation near Lille, and otherwise were the backbone of a decaying and disappearing France.

Monsieur Saint-Aulaire, essentially the artistic type, had views on music as well as the drama and society.

'Mozart,' he said pontifically, *'a fait une belle petite musiquette, mais, pour la vraie musique, donnez-moi Massenet.'*

[Mozart made pretty little tunes, but for real music give me Massenet.]

Monsieur and Madame Corre had never had time for music, but they had a piano and liked it when their young daughter-in-law, homesick in Paris to a pitiful degree, played Gottschalk and Nevin's 'Narcissus' in a lady-like way.

It is needless to say that The Navet had no music in whatever he had in place of a soul. His kind the world over do not go in for arts except to destroy them.

So the only men who sang with a will were Louis, the *garçon*, and the chestnut and oyster man from the Loire, and the only creditable performer on any musical instrument was Monsieur Monge who played hunting horns and the old-fashioned instrument like a Chinese hat. The best French composers had always been taken up first by the Germans, the kind of Germans now extinct or in hiding. That was true of the works of modern French painters, too. When the struggling German Republic in 1923 took over the former palace of the Crown Prince for an art museum, the new directors acquired a fine collection of Cézannes, Renoirs, Vlamincks, Utrillos, Picassos (nearly always confused with the 'French school' he practically destroyed), Braques, Matisses, and good lesser artists like Masson, Chirico and the fantastic Alsatian meat cutter, Hans Arp.

No so much could be said for any French museum. One of the last places the French impressionist got into was the Louvre.

The death of Jean de Reszke caused no flutter in the rue de la Huchette, whereas the death of the great actor, Lucien Guitry, whose only lapse from high art was Sacha, his son, was respectfully felt and acknowledged.

'All our great men are dying,' Monsieur Henri said, sadly. 'One hopes that some others are now being born.'

'Not likely,' cackled Madame Absalom.

When Rudolph Valentino died and fantastic reports about the demonstrations by American women in connection with the funeral of the great screen lover leaked into our quarters, well dressed up by the avid anti-American columnists who had a field day, again I had to proceed up my street as if I were running a gauntlet.

'Hey, American,' yelled Madame Absalom as I passed No. 10. 'What did that *type* have that other men have not? He must have rogered half the women in your country.'

By that time Madame Absalom and I were on such terms that I was able to reply: 'He would have passed you up, you old battleaxe.'

'If I'd have know when I was young what I know now,' the old woman said, 'I'd have *cocu mon* 'ex' every afternoon and morning. I wasn't so bad. Just like the rest, I suppose, when all is said and done.'

'Some are better than others, just the same,' said Monsieur Maurice, smiling and descending from his bicycle.

When I passed No. 27, the Épicerie Danton, I was hailed by a troubled Monsieur Corre, flanked by his porcelain Madame. They were not concerned with the defunct Sheik of Araby and Hollywood. Madame's Singer, or *San jhay*, had broken down, and since I had informed them it was of American origin, they had hoped I might know how to mend it. The Corres, like other middle-class Parisians and Frenchman, thought of the world as if it were a sort of dish, the bottom being France and all foreign lands and peoples being grouped together around the narrow slanting rim, so that stray objects and personalities slid down into their ken now and then. They expected all Americans to know one another, and to know all the answers about American occurrences and American machines.

The music shop at No. 26, owned by a non-musical bachelor named Gion who, like Madame Absalom, had received his means of livelihood by inheritance from an aunt, also had a small selection of early coloured engravings in the window. These Monsieur Gion picked up from clients who wanted to exchange them for sheet or bound music, and sold them to collectors, buyers from Right Bank art shops, and occasional stray foreigners like me. When I first saw the shop there was in the window, below a string of secondhand violins suspended like beautifully varnished hams above the level of the eye, a set of prints depicting the home life of the American *peaux rouges* or Indians. Broke as I was, I simply had to have them.

The Indians were very shapely, the women being built about like Gaby Deslys and the men like the Christian saint who is portrayed leaning against a Corinthian pillar being shot full of arrows without showing the strain. All of them were the colour of Josephine Baker, with a touch of lavender powder. The she-Indians were all in their late teens, wore bands round their foreheads to keep their hair in place, had rings and bracelets on their fingers, arms and ankles and skipped from place to place like Mary Pickford used to do before she was saved. The he-Indians fell into poses reminiscent of the Russian ballet, and in one of the best prints had strung hammocks of plaited deer sinews for the girls, who lay in them with one perfect leg exposed, while the braves swung the hammock gently.

My favourite was an old chief sending his sons off to war. He stood very straight and dignified, and the boys were lined up, in feathers and war paint, being embraced and kissed on both cheeks by the gruff old sachem, while squaws were turning their backs and weeping beneath trimmed willow trees. The engraver and artist, being a Parisian, had never seen an unpruned tree.

Monsieur Gion was a bloodless young man, something of the order of the floor-walker, M. Panaché. He expressed no political opinions, but one knew instinctively that those he had were all wrong. His mistress was an awkward, almost furtive, soft-spoken young girl who also was assistant in the store. This girl, Bernice, was an orphan who had worked in two department stores from which she had been fired for acting as the sisters in the orphanage had urged her to when approached by predatory males.

Monsieur Gion had hired her because she would work for two francs a day less than anyone else he had interviewed. She dusted well, which is essential in a music store. One day, however, when her hands were icy cold she dropped a violin worth 200 francs and got so rattled that, in trying to explain to the boss how it had happened, she stepped on the instrument and stove in the fragile belly.

From that day onward she did the dusting and kept house in a very faithful way for Monsieur Gion, sharing his room on the fourth floor of the Hôtel Normandie. Her pay ceased, and she learned how right the Sisters of Charity had been in warning her about original sin.

The very poor among the Parisians had learned that a certain poisonous drug which I shall not name, but which is obtainable without prescription in French and other drug stores, would, if administered a drop or two at a time, in a glass of white wine, make a woman quite ill for a few days, and sometimes produce a desirable result. Bernice was treated to this miraculous draught about three times a year, until queer things began happening to her digestion and her memory (never exceptionally good). This disturbed Monsieur Gion, who was afraid he might get himself into trouble. So he threw her out in 1932, after four years of unwedded non-bliss, and she tried to drown herself in the Seine, near the little park named after Henri IV, and merely caught pneumonia. Bernice looked so fresh and well after her long rest in the Hôtel Dieu, that Monsieur Gion took her back on one condition which practically removed the possibility of pregnancy.

There was no nonsense preached in France about the dignity of labour and not much outside the church concerning the possibility of being content and happy although poor. That might be possible in the country, but not in Paris. The daughters of the poor, if they were ugly, would naturally be drudges. If they were pretty, or not repulsive, it was assumed that they would amplify their incomes, and the family income more often than not, by furnishing what men seemed to need and for which they would pay them when they had to. The lucky girls, or the clever ones, landed kind and indulgent men. It was all part of the system, and helped keep it in gear until it fell apart. It was accepted as a matter of course. Whether it was better or worse than any other system is beyond my judgment. In many instances it seemed to work hardships, and in quite as many others it seemed to turn out delightfully, with resulting benefits to all concerned. It was a part of French thrift, of ecclesiastical compromise, of society highly civilized and poorly supplied with natural resources, of dangerous national boundaries and national enmities.

Madame Mariette, of *Le Panier Fleuri*, might permit old Armandine to get the hide whaled off her back for fifty francs, knowing the bruises would heal and that Armandine, at her age, could not make fifty francs as easily any other way. But the atmosphere of her establishment, from the point of view of the employees, was heavenly compared with that in Madame Durand's flower shop, Monsieur Gion's music shop, the sweatshop where

Madame Claire did piece work ten hours a day, or the office in the prefecture where Hortense Berthelot was employed.

Officially the bordel opened up at two o'clock in the afternoon, and remained open until two o'clock in the morning. But for men who had not gone to bed, or had found themselves restless and had time on their hands in the morning, one girl came in at ten o'clock, in modest street clothes, peeled them off, washed herself all over with the aid of a bidet, was given a perfunctory O.K. by the *sous-maîtresse* or assistant hostess who had early duty that day, and sat in a little triangular waiting room on a red velvet upholstered bench and chatted with the hostess until the bell in the hallway indicated that someone had entered without knocking, in obedience to the sign on the door.

The hostess, who was always fully and conservatively dressed, with the keys to the champagne closet dangling from her belt as a badge of office, would step into the hallway and greet the customer politely. '*Bonjour, Monsieur*,' she would say, or, if she knew him as a steady customer who liked a certain amount of familiarity, she would say, '*Bonjour, Monsieur Albert.*' Then she would usher him into a small reception-room or parlour across the hall from where the girl was waiting.

'Mademoiselle,' the hostess would call, in a carefully modulated voice.

Mireille or Mado or Susie or Daisy or Claude or Germaine would cross the hall and pause a moment, smiling brightly, in the doorway.

'*Bonjour*,' she would say to the man, or now and then sincerely pleased, '*Ah, c'est vous! Mais, vous êtes matinal aujourd'hui*' (Ah, it's you. My, you're up early to-day).

The visit was described as 'a little moment', *une demie-heure* or an 'hour', and was priced accordingly. For a short time, the client paid ten francs (about a shilling); a half hour cost twenty francs, and an hour thirty. The hostess mounted the short steep stairs with the happy pair, indicated which room they were to use: 'the red room', 'the blue room', 'the oriental room', etc., and left two small freshly laundered towels on the bed table.

Only white girls, not those in the 'heavy' class like Armandine, nor the little women who posed as schoolgirls, nor the coal-black Negress from Martinique named Dora, took their turn on early duty. Wandering drunks or fitful sleepers might or might not be in the mood for something unusual in size or colour, and the chance that a tiny restless girl would be the only one available when Monsieur had set his mind on a fat complaisant type was too great. So morning customers got medium-sized beauties and had to wait until two o'clock if they had bizarre ideas that day.

At two o'clock the downstairs waiting-room took on its lively air. Some of the girls slept in lofty little attic rooms upstairs in the establishment, but about half of them either had to meet their pimps and turn over the day's receipts at two in the morning or take a late bus or a taxi to their family homes. Even when business was dull they never read. The only literature on the premises was six or eight illegal books with illustrations tending to stimulate certain customers who liked to browse through an obscene chapter or two before settling down to business. The girls never read these. Neither did they peruse the 'album' which was kept on hand and passed out discreetly by the hostess when a client asked for it. The 'album' had a collection of photographs which left little or nothing to the imagination except to make one wonder, when half way through, what possibly could be left for the remaining pages to portray. To what extent the 'album' at Madame Mariette's place made things easier for fading clients I cannot say, but it changed the course of the life of a young Frenchman I knew who was attending the Sorbonne in the early 1920s. Jacques was brilliant but had no ambition and no plans for the use of his excellent mind. He was at school because his parents could pay for it and university life was more carefree and less onerous than a job in a bank or the executive offices of some factory. One day when he was idling away an afternoon at Mariette's, in perusing the 'album' he was struck with the infinite number of variations contained in a few simple acts involving two, three, and in extreme cases four parties. He began thinking in terms of numbers: permutations and combinations. That same evening he plunged avidly into his neglected mathematics textbooks and soon led his class in higher algebra and integral calculus. Today he is one of the most distinguished theoretical mathematicians in London and freely admits that he owes it all to Mariette.

One of the features of *Le Panier Fleuri* was what Mariette called 'the chamber of detached divertissement' in which a client (if he were well known or officially vouched for) might sit in an easy-chair, with a drink at his elbow, and watch through a hole in the wall, cleverly camouflaged by a figure in the flamboyant wallpaper and covered on the observer's side by a picture when not in use, the behaviour of unsuspecting fellow men who entered the 'red' room with the girl or girls of their choice. The girl or girls, of course, knew all about the red room, and when the grave-faced and dignified hostess led them thither, she or they chuckled inwardly and shed all inhibitions with the scant and flimsy garments they wore downstairs for display.

Many students of psychology and human behaviour patronized her chamber of detached divertissement, Madame Mariette told me. She had no affection for those professors who pretended a scientific interest in her spectacle because, when they had got through with their observations, instead of finishing the afternoon or evening in her salon they went to another one, in the rue de la Harpe or the rue Mazet, in order to leave with Mariette an illusion of sincerity in their detachment.

One client, who dressed like the late Berry Wall, used to show up every other Monday afternoon, that being the day of the doctor's visit. He would sit on the terrace of the Café de la Gare, sipping vermouth cassis, with the coins for payment of his drink already on the table. The moment he saw Dr. Clouet leave *Le Panier*, this gay old party would grab his gloves and stick and would hobble to No. 17. He knew that on Mondays the girls were forbidden by law to receive any clients before the doctor came, and it pleased the old boy to be the first on the order of the day. This man, during the years Consuela was with Mariette, chose her invariably and complained indignantly when she left Paris for Madrid. Consuela was a thin Spanish girl with an appealing dignified face, black hair piled high with a Spanish comb, and she was 'the bride' of the establishment. That is to say, she did not appear in the line-up with the other girls when a chance customer arrived, but waited in a dim room for the initiated who were hard to please. She wore a white bridal gown, a white lace mantilla, long white gloves and carried a bouquet of small rosebuds and forget-me-nots (artificial but very bridal).

One of the most popular specialities at Mariette's was a Scandinavian type of blonde who dyed her hair, and I mean all of it, pale green and appeared naked except for a transparent cellophane raincoat tinted green.

All this was for the trade. The girls themselves were much like any other girls. The same ones used to work for a while in the cheaper houses like Mariette's, where things were more lively, and then would be graduated to the high-class houses in the Montholon or Madeleine or Étoile quarters and receive one hundred francs instead of ten for the same *quid pro quo*. They made about the same amount of money, since at Mariette's there was more activity, and they preferred that, not because they enjoyed it, but because in the expensive houses they had to wear expensive clothes and be careful with them, and were obliged to watch their grammar. The cheap busy places were less 'lonesome'.

Let no man think that he and his reactions were not described gleefully and in piquant detail in that red plush waiting-room where the waiting girls gathered. Generally speaking the girls got along with one another. If one girl got in trouble or needed money, or was bereaved or discarded by a lover she doted on, the others rallied round. They all knew that if two girls in a house took a dislike to each other, and could not control it and be polite, one would have to go. Men reacted badly to an atmosphere of discord. And the one the Madame would send away would invariably be the one who was least popular with the clients.

I liked Madame Mariette. I think of her as a friend, an interesting and beautiful woman with genuine understanding, wide experience and something deep inside her that no man had yet aroused or even touched and but rarely suspected. In our street she was second to none, unless it was Monsieur Henri, in her love and solicitude for France. Of her profession, which many despise and deplore, this clear-eyed shapely woman was neither ashamed nor proud. It existed. It was wanted. She tried to direct her establishment efficiently and well. No one was ever clipped at Mariette's, and most of her clients remained her customers for years. But when France's Mr. Blum knuckled under to England's appeasers and stood idly by while the decent men and women of Spain were destroyed and martyrized, Madame Mariette wept and bit her lips constantly for shame, the deep fundamental kind of shame that sweeps from head to foot and through all the nerves and fingers and intestines and glands like a foul disease made instantaneous. By the time Munich came along, her eyes had no more tears but were hot and dry and smarted.

What fascinated me most about *Le Panier Fleuri*, after Mariette and the others had accepted me as a neighbour and a comrade, was the little record book and what it contained in the way of statistics. I tried to look at the astonishing Mireille with dispassionate scientific eye and decide why it was that, day in and day out, in sunshine or in rain, in May or in December, about three-fifths of the men in search of physical and spiritual solace would, when eight shapely, sweet, skilled and accommodating girls were lined up before them, nod or point or smile toward Mireille. Mireille was not the most attractive, from the magazine-cover standpoint. In fact, she was somewhat bony, lean, with long feet and hands and breasts slightly shrunken. Her face was not beautiful, and not particularly interesting. True, her eyes were large and the lashes were long and curved, but they did not reveal her dry sense of humour or her perverse and very ribald wit. Her voice was unforgettable, but a large percentage of the clients had never heard it when they selected her for the first time.

In the case of most of the girls, clients stuck with them two or three visits, then tactfully switched to a contrasting type. Not so with Mireille. They would have no other, even if they had to wait, which all of them detested.

Conversely, there was one little girl, a small *chic* brunette who had had one baby without leaving a mark, and who could have served as a model for any commercial artist. As Mariette expressed it, she was '*extrèmement gentille et caressante*'. Her name was Mado, and her average was the lowest in the house, come what may. Every man who chose her liked her, assured Madame that Mado was very nice, but they did not want her again.

In all public or private lupanars, there was always one favourite, another badly out of luck, while the rest of the girls maintained a fair average. In order to keep their unfortunate sister in funds, each girl, when asked by a man which among the others she preferred to have with her on a 'double date' said promptly, 'Mado', and promised all sorts of hitherto undreamed-of delights.

The girls of *Le Panier Fleuri* grossed about 150 francs apiece per day, half of which went to Mariette, who footed the bills of the establishment, furnished the meals (and excellent ones) in the attic dining-room, arranged police protection and gave the place its personality and reputation for fair play. Her profit as owner and proprietress amounted to about 100,000 francs a year (from £400 to £500). This she doubled by tips on the market and the exchange received from bankers who patronized her place.

Mireille averaged about 65,000 francs a year; poor Mado had to struggle along with 12,000, as did Monsieur Frémont, the letter carrier, Hortense Berthelot and others of our acquaintance who worked for a living.

17

THE CARD THAT HAS SLIPPED FROM THE DECK OF THE PAST

The reader already knows how little the neighbourhood grocery in the rue de la Huchette resembles an A and P in America, M. Corre having been surrounded by specialists who took care of the meat, fish, milk and dairy products, vegetables, delicatessen, etc. It was equally astonishing to the American observer how many more articles than might have been expected were to be found at No. 4 in the store of the *marchand de couleurs* or paint store. Like the carpenter at No. 3, Monsieur Villières, the paint dealer, lived among his neighbours amicably without expressing his political or religious convictions. Monsieur Villières carried his non-partisanship to a degree of refinement which made a purchase in his shop quite difficult at times. He would not choose between rival brands of brads or screws, or advise a customer about a suitable colour for woodwork. Patterns and thicknesses of oilcloth all had their virtues and drawbacks, nicely balanced, in his cautious mind.

Monsieur Villières carried small tools and minor items of hardware, artists' materials and draughtsmen's supplies, school supplies, flower and vegetable seeds, what the French mistook for modern office supplies and bookkeeping equipment, toys, jigsaws puzzles, novelties that mooed like cows when concealed in drawers, tin frogs that bided their time before leaping disconcertingly into the air, jack straws, chess and draughts (French style), dominoes, household disinfectants, furniture polish, machine oil — the list is inexhaustible. Furthermore, Monsieur Villières knew exactly what was in the shop and where to find it. The customer had to know and say just what he wanted. In that respect he was given no help whatsoever. Once the client had stated his desire or pleasure, the paint man would respond, even if he knew the kind of hook the chap was buying would not fit the eyes already in his possession. His not to reason why.

His personal life consisted of meals at the Hôtel du Caveau, during which he was careful not to raise his eyebrows no matter what was being said at the bar, evenings occupied with endless inventories of his stock, his eight hours on a cot in the back room, now and then a bath in his portable tub (which he rented out for a small fee to neighbourhood exponents of bathing, of which there were not many). He attended an American Western, or Chaplin movie whenever one came to the neighbourhood cinema on the boulevard St. Michel, enjoyed old Armandine every fortnight at half past eight, and spent alternate Sundays with relatives in St. Germain.

The paint dealer simply doted on counting camel's hair brushes, boxes of drawing-pins, the three tubes of a most unpleasant oil colour called 'Italian pink', not one of which had been sold in twenty years of strict application to business, and whatever else was on his shelves. He proceeded methodically, wrote figures in his ledger, checked them with notations he had slipped into the cash drawer during the day, and considered that all was well with the world when the whole proved to be equal to the sum of its parts, and vice versa. The only information he ever volunteered to me, in the course of sixteen years' acquaintance, was a flat statement to the effect that one could not mix aniline dyes but had to use them as they had been created in the package. This proved to be erroneous, and I was tempted to tell him so. Some good instinct halted me in time. One had to respect the beliefs of others and not continually be setting folks to right about this or that, if one wished to live serenely in Paris.

In the canning or preserving season, taken very seriously in thrifty France, in Paris as well as in the country, every *marchand de couleurs* trotted out a most beautiful array of huge copper and bronze kettles which he rented to housewives and others for two francs a day. I rented one once for two months and kept it on a table in my attic room, so beautiful did the otherwise unsightly objects around me appear in resplendent reflection. This bothered Monsieur Villières more than anything that had happened to him since World War I. I paid regularly, by the week, in order to enjoy his perplexity. I assured him that I was using his marvellous example of the coppersmith's lost art for no ulterior or unworthy purpose, that I never bathed in it, or used it as a chamber-pot. I liked the look of it, that was all.

Undoubtedly I contributed to the French belief that all Americans are crazy.

Imagine my surprise when, one day at the Caveau, Monsieur Villières, with flushed face and indignant eyes, stopped at the bar on his way to the luncheon table with a weekly paper clutched in his hand. He confronted me with such asperity and personal reproachfulness in his manner and tone that I was taken aback, as were my drinking companions, the chestnut vendor, Monsieur Frémont, and the *garçon*, Georges.

'This is an outrage,' the paint man said, beating the bar with his folded periodical. 'America is barbarous and uncivilized.'

As soon as I could, I ascertained the cause of this unique spasm of partisanship. One glance at the paper made it all too plain. Charlie Chaplin was in trouble. He was, according to the text, being victimized and persecuted and robbed by a designing woman who had used her young daughter as bait, bamboozled the world's greatest pantomime artist into marriage with the child, and now was demanding a huge fortune out of Charlie's earnings.

The way in which the American male seemed to be pushed around by his womenfolk left Parisians goggle-eyed. There was a feeble women's suffrage movement in France, but it never came to anything because French men and women did not think in terms of abstract justice. None of the sentimental arguments in favour of sex equality had much weight in France. Clever women got everything they wanted, if they were lucky, and often manipulated high statesmen, financiers and stream-lined executives as if the men were marionettes. The French wife did not think the end of the world had come if her man made an occasional trip to the neighbourhood bordel. She did not expect to live without work or worry for ever afterwards if she caught him in an hotel room with another woman standing by in *déshabillé*. What she was to get, under any and all circumstances, was carefully specified in a marriage contract written by the head of the family and the head of her husband's family.

Men in public life, except clergymen, did not have to scuttle and hide like waterbugs if they felt the urge for some good loose feminine society. I never heard a Frenchwoman complain about any action of her husband's that she did not know about. Most of them knew just how much or how little of a hold they had on their man, and arranged their lives accordingly. If a jealous woman lost her head and shot an unfaithful lover, a French jury, 999,999 times out of 1,000,000, would acquit her, and in the remaining instance the President of the Republic would pardon her. That this had any deterrent effect on men's philandering was not noticeable.

Charlie Chaplin's predicament was kept in the public eye of Paris several days, and the comment was uniformly sympathetic with Charlie, indignant toward the mother, and scarcely mentioned the girl, who was thought of as a sort of stage 'property' which could serve in one kind of show as well as another. I saw the chestnut vendor staring with wrinkled brow at a newspaper cut depicting the girl wife of the comedian one day.

'I've picked up better ones than that in the place Zacherie on the 14th of July,' he said.

Pierre Vautier expressed the neighbourhood idea of middle-aged American females when shown a photograph of a club woman from Ohio or Wisconsin.

'What impudence!' Pierre exclaimed.

'The French they are a funny race,' is a household word in America. Having witnessed the American Legion parade in Paris (on the day of Isadora Duncan's funeral), I began to understand that we are as comical as anyone could be.

Something deterred me from taking Hyacinthe Goujon to see that Legion performance, where drunken veterans in miscellaneous costumes that had everything except art and imagination streamed and staggered along, with female drum majors who would not have been allowed to polish door-knobs in the Moulin Rouge. Instead I escorted Madame Frémont and Yvonne, and neither of them laughed or cried when those middle-aged men, looking more incongruous when they had preserved part of an athletic shape than when they had let themselves go, gave one of the world's most amazing exhibitions of goodwill and bad taste. The ex-doughboy faces in a foreign setting looked almost depraved; the costumes were ill-chosen; the average veteran wasn't drunk enough to be clownish or sober enough to be dignified. But, if neither Mlle. nor Mme. Frémont brushed tears from her eyes, I must admit that I did. For there was something in the beat of that old march step, echoing between French buildings, some relentless and jaunty and effective rhythm in the drums, that made me see my former comrades as they had been in khaki, years before. I remembered standing in the door of a goods truck in a troop train, very early in the morning, in some region of France where the cattle were snow white in green fields, and an old peasant woman, seeing strong young men swarming over that string of waggons, dropped down on her knees in gratitude to pray, as naturally as she would have reached for a pitchfork.

About the time the Legion was parading in Paris, Briand and Kellogg were outlawing war, by means of a series of complicated multilateral pacts which now are useful, one hopes, for carpet lining. France accepted the Kellogg plan (which before it had become apparent that it was to prove a dud had been called the Briand plan) with the reservation that France should have 'the right to fight' if the Rhineland non-military zone were militarized.

The rue de la Huchette knew only this about the American presidential campaign; namely, that Al Smith habitually wore a brown '*chapeau melon*' and that he was against Prohibition, as who wasn't.

'Smith can't be elected because he is a Catholic,' I said to Monsieur Monge, who was all for Al and a glass of wine with his meals.

Monsieur Monge tried to remember whether Papa Doumergue, then President of the French Republic, was a Catholic or a freethinker. He could not be sure, and neither could anyone else in the bar.

I went on further to say that Al habitually mispronounced some well-known American words when campaigning over the T.S.F.

'That's nothing,' said Madame Berthelot. 'I heard Tardieu the other day and he made three mistakes in syntax. Blum had good schooling, it seems. He makes practically no mistakes at all.'

'All Jews make a mistake in being born,' The Navet said. 'It makes life hard for them and for us.'

Somehow the fall of Jericho does not seem as remote as the carefree 1920s. One has long lived with the fact that those walls came tumbling down. Likewise we accept the fact that a hero's dead body was dragged around the ramparts of Troy. Not so familiar is the fearful twilight over France. I can hear those voices in the rue de la Huchette. Blindfolded I could identify the clasp of Madame Berthelot's gloved hand, the tough palm of the chestnut vendor, the intonations of little Hyacinthe's lost voice, the life of Mireille's unquenchable spirit. Of Monsieur Henri Julliard I think each day with gratitude. Or is it gratitude to death itself? Monsieur Henri, who had lived so well, knew just when to die.

I am telling you in advance that Henri Julliard died while dying was still good, because that is satisfying news, and so much I have to tell will undermine your faith in evolution.

That remote and historical post-war period (1918–1930) has slipped from the pack of time and lies face downwards on the floor. For when the 1920s collapsed and fell, they took with them all that was worthwhile in the nineteenth century.

In 1929, Poincaré, the only living mathematician who could not figure out that what went up must come down and that money is labour (nothing more or less), was still at what one calls loosely 'the helm' of France. He had a majority of two or three votes in the Chamber, the support of the pactingest politician in the world (Aristide Briand) and a financier named Charon who had one of the softest hands under a hen of any gent who ever balanced a budget.

It was during 1929 that two new figures appeared in the Chamber of Deputies both destined to play important, if ignoble, rôles in French affairs. No. 1 was Léon Blum, and the other was Marty, the Communist who led the French Black Sea Revolt. In the German elections of that period, both the Communist and the Hitler party made gains at the expense of the centre. In England, Ramsay MacDonald got in again, having proved to the ruling clique that he was the world's worst false alarm as a labour leader. In the United States, in case you don't remember, the camphorous sage from Vermont was in the White House and was busily saying nothing, because he could think of nothing whatever to say.

Marshal Foch died and was given a magnificent state funeral. Ambassador Herrick died, and with him the last vestige of Franco-American co-operation or understanding. Then, when everyone in Paris was weary of superlatives having to do with death or internment, an obscure marshal named Sarrail discovered two years late that he had passed the Biblical age. All the properties and phrases had to be trotted out again for his public funeral.

Dr. Stresemann, who had agreed with Briand to end Franco-German wars, died and got less notice than Sergei Diaghilev of the Russian ballet. The *Bremen* made her maiden trip to New York and set up a speed record. General Maginot declared that the Franco-German frontier must be fortified on the French side before the Rhineland could be safely evacuated.

In the Radical-Socialist Party, a hot contest was going on which kept Monsieur Noël, the Satyr, and Monsieur Monge, the horse butcher, on their toes. Herriot, the Lyons local politician-littérateur, an amiable gentleman who came about as close to being honest as a practical statesman can, was opposed for the leadership of the powerful conservative centre party by a baker's son named Daladier. There was practically nothing left of Socialism in the Radical-Socialist Party, and Daladier wanted even less of it. Daladier was a non-prepossessing man with little personal charm or intellectual distinction, but he had never been Premier and had therefore made fewer enemies than Herriot, who had held the office several times.

The three 'radical-socialists' on our street all voted for Herriot — and Daladier won. Little did anyone suspect what that would mean to France or even Czechoslovakia. To The Navet and Monsieur Panaché, the beef butcher, Monsieur Saint-Aulaire, Madame Durand the florist, and even the inoffensive Monsieur and Madame Corre, Daladier was a dangerous radical who would undermine business and the home. On the other hand, to Milka and the chestnut vendor, Daladier was beneath contempt as a reactionary blunderer who was in public life because working in a baker's shop was harder and less profitable. Daladier made a bid for the premiership and lost because Briand would not play ball with him. So Tardieu, a reactionary patriot who believed in big business, got in, just after Clemenceau, the Tiger, died. Hoover became President of the United States, and Senator Edge came to Paris as Ambassador. The Parisians never even learned his name.

My connection with the press entitled me to tickets for various state funerals and other functions. The stirring pageant when Foch was laid away was made to order for Hyacinthe. We stood side by side on a balcony in the rue de Rivoli and saw the procession pass three stories below. There is nothing I can say that will describe how my companion of the day reacted, when the dead Marshal's snow-white horse, blanketed with a flowing black robe, and riderless, was led past, toward the place de la Concorde. Cardinals marched in their red trappings, the Coldstream Guards, shipped over for the purpose, wore their bearskin shakos. Crack French troops marched with their nervous hurried step. They kept time with the heart beats of a thirteen-year-old girl, becomingly pale, most tastefully dressed in deepest black, not Joan of Arc, but a daughter of France who had sprung from her decaying class like an orchid in a tropical swamp.

When the lesser marshal named Sarrail had his turn I could **not** resist taking Mireille. When she lighted a ready-made cigarette, not far from the casket, while a solemn part of the ceremony was in progress, my first impulse was to take it from her gently and step on it, eyeing the police and military guards and hoping for the best. My second and sounder impulse was to mind my own business.

While spending freely on the epidemic of public funerals the Government of France made spasmodic attempts at minor economies, one of which alarmed the Paris police department to such an extent that, after a lively tilt in the newspapers which spread to all our neighbourhood cafés, the plan was promptly abandoned. The French army had on hand several hundred thousand rifles of obsolete types. In fact, that was about the only kind of rifles available for the national defence. In order to cash in on the old-fashioned shooting irons, some ordnance officers, backed by the Deputies in the Chamber who liked to reduce mounting taxes, proposed a huge national bargain sale at which the old rifles were to be auctioned off to the the highest bidders.

The police commissioner howled to heaven, and his arguments found favour with propertied middle-class citizens who already had weapons. Factory owners and executives joined in the protest. These prudent menbers scented sure disaster, if every Tom, Dick and Harry could purchase a gun. The weapon might not stand in competitive test with those new ones Germany was manufacturing in open secrecy, but it would still be effective in riots and uprisings in the narrow city streets.

What became of the obsolete firearms was never disclosed, but they were not put up to public auction.

What had become of French unity, security, solidarity, and spirit is today more apparent than it was then. Clemenceau had sabotaged the only promising world peace proposal since the Sermon on the Mount. The bunglers of the Quai d'Orsay abused all of France's former allies. They had failed in an attempt to grab the Ruhr, the Rhineland and the Saar. France was economically unsound, financially bankrupt, morally ill and physically tottering. From a first-class power she had slipped to a third-class relic.

How was this débâcle reflected in the rue de la Huchette?

Meat was higher and tougher, and the families in average circumstances could not afford it more than twice a week.

Across the street from the meat shop, piety collected dust in the windows. It is not before, but after, wars and national collapses that piety abounds.

At No. 4 less paint was sold; inventories, consequently, became simpler.

At No. 3 timber was prohibitive in price, hence little carpenter work was attempted. One of the two apprentices was sacked.

At No. 6 expensive sausages and delicatessen became unsaleable.

At No. 5 hotel bills were harder to collect, and no tourists came to the cabaret.

At No. 10 wool and cotton touched fantastic all-time heights. So did Madame Absalom's invective.

At No. 9 Dorlan, the bookbinder, scarcely noticed any change. His clients were eccentric anyway.

At No. 12 milk was paler, eggs smaller and dirtier. The delivery girl tried what all the men had long been after and was not impressed.

At No. 15 the Lanier *clandestin* raised prices from 5 to 10 francs. Twenty per cent drop in volume of trade. Laundry prices also doubled.

At No. 14 the pay received by the police officers had shrunk so much in relation to the cost of living that the wife of one of the officers, unable to buy pretty underwear, formed the habit of picking up rich gentlemen in department stores. The family life became insupportable.

At No. 17 the neighbourhood men who worked for wages stopped patronizing *Le Panier Fleuri*, which attracted increasingly well-to-do clients from the textile manufacturers and dealers near the Chatelet and the boulevard Sebastopol.

At No. 16 an Englishwoman at No. 25 (third floor) complained that the bread left at her door each morning was not wrapped in paper, and therefore was dirty. Thereafter the delivery girl carried inside her blouse, next to her rather clear skin, a sheet of newspaper, with which she wrapped Madame Spook's loaf before standing it against the door. Madame Spook's real name was Root, but the French could not seem to manage that.

At No. 18 Sara's rich uncle from the Temple quarter sent her two clients, distant cousins from Germany who wished to transfer some assets out of Germany, in case the anti-Jewish feeling mounted.

At No. 19 the son of M. and Mme. Luneville left the drapery shop to begin his eighteen months of military service. Mme. Luneville, who had been a World War I bride, wept when she saw Jacques in uniform. Her veteran husband rebuked her.

At No. 20 Julien, the barber, received a call from his old employer, Monsieur Riess, the famous hairdresser. Riess told him about the American bank holiday which had frightened away his best paying clients from abroad. The old man was puzzled and discouraged. Money was no good anywhere, he said.

At No. 21 Monsieur Saint-Aulaire found himself overstocked with horizon-blue material, the Chamber having agreed that French soldiers and officers should wear khaki in future. This, like all modern innovations, the spade-bearded tailor deplored.

At No. 22 the cleaner and dyer had less cleaning and more dyeing to do. This was always true in hard times, he said. So he raised his prices for dyeing to make up for the cleaning he lost.

At No. 23 Madame Durand discharged Amélie, her nineteen-year-old clerk and assistant, for having angered a steady client by refusing to spend a night in the country with him.

At No. 24 M. Dominique made a journey to Bayonne to buy stamp collections from Jesuit exiles from Spain, who needed ready cash. He found some very good bargains.

At No. 25 André, the coalman, intending to go to the Auvergne for the first time in eighteen years, to attend his sister's funeral, got on the wrong train at Langres and found himself at Bourbon-les-Bains. The stationmaster would not let him sleep in the depot after two. The park was closed, so he walked back and forth on the platform, then took the morning train back to Paris. He was non-communicative for several days after he got home and once spoke crossly to his little son.

At No. 26 Bernice, because trade fell off in the music shop, started embroidering on a piece-work basis and used the proceeds to buy food for M. Gion, knowing that it would make him sullen and harsh if he had to tap his money in the bank. Because M. Gion did not like her to use the electric light when he was away, she worked at the window, in the glow of a street lamp. This made it necessary for her to wear spectacles, which she purchased for ten francs, selecting them from an open basket of assorted glasses on a counter in the Bon Marché.

At No. 27 M. and Mme. Corre, who had planned to take a commodious apartment in the avenue du Maine after their son was married and took over the grocery, decided to be content, instead, when the time came, with a smaller apartment in the rue du Bac.

At No. 28 the goldfish trade, always desultory, was slow in reflecting the general depression. Maurice discovered Fenimore Cooper, and, for once, tried to get another book by an author he had chanced upon. This he was unable to do along the quai.

At No. 29 Dr. Clouet attended a meeting of French physicians and voted in favour of restricting sales of iodine to Germany. He would have voted with equal relish to restrict the sale of anything to Germany.

At No. 32 The Navet wangled a rise in pay by joining a secret organization against Communism, favoured by Chiappe, the police commissioner, and dedicated to the proposition that all men are not born free and by no means equal.

At the Brasserie Dalmatienne, which belonged to the boulevard and was patronized by prosperous Serbs and other Balkan people, the police were on watch with instructions to pick up foreigners who might be reds and did not have identity cards. The Serbs in this café were reactionary, not Red, but the police did not know the difference, where Slavs were concerned.

At the Café St. Michel, when customers complained that the crescent rolls were smaller than before, Mme. Trévise blamed War Minister Maginot, who had just asked for twelve billion francs yearly for the army.

18

OF WESTERN CULTURE

Once in Dorchester, Massachusetts, lived a huge fat undertaker, a veritable Man Mountain Dean *sans* whiskers, who had a beautiful black cat. The cat was sleek and well-fed, with glossy fur and agate-yellow eyes. When business was slack, the undertaker used to doze for hours in a swivel chair, his feet on a littered roll-top desk, in full view of the passing crowds from the elevated railroad terminal near by. The cat, stretched comfortably on her master's commodious belly, slept when it pleased her, and at other times followed the movements, left to right, of the stream of pedestrians that never seemed to dwindle during daylight hours.

When the undertaker died, and was stretched out in his back room among the materials and implements of his lugubrious trade, the black cat paid no attention whatsoever to the body, but paced nervously back and forth, tail twitching, yellow eyes distended peevishly, in front of the empty swivel chair. From time to time she uttered a soft complaining cry.

A discerning friend of mine, observing this, pointed out to me that the cat had thought of the deceased mortician not as a person but a place. The place was gone.

The attitude of the average foreigner toward Paris and its people was much like that of the undertaker's cat. The city was a refuge. That it was staffed with people who, beneath their inefficient exteriors, were toiling and aspiring human beings escaped the casual visitors.

It was the sad-eyed Noël, the taxidermist, who said one evening in 1931: 'If France goes down, so much of Western culture will go too.'

Monsieur Noël and his two friends, Monsieur Monge, the horse butcher, and the maligned Satyr, were among those in our little street who were concerned with culture and with France.

As my companions knew, I was planning just then to leave Paris very soon for Spain and what turned out to be the most soul-stirring adventure of my disorderly life. Each one of my French friends envied me, in a way, but most of them would not have travelled if they could.

'The French do not travel,' Monsieur de Malancourt said to me. And he added: 'Why should they?'

There was little I could say in reply. But it always gave me an odd sensation when I talked with Frenchmen about foreign lands, even if they had been to the countries in question. It was as if I and they were speaking, simultaneously, of two different entities, both of which were removed from what is loosely known as reality.

Pierre Vautier, who, the moment he had broken loose from his family ties, had developed mentally before our eyes, and who thought in terms of the arts, took up Monsieur Noël's remark about the decline of Western culture.

Being primarily interested in painting, Pierre started with that. France, he said, had taken over the art of painting from the Italians with Poussin in the seventeenth century. Like so many other amateurs of painting, young Vautier ignored the Spanish development in that field, which reflects as truly the course of history and world and national affairs, believing that all Spanish painting had been done by El Greco, Velasquez and Goya, and had died in Napoleon's time.

Pierre was eloquent in his résumé of French achievements with palette and brush, and he was well informed. But when he remarked that the Italians had civilized the French, and that Poussin, the first great French painter, had learned painting in Rome, Father Panarioux spoke up gently from the doorway.

'You're forgetting Clement Vautel,' the priest said. Vautel was a wandering painter, almost a tramp, who went from village to village and earned small sums by repairing church decorations or painting murals of his own on chapel walls. Vautel had visited Poussin's native village in Normandy when Poussin was twelve years old and had let the boy clean his brushes and watch him while he worked. The old vagrant also did one job in Paris, a mural which still is intact in St. Germain Des Prés and which shows many of the salient characteristics of Poussin's best painting, notably *le cri parmi les gris*.

'So French painting may be French after all,' the priest said, smiling.

Pierre told of Claude Lorrain, and described the blossoming of French genius in the hands of Watteau, Fragonard, Chardin, David, Ingres, Courbet, Corot and Delacroix. His eyes shone and his voice trembled when he got to the Impressionists, who let sunlight into art (in the path of the pioneer Claude Lorrain). He spoke of Manet, Monet, then — nearer home — Renoir and the great Cézanne. He told of Gauguin and Van Gogh, of the moderns Derain, Vlaminck, Utrillo. But there he struck the snag that made Henri Julliard, who had never seen the inside of the Louvre or the galleries in the rue la Boëtie except on Sunday mornings, look worried and puff at his pipe.

For modern painting, beginning with World War I, had been taken in hand, revolutionized and stamped with the vigour of his race by a Spaniard named Picasso. And the French petered out. It is true, said Pierre, that Picasso has a studio in Paris and that his paintings were sold by the yard by dealers of France. His art is Spanish, nevertheless, and what few Frenchmen have not thrown up the sponge are influenced by Picasso to a degree which amounts to imitation. French painting, glorious as it was, will have on its tombstone the dates 1594 (Nicholas Poussin) to 1914, when Picasso came forward with his first 'cubistic' landscape.

'After all,' said Thérèse the cook, who was drunk but attentive, 'what is painting? One can't eat it, or even make a living at it, unless one has pull.' She had fed too many art students, on the cuff, in her time.

Concerning music, the floor was held by Monsieur Monge, purveyor of horse meat and the world's best performer on some kind of antique horn. He was aided and prompted by the Satyr and Monsieur Noël. The Society for the Preservation of Ancient Instruments, it seemed, took the long view in connection with its art and, before and after hours of ancient practice, played 'for fun' whatever scores the leader could obtain from the contemporary 'Six' and other living French composers.

The great misunderstood genius of modern French music (although he did his best work in the 1860s) was Berlioz. He was ridiculed and neglected by his contemporary Parisians and had to go to the Rhineland for his first success. Liszt stood up in his might in his theatre box in Budapest and roared for Berlioz, carrying with him the Hungarian crowds. But the French Government refused to pay for the great Mass evoking the resurrection and the life, and, even in the year 1931, sloppily played Beethoven numbers were seldom set aside to make room for Berlioz in French concert halls. The once great French opera, had, for lack of funds, become a travesty. Rameau and Couperin were 'revived' from time to time and atrociously misinterpreted.

Debussy? When it came to Debussy, Monsieur Monge grew lyrical, and the faces of my friends were alight with hope. But, said the horse butcher, Debussy's genius (which was prophetic of the impressionist movement in all the arts), led into a *cul de sac*.

'Debussy,' said Monsieur Monge, 'did all there was of its kind. No use to imitate or copy. His music was fresh, inspiring — in a word, it was French. But it had a beginning, a middle and an end — a verdant island around which flows the main stream.'

'Satie?' suggested young Vautier.

'The best toy music (*musiquette*),' said the Satyr. 'That is all. It goes well with motion pictures.'

Ravel, according to our academy of the rue de la Huchette, brought into France an African and Spanish influence as Manet did into French painting. He was good, but of the nineteenth century, which 'the big shots' of European governments (officials, financial and otherwise) were out to sink without trace.

The Six? Honegger (with his 'King David' on the one hand and his 'Locomotive' on the other), Poulenc, Auric, Milhaud, Durey and Tailleferre. Jacques Benoit-Mechin, who wrote tone poems about South America? The music after World War No. I?

It was entertaining, derivative and slight. On a programme with an early masterpiece like Monteclaire's *Plaisirs Champêtres* it sounded like the decorations on a department-store Christmas tree.

Of literature?

Another drink all round, and while Georges the *garçon* did fine feats of serving to supplement Monsieur Henri's masterful pouring, the eyes of our company turned first to young Vautier, who deferred to Monsieur de Malancourt.

'Alas,' said Monsieur de Malancourt, looking slightly ashamed. 'I haven't got a step beyond Proust. And *his* marvellous works, I must confess, were brought to my attention by a schoolgirl in my apartment house, a young girl, I assure you, my friends, who should be locked behind convent walls for the good of her soul and my own, and God knows how many others.' He glanced at me uneasily as he was speaking, knowing that I knew he was referring to Hyacinthe Goujon, at that moment staring thoughtfully at the ceiling in her still virginal bedroom on the third floor of No. 32.

Now in that small smoky bar-room, there were perhaps six of us who had read Marcel Proust. Pierre, Milka (with impatience because Proust was class-conscious in the unapproved way, that is, from birth quite snobbish and aesthetic), Madame Berthelot (who read behind official ledgers and files, when business was dull in the prefecture), Maurice, the goldfish man, who had chanced upon *Sodom and Gomorrah* on the second-hand bookstalls, Monsieur de Malancourt and your author. But even the cook Thérèse had heard of Proust and knew he was a Frenchman and of the élite.

'A genius is neither an invalid nor a pederast,' said Monsieur de Malancourt. 'He transcends all disabilities.'

'*Ce n'est pas les pédérastes qui manquent*,' said Thérèse.

The priest glanced at her disapprovingly and smiled.

'A genius makes no mistakes,' I quoted from Joyce. 'His errors are the portals of discovery.'

'It would be better if your geniuses were less arrogant and more humble,' said Father Panarioux. 'And, furthermore, a genius does not flaunt his twisted sex except unconsciously, as an ambi-sexual genius does. In the days when Frenchmen were more vigorous, and content with wholesome sins for which they could be forgiven with less distaste, French writers were not preoccupied with vagueness or monstrosities. There was something quite solid in between. A Christian reading Proust will find much truth and exact observation, precisely expressed with care and good taste. Sin is not glorified — true, it is not castigated, either. That would interrupt the flow.

'The result of modern corruption will be,' the priest continued, 'that our artists and then our countrymen will turn from warmth and sentiment altogether. They will become hard and Godless, without scruples or pity.'

'Our enemies are that way already, or so they would have us believe,' said Henri Julliard.

'Poor men,' the priest said, sadly.

'The bastards,' said Thérèse.

Céline's *Voyage au Bout de la Nuit* had not yet shocked the world with its uncompromising vista of Paris, New York and Detroit.

Rolland had doddered into a senile pacifism. Gide was in a *cul de sac*; de Montherlant deal only with a devastated aristocracy. The writer with the widest historical scope was Jules Romains. It still remained for a young man who wrote so simply that his prose was disarming to achieve the utmost in brutal prophecy, and portray, in advance of its general appearance, the fascist type in *The Young European*.

In the Caveau bar that night, I was the only one who had read Pierre Drieu La Rochelle; so I produced a copy of *The Young European* and handed it to Mme. Berthelot, who, shuddering, read passages like the following:

'Man need never have left the forest. He is a degenerate nostalgic animal.'

'The violence of men! They are born only for war, as women are made to have children. All the rest is a tardy detail of the imagination which has already shot its bolt.'

'I felt only the civilized side of war, in that odour of feet which pervades all monasteries, that rancid smell of men alone.'

'I had seen no women for several months. A large girl entered my office each morning (in America) . . . Here was the great white race I had sought throughout the world. I no longer looked at her face. Her features merely prolonged the long lines of her body . . . I brought her a love from Europe, precise and tender.'

'The skyscraper seemed no higher to me than the trajectory of our cannon and this mass of humanity hurled itself to the assault of unknown impregnable positions in blind columns, obeying an absurd order dictated by an anonymous telephone. I was not astonished by the grandeur of the American material apparatus, since the war had sickened me forever with the prestige of masses. I was intrigued only by the sight of so many wholesome bodies . . . I turned the great body of my wife over and over, admiring those limbs firm with exercise, the calves of her legs, her thighs, her shoulders. . . . One evening I did not return home.'

'It is necessary to have killed with the hands in order to understand life. The only life of which men are capable, I tell you again, is the spilling of blood: murder and coitus. All the rest is decadence.'

(This was written in 1926, about the time that Mothers' Day was first celebrated in France.)

I have seldom seen a man with a sadder face than that of Father Panarioux when Hortense finished reading, but he stepped resolutely forward and copied on a slip of paper the name of the author and the book.

Jules Romains, after starting out adventurously, gave up looking for new paths and tried to be Balzac, Zola *and* Proust. He lacked the incisiveness of the first, the fire of the second, and the sensitivity of the third. His *Men of Good Will* is a work of patience. Of the Nobel prize winner, Roger Martin Du Gard, it need only be said that his forceful work centres around the period of the Dreyfus case. The contemporary problems he has passed by without a sign of awareness.

In World War I, Monsieur Henri had read *Le Feu* of Barbusse, as many

Americans did. Barbusse's effectiveness stopped with that indictment of force.

The man who is most likely to match the work of the nineteenth century giants is Louis Aragon, but his talent is scattered and his contempt for the race too near the surface of his prose. After years as a Surrealist clown, he did heroic work as editor of the newspaper *Ce Soir*, presenting the Communist view with clarity and brilliance. Only when confronted with the Hitler-Stalin pact did he flounder and shelve his intelligence.

Malraux went to China and wrote *Les Conquérants* before he had had time to digest his observations. Six years later he made a splendid work of the same material, under the title *La Condition Humaine*. He went to Spain and turned out *L'Espoir*.

François Mauriac, a Catholic, wrote of the decline of Catholicism and took a brave stand for the Spanish republicans. He is silent now.

Morand was never worth mentioning; Duhamel was a phoney who hoodwinked the Americans but never the French; Cocteau was a playboy and good light entertainment; Cendrars a fascist dupe; Jean-Richard Bloch essentially a journalist. Maurois was superficial enough for the English and never found out what his century was like.

The survey makes it all too clear that France had no twentieth-century Proust, not even a Gide, who belongs before World War I; not even a poet to compare with Paul Valery. Literary giants must have a solid country under them, or the stables of Hercules.

An exception to the general decline in France's share of Western culture was the cinema. The medium was perfectly suited to the modern French temperament, to their instinctive taste and quick reactions, their adult approach to life, their wit and adaptability. Georges Melies turned out the first story-films in 1912, with Sarah Bernhardt as co-pioneer. On their trials and errors much has been built that is sound. The first World War gave the producers, directors, writers and actors a change of occupation and Hollywood four years in which to demonstrate what should not be done. Immediately after the armistice, the French took the lead with Abel Gance, Louis Delluc, Marcel l'Herbier and René Clair.

Even the Clair contributions that have been stolen or imitated elsewhere have increased his stature. His wit and finesse no one could borrow or debauch, until he was forced to submit to the Hollywood conventions. Then he debauched himself. His *Chapeau de Paille d'Italie*, *Sous Les Toits de Paris*, *A Nous la Liberté* (which Chaplin took over in *Modern Times*), *Le Dernier Milliardaire* are film classics such as America could never produce.

With the best French directors, the play is the thing. Not only Clair and Renoir, but Duvivier, Chénal, Carné, and Feyder, respect the writers like Giono, Jacques Prévert (*Quai des Brumes*) not to mention Anatole France. The French producers were willing to give cultured adults a break, and not make films exclusively for backward children. When the output was bad, it was consciously bad, and not standardized mediocrity.

The best French films reflected the most interesting French life in one or many of its phases. The characters were not automatons, their motives were not trite or over-simplified, their words were not wisecracks like raisins in a dough of banalities.

Bergson's philosophy, based on the impulse of living (*élan vital*) and the conception that one creates whenever one acts freely, is essentially a product of the best thought of the nineteenth century, and dates before World War I. It is the antithesis of the fascist idea, the most dangerous doctrine for a totalitarian state. No philosophy comparable to Bergson's sprang from the post-war twenties or the pre-war thirties. It breathes of the life of France in the days of the now dead Third Republic.

The restaurants of France, which led the world during the nineteenth century, came into being with the revolution, an outgrowth of republicanism. As freedom faded, so did the restaurants, and with the Third Republic they died. In no totalitarian country is good eating encouraged, but only the kind of food that makes for soldierly stamina without mental health or elasticity. A restaurant was a meeting-place, and meetings are taboo.

The famous restaurants of Paris which flourished before World War I — Boulanger, Verdier, Legacque, Les Frères Provençaux, the Café Anglais, Véforn, Café de Paris, La Vachette, Bignon, La Maison d'Or, Philippe, Brébant, to name but a few of the leaders — were creative institutions. The famous chefs, such as Véry, André, Terrail, Casimir, Mourier, Burdel and other artists, did not merely turn out copies of the great creations of Bechamel, Parmentier and the giants of the monarchy. They made contributions of their own. Two revolutionary writers and philosophers, Brillat-Savarin and Grimrod de la Reynière, made food articulate. Gauclair perfected *aioli*; old Alfred Prunier learned to cook oysters; Close invented *pâté de foie gras*.

Between World War I and World War II there were fine restuarants in Paris, like Pharamond's in the market district, Foyot's and Prunier's and Lapérouse, Weber's, Larue, the Café de Paris, the Tour d'Argent, Chez Francis, etc., and most of them were hangovers from pre-war days. But they lost their republican quality and became hangouts of the newly rich. They kept up the quality of pre-war food but evolved few new sauces or dishes. Like piano music, the last of which was written in 1870, French cooking coasted along on its former greatness, marvellous but not living or modern.

No restaurateurs in the 1920s or 1930s had had the stature of old M. Frédéric (Delvan), or Gauclair, or old Marguery or Noël Peter. Escoffier, the last of the major chefs, died in 1935. No successor is in line. Neither will there be any young man to take the place of such a *maître d'hôtel* as Ollivier of the Ritz.

French cooking, like French painting, music and literature, was cherished by the monarchy and adapted itself to the Republic. All these arts, by stagnating and dying after World War I, foretold the fall of France.

French couture reached its artistic apogee in the years immediately preceding World War I; it achieved its greatest commercial success and the maximum of its influence on world fashions in the early twenties. In the years just before World War II, Parisian dress houses had become a fair of samples which buyers bought piecemeal, pooling their purchases so as to pay less and reduce the cost of copying. From the eighteenth century, when Rose Bertin, whose most famous client was Marie Antoinette, decreed styles, through the period dominated by Charles Frederick Worth, who was the first to display creations on live mannequins and induced the Empress Eugénie to wear a dress made of Lyons silk, to the time of Paul Poiret, the leadership of the fashion world remained in France. Poiret was the first to make use of modern artists. Under the influence of Bakst he restored brilliant colours to fashion and released women from the armour of corsets and petticoats. By the introduction of the short skirt Poiret gave impetus to the present hosiery industry.

Chanel created the one-piece jersey dress. This started a trend that eventually developed into modern sports clothes. The influence of Jeanne Lanvin, Jean Patou, Lucien Lelong and Molyneux on fashion was to feminize it. Schiaparelli, with a thought for her less attractive sisters, provided ornaments and surrealist gadgets that distracted attention from the face — when necessary.

The French couturiers borrowed without stint from their fellow-artists, and used colour and form as lavishly for their creations.

Unlike the United States and Germany, where scientific education has run so far ahead of artistic culture and general knowledge that adults with the mentality of children are playing with phenomenally powerful toys, France laid emphasis on matters of the spirit and let modern science go hang. A few brilliant exceptions among French scientists, therefore, had to work under handicaps imposed by an indifferent public and a penny-pinching Government. Pasteur, in pioneer days, was hooted and obstructed. Joliot had to squander his invaluable time raising money for his *cyclotron*, which cost about one-eighth as much as a small destroyer. The entire French appropriation for scientific research after World War I was about 2,000,000 francs, and there was no crop of private millionaires to rally round. In 1924, when World War I's victory had slipped away, Emil Borel, the famous mathematician, persuaded Parliament to set aside a special tax for the support of laboratories. About that time, the Rothschilds, alarmed because their interests in France were falling behind their interests in other countries where science was encouraged, created a foundation of 10,000,000 francs for fellowships, and thus aided the work of the chemist, André Job; the physicist, Claude Bernard; and the distinguished scientists, Jean Perrin, Pierre Garerd and André Meyer.

In 1930, long after it was too late, Herriot, then Premier, got across an annual appropriation of 5,000,000 francs for encouragement to science. This amount, about £250,000, represents the receipts of the Child's restaurants in New York for about four weeks.

In 1935, the French deputies took a long step backwards, and in the interest of economy, abolished the Borel tax. In 1936, Leon Blum appointed Irene Joliot-Curie under-secretary of scientific research, and in 1937, the budget for modern science was boosted to 32,500,000 francs. An observatory for astrophysics was set up at Forealquier; a national chemical institution was started at Ivry; a laboratory for atomic transformation in connection with the Collège de France, a laboratory for low temperatures at Bellevue, and a magnificent collection of documents known as the 'Institut des Textes,' all were established just in time for Hitler to grab them, transport their contents into Germany, and where that was not possible, to replace their personnel with storm professors from the Reich.

19

THE CENTRAL MARKETS

Perhaps the most vital part of Paris the Germans have soiled and ruined was Les Halles, or the central market, which belonged to all quarters and streets alike and from which the rue de la Huchette, like the others, got its sustenance. I mean the city acres between the rue de Louvre and the boulevard Sebastopol, extending west from the rue de Rivoli all the way to the rue Étienne Marcel, where fresh food — fruit, cheese, eggs, vegetables, meat, fish, game and poultry — poured in daily from the fertile countryside and was distributed and sold to the hotels and restaurants, as well as the little local markets, and, without formality, to the lucky retail pedestrian who chanced to be out that night or who got up with the sun in the morning.

The above-mentioned parcel of former France had colours and shapes as exciting as the walls of the renowned long gallery of the Louvre Museum, had movement that exceeded in grace the undulations of Loie Fuller's pastel robes, had vigour surpassing the action of molecules under a microscope, smells that put to shame the scent shops and verdant gardens — also brutality, avarice, stench, confusion. In short, the foremost necessity and historical privilege of mankind known as food.

That at two in the morning one could stand in the shadow of the flying bastions of St. Eustache (where the Christmas music was so inspiring that tickets were sold at least one year in advance) and could, if one could bear it, look south-eastward. The fragrance of wild strawberries forced one to breathe deeply and to lower the lids of one's eyes. There were in the middle distance lanes between pyramids of carrots under lamplight (henna by orange by green by gold) and of stacked cauliflower (buff and cream with blue-grass setting), but first — the strawberries!

France, in her wisdom, ordained that all strawberries for miles and kilometres around should convene near a grand old church just after midnight, and should be ranged there neatly in straw baskets or in boxes, garnished greenly with their leaves. If one man can smell one wild strawberry at a distance of eight inches, how far can four million men enjoy the perfume of one million five hundred thousand strawberies with cool leaves all round, laid out on ancient cobblestones?

I know many tourists and even foreign residents of Paris who rode through the market district in the daytime fairly often, seeing nothing but shabby stores and sheds on uninteresting and not quite tidy streets. There was traffic in the day, and retail business of a sort, but no fresh food in sight. The miracle of each time of darkness was hauled, swept, washed and brushed away before nine o'clock in daylight. The farmers and produce men had by that time scattered back into the country, on roads like the spokes of a wagon wheel, with Paris as the hub. To come in before midnight and depart when their stuff was sold or stored, these citizens of France who made such a solid contribution employed a multitude of vehicles of widely assorted kinds, periods and conditions of practicability and servitude.

It was a pleasant reassuring sight to see streaming into Paris in the late evening, and departing in the early morning over avenues and bridges whose names were known round the world, the farmers and outdoor workers driving enormous stallions between high heavy shafts, made slightly more tractable by heavy collars and double-plated harness. These vegetable and produce carts were not exactly of our century. A number of them rumbled past our little street on the Boul' Mich' end and crossed the pont St. Michel. Others jolted by the eastern extremity of the rue and crossed the two bridges ahead of the rue Deux Ponts. In the late thirties, many of these horse-drawn supply chairots were replaced with cheap trucks, burning an atrocious-smelling petrol which counteracted the earth and vegetable odours.

At midnight the rue Montmartre and the rue de Montorgueil just northward and all the streets around Les Halles were lined with carts in front of which and on which stallions and peasants were slumbering. Some had been unloaded, but most of them were awaiting their turn. In some of the small or cheap restaurants near by, an upstairs room was provided where incoming farmers could snatch an hour or two, sitting tightly side by side on a bench with their elbows on a rope or a rail. The food in all the market restaurants was good. It had to be for hungry farmers and jolly produce dealers.

The beef and mutton were displayed in huge high-roofed sheds like giant airplane hangers, suet and flesh and tubs of blood, and miles of tripe and lights and livers, hung from hooks in endless files and rows. If Rembrandt found one carcase notable and paintable, who would sneer at fifty thousand? Butchers, roustabouts and helpers, cashiers and clerks, women whose faces and hands were ruddy from exposure, toiled steadily in the lamplight amid sharp shadows and customers in inexhaustible throngs. At 5 a.m. on certain days one would see there the surly Monsieur Salmon, the butcher from No. 2 rue de la Huchette, complaining and pinching pennies as he made his purchases, but using good business judgment and getting the most for his coin.

Along the rue Ferronnerie were waiting in line the barrow men and women who would appear in the rue de la Huchette and the rue Zacharie as soon as the inhabitants got up and were ready to buy their day's provender. The chestnut man (who sold oysters, clams and periwinkles, as well as pistachio nuts, castañas and the very best peanuts from Perpignan) frequented a small bar called the Café Jean Bart, an excellent spot for a nocturnal drink or snack. Around the counter, and seated at the tables in the main room of the Jean Bart, were men and women who worked in the markets near by. Not infrequently one saw the old red stocking cap of the French revolutionaries, and more often wide blue sashes and wooden sabots. The back room was devoted to occasional tourists, for whom the prices were slightly raised, and the neighbourhood whores who worked in the four o'clock houses across the rue du Louvre and in the Quartier St. Paul, or across the Seine in the rue des Rosiers. The pimps drifted in, sleekly dressed in tight-fitting coats and coloured mufflers, or with secondhand army raincoats if the weather were inclement, arriving about a quarter to four. In case of heavy rain, they brought rubbers or umbrellas for their non-foresighted providers.

Everybody in that neighbourhood ate heartily and well, excepting the trembling ill-smelling vagrants the police had chased out from under bridges. They had to pick up what they could, which somehow kept them alive.

On the morning the death of Willette, the famous cartoonist, was announced in the press, I met l'Hibou (the owl) as he was sitting on the stone doorstep of No. 30 rue de la Huchette, the semi-religious publishing house. It was about five minutes to two. L'Hibou was not a sound sleeper. He was the one among the throng of vagrants who had chosen our street as his own, that is, for a sleeping place. On the pavement, snug against No. 30, was a grille covering a vent from the Métro, or tube; from this issued a sluggish current of air that was warm and had been purified somewhat, let us hope, in rising from the depths of the St. Michel station to the level of the ground. This was l'Hibou's bed, and pedestrians on the northern pavement (not more than two and one-half feet wide) were careful to step around this slumbering form when walking that way between the hours of eleven at night and two in the morning.

It was noteworthy of l'Hibou that he considered himself entitled to his share of public service, for on the occasions when he woke before the hour of tramp's reveille, when the police throughout the city roused sleeping tramps and started them toward the central markets to rustle scraps of food, our rue de la Huchette representative among the hoboes would sit calmly on the publisher's doorstep and wait to be summoned in the formal way. Consequently, some cop had to walk all the way from the police station at No. 14 to the publishing house at No. 30 in order to do the job. The dialogues that resulted nightly have been lost to posterity, but I had the luck to overhear one now and then.

The cop, sometimes the sarcastic *Agent* Benoist who had trouble with his liver, would stride self-consciously along the narrow stone-paved pavement, listening to his own footsteps and their echoes. Formerly the police had shouted to l'Hibou across several intervening street numbers, but the residents had complained about that, since it broke their sleep, and l'Hibou would never recognize the validity of an order to move on if it were delivered at an unconventional distance. He had done his military service just after World War I, mostly in Coblenz and Ehrenbreitstein (where the guardhouse was), and he knew that a man should be addressed from not more than four paces, when given the orders of the day.

'*Dis donc, toi. Tu as bien reposé?*' *Agent* Benoist would inquire, rocking back and forth on the heels of his well-polished regulation shoes.

'*Pas mal, je vous remercie*,' l'Hibou would reply.

Agent Benoist: 'Then get your dirty arse to hell out of here! Why can't you vamoose of your own accord, when the clock strikes? Why do I have to come out in the cold . . . ?'

L'Hibou: 'Monsieur, you have a frivolous idea of duty. Come out in the cold indeed! The public is not paying you to toast your *derrière* on a brazier. You should be out of doors, making life complicated for the helpless and homeless whom nightly you abuse, while the rich, Monsieur . . .'

Madame Absalom (from the second floor window of No. 28, where she slept): '*Alors, bavardeurs. Est-ce que vous allez trompeter pendant toute la nuit, pour embêter les gens honnêtes? Foutez le camp, tous les deux. Vous valez également à deux fois rien.*' (Now then, windbags. Do you intend to trumpet all night, to annoy honest folk? Scram, both of you. You are equally not worth a whoop!)

Agent Benoist (with severity): 'Madame, My duty . . .'

At that l'Hibou would break out with derisive laughter.

L'Hibou. 'I know where you do your duty, Monsieur l'Agent. Up against the door of No. 15 rue Zacharie. One of these nights that trollop will get the door latch in her behind and you'll have to . . .'

Madame Absalom (nightcap appearing at window, gleefully): 'Respect yourselves. What kind of talk is that for a serious woman's ears?'

What l'Hibou suggested, with exaggerated politeness, that Madame Absalom should do with her ears, had best be omitted from this *reportage*.

On the night or morning of which I started to write, I found l'Hibou, who was usually quite self-possessed if not gay, sitting dejectedly on the doorstep staring at an early edition of the *Petit Journal*. Tears were coursing down his cheeks. Because they furrowed the dust from the tube exhaust, they were more easily discernible.

'Something wrong.?' I asked.

'*Il est mort*,' said l'Hibou simply, and bowed his head. '*Un grand homme*,' he continued. '*Il n'y en a plus comme lui en France, Monsieur* Heliot (that was as near as any Frenchman could come to Elliot). *Nous sommes tombés dans les jours maigres . . .*'

I wish I could convey the elegant way in which he growled out the words like '*maigres*'. Villon, in reciting '*Ma pauvre mère*,' could not have hit a richer diapason. Briand would have been jealous.

(In translation, l'Hibou said: 'He is dead! A great man! There are no more like him in France, Monsieur Heliot. — We have fallen on lean days.')

'Who is dead?' I asked. I had within an hour made up the old *Tribune's* front page and the only death of note was that of Willette. 'You mean Willette?' I added, puzzled.

L'Hibou rose with dramatic weariness. 'Who else?' he asked. '*Ah, les gosses!* The poor kids of Montmartre! Who will now interpret them, their laughter, their pranks, their heartbreaks, to the world?'

L'Hibou and his small circle of friends and social equals who gathered around the open fire on the riverside between the pont du Louvre and the pont du Carrousel passed over the political news of national and world affairs with scant attention. But whatever was Parisian, like the cartoons of Willette, belonged to them.

Once I told Henri Julliard that I had never had enough mushrooms at one time. Mushrooms, undoubtedly the miraculous manna of Holy Writ, are used for garniture, are chopped and lost in sauces and omelets, on rare days are stuffed and roasted and served on toast. But I had always had in mind a meal consisting mostly of mushrooms, fresh from the earth and replete with earthy tastes and odours.

'Come with me,' said Monsieur Henri.

It was about four o'clock in the morning, just as the sky behind Notre Dame was clearing to form an impressive morning background for that majestic example of French Gothic art. That air was crisp and cool, the timeless city (we thought) was silent and slumbering. In heavy darkness the street lamps of Paris, along important avenues or boulevards and across bridges of the Seine, glowed alternately with a pink and lemon tone. Every other lamp gave out pink-toned light, and the odd ones were tinged with yellow. As dawn approached, those contrasting colours drew nearer to each other, as if seeking a common factor. Instead of heading for the Châtelet, toward the central area of Les Halles, my No. 1 Frenchman led me westward to the rue du Louvre. I remember that we both halted, on the same strong impulse, to look at the large beds of *fleurs de lys* (blue iris) that beautified the northern end of the former palace of the Bourbons, in the days of the Third Republic the most important national museum. There was something in the slowly blending light, a combination of natural pre-sunrise and dwindling artificiality of man-made incandescence, that caused shades of blue to radiate, on the borderline between warmth and coolness, and make one feel that, in stumbling around the world for many years, and seeing red and yellow, one had overlooked the essence of blueness, because of its remoteness in the sky.

'*Formidable!*' was Monsieur Henri's comment.

The official gardener, a most competent one, must have been near by because the black soil around the iris plants had been trowelled and its fragrance (for the hardy) was an excellent preparation for what I was about to experience.

Ironically enough, the space in Les Halles devoted to heaven-sent mushrooms is backed up against the Bourse, where men toil and moil for paper which they make believe is gold. There, in a clear area about fifty yards square, were mushrooms displayed in boxes and baskets — not only the common or restaurant variety (*Agaricus campestris*), but pungent little *cèpes* from the south that incite to abandon and the wholesomeness of sin, large pine-needle mushrooms from up near Lille, the special medium mushrooms from outside Rouen with the flesh tones of Jeanne d'Arc to be ravished by irreverent teeth and swallowed as substitute magic. Twenty-five hundred square yards of mushrooms back to back, as neatly matched as dancers by Degas, each basketful consistent, clean (without washing), and with a brimming convex surface, like a cream-coloured sea.

'*C'est bien la France*,' said Monsieur Henri. 'How do you do this in America?'

I tried to describe the Washington market in New York, the Fulton fish market, the Faneuil Hall area in Boston, the markets of Mexico City, to which barefooted Indians come from many miles with desert cacti. But nowhere else in the pre-war world was there a square, backed up by a temple of Mammon like a roundhouse, where at dawn those interested in mushrooms met together, and found assembled for their benefit all the mushrooms that had sprung up and been picked and brushed with understanding fingers and placed just so in clean and uniform containers.

I hope some day when the damage done by tanks, tractors, trucks, artillery and the tramp of foreign feet over fields and farms is computed that the statisticians will add an item for the ruined mushrooms.

In France, as in Spain, but to a lesser degree, the outside of old churches was likely to be beautiful. The edifices had been well designed by men who knew what they were doing and felt it, too. Unfortunately, the interior was likely to be packed with the tawdriest of gimcracks, of cheap material with a cheaper veneer, showing taste that surpassed the grotesque. In Les Halles, the buildings were ugly and shoddy, *per se*, while the sheer loveliness of what was inside took one's breath away. To reach the central area, one plunged into the teeming markets, in lamplight or thin daylight, from the rue de Rivoli. One abandoned one's taxi near a series of shops in front of which were crates of doves and pigeons, clucking hens behind lathe-work, roosters of henna, with vermilion combs, sardonyx eyes, old ivory beaks, Rousseau (the Douanier) tails, and on their necks a turquoise sheen, squat ducks, obese frogs, prone sleeping puppies, love birds, parakeets, and frequently, in small tanks equipped with moss and stones, some tiny turtles.

Between poultry and pet shops a narrow alley led westward to a small street where barrows were being loaded. Suddenly one was aware of a ravine of colour, variegated and profuse, fragrant above human and vegetable smells, velvet in tone, suffused with green and revealing a semblance of order. I refer to a passageway between two sheds where cut flowers were on display.

There one frequently met Julien the barber, who, because he had a feud with Albertine Durand at No. 32, would not buy from her the small bouquet M. Riess, the master coiffeur, had taught him should grace any well-appointed ladies' and gents' hairdressing parlour. Julien had some kind of kidney trouble that woke him, if he was lucky, very early in the morning. Since he was a sensitive man, the general air of oncoming disaster in the Paris atmosphere prevented him from going back to sleep again. So he left his handsome wife (who was equally restless at the beginning of the night but who slept like death itself in the morning) and passed the time wandering round the markets, until the Café St. Michel opened.

Julien's quarrel with Mme. Durand arose over a bunch of dahlias. He bought them (six in all, of purple and garnet shades) from Jacqueline, a lame girl who worked for the exigent Albertine about ten days. The dahlias wilted almost before Julien got them to his shop in No. 20. He complained and took them back, which threw Mme. Durand into a white-hot rage. She fired the crippled Jacqueline on the spot for having failed to burn the dahlia stems after she had broken them off to the length indicated by Julien, but madame did not offer to give Julien his money back. Instead, she gave him a bunch of yesterday's petunias which didn't last long either.

From that time on, dahlias were Julien's favourite flower and he had a few in his shop every day in the long dahlia season. He found that practically none of his clients knew that dahlias will wilt, if the broken-off stems are not treated with heat. He loved to collect such odd bits of information and give them out gratis to his customers. When he learned from Monsieur Luttenschlager, who sold prayer books and crucifixes (increasingly less often), that rabbits do not drink, either milk or water or anything whatsoever, Julien added this fact to his repertoire. No client Julien esteemed was deprived of this jewel of knowledge. I did my best to stock Julien with a few Americana, such as the Kentucky breakfast (straight whisky and raw beefsteak), scented and tinted bathroom tissue, and the requirement that couples renting rooms for short periods in American hotels be equipped with suitcases, which could be rented cheaply, loaded down with a few bricks and wadded newspapers, in pawnshops near the large terminal railway stations. What really got Julien down, however, was my insistence that playing-cards, sheet music and typewriter ribbons were on sale in United States pharmacies.

Upon entering the market shed with the galvanized roof beside the alley filled with flowers, one found on gently inclined counters prodigious numbers and assorted specimens of fish of the sea, not to mention lakes, ponds, brooks and rivers and even hatcheries.

Salt-water fish streamed into Les Halles from the Channel ports, and the Mediterranean. Cod, or *morue*, came to France by the boatload from Iceland and Newfoundland. Trout were shipped from the Vosges, the Pyrenees and Alps and the streams amd mountains of Alsace-Lorraine. Eels came from Brittany, the long low marshes, or from Normandy, a region rich in foodstuffs of all kinds and inhabited by the world's hardiest *gourmets*.

So in the great shed in Les Halles one saw the shapes and colours and patterns of sea creatures from the Maritime Provinces. The great *langouste* (large crayfish), one of the best of shellfish, the *homard*, huge pink crabs, turquoise king crabs, transparent soft-shelled crabs, the small flat but tasty European oysters ranging from the green-tinged Portuguese to the marennes and the matchless belons (pride of Prunier's). Ugly John Dorys with faces like Raimu, bluefish with faces like Hoover, silver melts, *dorade* with golden flecks of false sunshine to camouflage their predatory eyes, slabs of smoked haddock, skates and sting rays and Portuguese men-of-war; a dozen kinds and sizes of shrimps, crayfish, cockles and periwinkles; mussels of Tyrian purple; steak salmon; *lotte* (the only fresh-water fish fit for chowder); flat turbot; philosophic eels in plate-glass tanks; *calmars* or ink-fish; roguish young sharks which seemed to be slumbering; mackerel (God's idea of quantity production) perfectly matched and matchlessly marked.

The soles, being tough enough to be mauled by waiters and having boneless fillets to be served with sauce, were bought by the large hotels and restaurants, which did their best with them. The sweet flounders, but more breakable, went to housewives' kitchens.

Importunate hardy women sang hoarse praises of their wares as one passed from counter to counter, for when Nature has produced a school of mackerel impossible to distinguish one from the other, the personal element enters into salesmanship. The local fish shop of the rue de la Huchette was just around the corner, in the truly provincial rue Zacharie. Quite naturally, none of the small merchants of our street wanted a fish shop (with elementary ideas of icing) next door or fifteen feet away across the street.

Thérèse, the cook at the Caveau, was fond of fish, because it stimulated her thirst. She prepared fish in a talented manner. Nightly she would leave her door open so that Monsieur Henri could shake her by the shoulder in the morning (about 5.30), knowing that a mere banging on the panel or a siren or artillery fire would never rouse her from her drunken sleep. Like so many manless women, Thérèse was extraordinarily sensitive and hostile to the masculine touch. Had anyone but Monsieur Henri put his hand on her bare shoulder (she slept in her low-cut chemise) he might have lost his life. An unsuspecting client of the hotel, good-naturedly drunk, had pinched her once as she passed with a dish of stew and had remembered the incident dimly but with almost pious regret for years afterwards.

The day, for Thérèse, began with a tug at her shoulder, a bleary opening of protesting eyes, and the sight of the fine Savoyard countenance of Henri Julliard. Very often he would linger while she struggled out of bed and into the rest of her clothes, talking casually about the weather, or the menu for the day. Down at the bar, he would serve her coffee spiked with rum. Then she would grab her huge basket and start on foot for the market. At the Café Jean Bart, she would pause for a glass of red wine and a word with the chestnut man, whom she treated like a comrade. Then she would buy her vegetables along the street. The loafer of her choice would follow her from stand to stand with a barrow and would be taken under her wing into the various bars at which she stopped to refresh herself *en route*. Fruit, vegetables and other bulky and perishable supplies would be entrusted to the tramp and his barrow, but the precious meat, fish and poultry she lugged in her own large basket. By the time she got back to the rue de la Huchette, Thérèse was feeling warm inside and all right with the world, and the tramp was even more so. But whatever had been on Monsieur Henri's list was on hand and intact, if it were obtainable, and if not, something just as good.

In the market shed of incomparable beauty, the zone between the fish and the fruit was given over to the kingdom of poultry. There the fowls of the air, by long habit or coercion grounded, were ranged side by side, and row on row, bereft of feathers and showing thin tender skin and plump meat beneath and just enough fat and not too much. Their eyes were closed; their necks and heads showed resignation and a long sweet last repose. Their very neat feet were tucked under them. The fryers and roasters of Bresse, browned over poplar and willow twigs, impaled on spits, cooked in ovens or boiled or served cold on cool plates in the heat of the day; the birds paired with bottles that aided in seductions and persuasions, that gladdened little children on Sunday, that bolstered convalescents in the grim Hôtel Dieu, that yielded broth and curry, that graced expensive banquets — all are now a mirage of forsaken years of plenty.

20

A BEVY OF REDS

Even in the late 1920s, while France was still assumed to be a first-class power, by Frenchmen and others, the Communists had started making themselves unnecessarily conspicuous and unpopular. If there is contained in the works of Karl Marx an admonition to his followers to make life hard for themselves and to add to the almost insuperable difficulties attendant on social reform the handicap of offensive personalities, it has escaped my cursory examination. Nevertheless, in all countries I have visited, and in the United States where I properly belong, the so-called Reds have conspired, perhaps unwittingly, with reactionary traitors and die-hards to place the blame on Communists for all of man's ineptitudes and Nature's sorrows. They will never utter a word but hem and haw when a clear explanation or avowal would be helpful, and it is impossible for them to keep their traps shut when discretion would be the better part, not only of valour, but of strategy and tactics as well.

A group of talented literary clowns known as Surrealists, with an associated handful of painters whose works are just now fitting into the consciousness of New York (sixteen years after their purposes have been served) adopted in 1926 a policy of protest. Members of the group, including such outstanding and authentic talents as Louis Aragon, Paul Eluard, the painters Masson, Chirico and others, and led by a windbag named André Breton (who could write like hell when he wanted to) were not encouraged to write or paint too much. It was passé, Breton decided, to spend one's time making beautiful objects. Instead they issued manifestoes concerning this or that, and into them went so much wit and perversity that invariably they stirred up a squall. The only Communists, at that time, in our little street were Milka, the Serbian student, her lover and disciple, Stefan Koltko, and later, Pierre Vautier.

Pierre's conversion from being the wayward son of a rich aristocrat and manufacturer to a champion of the prisoners of starvation took place in a charismatic way (for Paris of that period). The boy detested military life and engineering and he had always disliked his father, who exploited his employees in a bald-faced and arrogant manner that should have offended less sensitive men than Marx. When Pierre found refuge in the art gallery infested with homosexuals, their combined influence disrupted his wholesome liaison with Mary the Greek. The group of painters whose work was shown in the Galerie Peret included several minor Surrealists and others who were independents. Along about 1926, André Breton decided that his followers could not permit their works to be exhibited in galleries which also included conservatives, or still worse, non-Surrealist radicals. Bertrand Brun, proprietor of the Galerie Peret, who had succeeded Mary the Greek in Pierre's warm affections, had to make a choice. For various reasons he elected to become pure Surrealist.

Then Breton made another grandstand play. The Communist Party in France had been founded and nurtured in its infancy, as in other countries, by a few exiles and refugees with no special interest in France but only solicitude for the workers of the world. Discontented French industrial workers, in small numbers, were induced to join and did so, principally because the other parties were obviously so corrupt and ineffectual. To this unfortunate nucleus, the Surrealists decided to attach themselves, and proclaimed themselves Communists in a bombastic manner by public manifesto. The only hitch was that Moscow would have none of them, and let this be known.

Years later, after tragic events and longer experience, more calmly assimilated, a few of the former Surrealists became bona-fide Communists, and some of them, like Aragon, did heroic work. Breton, the pontifical sachem, turned to Trotsky and became an enemy. Most of the Surrealists eased themselves back into the *intelligentsia* or the bourgeoisie, or both, and now are indistinguishable from other French citizens.

Pierre Vautier was a fine intelligent young man. His effeminate instincts were congenial and had been fostered by an idiotic doting mother, and were brought into high relief by a mutton-headed obstinate father who was not an impressive example of mankind. In spite of their differences in breeding and temperament, not to mention race, nationality and point of view, Pierre did his best to maintain solidarity with Milka and Stefan, his fellow Reds, after Breton had read him and his gallery into the party. I have seen him turn white with embarrassment when his comrades exhibited abrupt and bad manners. I observed with what effort he bore with the odour of Stefan's unwashed body and infrequently laundered clothes. Had there been a barricade, just then, Pierre would have defended it calmly. Later, his behaviour in the valley of the shadow of death entitled him to forgiveness and acceptance by the most bigoted and righteous of his critics.

But from 1926 until the end, Pierre's days and nights were beset with problems far wiser and older men could not have batted back and forth between conflicting theories, facts and policies like tennis balls in a champion doubles match. He knew the rottenness of his class, and hoped the workers would prove sounder and better, as they did.

His first jolt was when his *Führer* (M. Breton) forced his lover (M. Brun) to eject the works of Pierre's friends whom I need not name from the Galerie Peret. That he swallowed in the name of discipline, group discipline. When he was read into the Communist Party with his brother Surrealists, he went humbly to Milka, who was nothing if not articulate, and sat at her feet for hours, while she tried to make him class-conscious (which he was) and politically minded (which he was not). Pierre, having lived in an atmosphere of petty jealouses all his life, was warmed and impressed because Stefan showed no jealousy when Milka took him under her shapely wing and was closeted with him far into the night and sometimes all night. Milka had a theory that a two-sided conversation is infinitely more effective than a three-cornered one. So she banished Stefan during Pierre's apprenticeship and let him do Party work in the rue des Écoles while she was supplementing Pierre's education. The spice of jealousy, however, was amply supplied by M. Brun, who, although technically a comrade by force of Breton's decree, nearly lost his mind. On two occasions he stormed into the Caveau, rushed hatless upstairs and burst into the room where Pierre and Milka were deep in Party lore. Both times they had their clothes on and were sitting at least a foot apart, but that did not comfort M. Brun.

A short time afterward, when the Surrealists discovered that they were not, in fact, Communists and that Moscow was leery of their antics, Pierre went through a double crisis which faded the roses on his cheeks and cost him at least ten pounds of much-needed weight. M. Brun was ecstatic. Pierre, he believed, would now put that foreign menace and her mackerel in their places and spend all his evenings with him. He had not reckoned with Pierre's sterling qualities. For Milka's eloquent interpretations of Marx had taken root in Pierre's logical mind. He could not discard them at the casual behest of an absent chief — even Joe Stalin, himself.

The result was a soul-storm such as only homosexual young Frenchmen can achieve, but it resulted in a victory of Milka over Brun and the loss of Pierre's job. The pay had been small but steady, and was all Pierre had had with which to eat.

Milka came through splendidly. She vouched for Pierre as a promising convert, notwithstanding his Surrealist affiliations (which were shattered by the influential Brun) and got him into the C.P. rank and file through regular channels. For the sake of economy, since every franc was needed for the cause, she persuaded Pierre to give up his expensive room, which cost £1 10s. a month, and move in with her and Stefan. This he did, at what cost to his squeamishness about perfumes and sartorial elegance no one else will ever know. There was only one double bed and a moth-eaten upholstered chair, and what the trio did or how they managed, I have no idea. I wondered from time to time but could not, with delicacy, inquire directly. Georges insisted that they all slept together, most often with Milka in the middle, also that Milka mothered and lectured her two room mates and kept them both busy from morning until night. Once in a while, when stray comrades entered the Caveau by the side entrance, Milka would send both Pierre and Stefan down to the bar while she conferred on matters too desperate for their ears.

Mary the Greek, who had been reduced to prostitution and was allowed to sit in a dingy café in the rue St. André des Arts from six in the evening until two in the morning, did not rebuke Pierre openly, but she whispered insidious things about Milka and sang sad maudlin songs in her cups every night. Her drinking interfered somewhat with her trade, for which she was not at all suited. But since she was patient, her face and body beautiful, and in spite of the fact that she had only one skirt and two blouses, she made enough in good weeks to pay her rent and board to Monsieur Henri. Marie wanted to eject her while she still was not quite destitute, knowing Monsieur Henri would never do it later when she became entirely helpless.

An example of Red tact occurred early in 1931, and put Pierre on an uncomfortable spot in the Caveau bar. The beloved Marshal Joffre died, and while public feeling for and gratitude to the grand old soldier was at its height, the handful of Communists in the Chamber of Deputies refused to join in a eulogy. Nothing whatever was gained for the prisoners of starvation by such a surly gesture, and its effect was to inflame public opinion against all the sound causes the Communists were favouring at the time or would sponsor in the future. Milka, in private, to me, excused the blunder on the ground that the French were only in the kindergarten stage, as far as Marxism was concerned. It was the country in which the middle class was the stuffiest and most influential, she said, with more justice than relevance. Pierre was acutely sick, and for days did not show himself in the street; so the kind-hearted Stefan, to cheer him up, took a bath and had his hair cut and promised to be neater in the future, which he sincerely tried to do.

It appeared to me and nearly everyone in the rue de la Huchette that reform and regeneration of society was retarded when small minorities with some good ideas (and a lot of absurd ones) did everything they could from day to day to antagonize that great body of non-partisan citizens without whom no action can be made to stick. Nevertheless, the French C.P. overlooked not the minutest opportunity to make itself loathed and detested. From its inception until this very day, the American C.P. has followed suit, with the exception of a short period in 1936 when, acting on instructions from above, the American comrades whooped it up for 'democracy'.

For the last fifteen years in France, every pretext furnished by events large or small has started the so-called government on a Red hunt which has helped camouflage the real issues. In the rue de la Huchette the general feeling was so strong against Communists that it would be simpler to list those who tolerated them than to enumerate their enemies. Of course, Henri Julliard, humanitarian that he was, was willing for everyone to have his say, and would listen respectfully even if he were not taken in. So would Mme. Berthelot.

Monsieur Henri, it is true, housed all three of the Communists in our street, and defended them against flank attacks by The Navet and his henchman, the floorwalker Panaché.

Maurice, the goldfish man, who was accidentally martyred in the name of Lenin, Marx and Stalin, had a smile for everyone and listened just as respectfully when Milka held forth against class compromise between workers and employers as when The Navet insisted that he had inside information to the effect that munition makers like Schneider spent all their profits, and more, in patriotic and charitable endeavour, while labour leaders drew down fabulous salaries and sat with their feet on desks of pure mahogany, with 100-franc courtesans, half-dressed, as office help and thugs out in the alleys, garrotting helpless respectable citizens who refused to let themselves be blackmailed.

'Those *maudit* Reds are no worse than the rest,' Maurice said, but he added, with characteristic emphasis, 'and no better, either.'

21
MENE MENE TEKEL

The people of the rue de la Huchette were fairly representative of Parisians and other Frenchmen who lived in cities. The *garçons*, chambermaids and many vegetable and fruit peddlers were peasants. They treated our street as if it were a lane in the country and were bewildered by gas light, telephones and the traffic in the place St. Michel.

It was necessary to walk only a few minutes towards the place St. Germain or the Ile de la Cité or into Notre Dame, when it was open, to find French people with more money than those in the rue de la Huchette. On the other hand, a shorter trip across the rue des Deux Ponts would take one to a quarter that was even poorer, probably poorer than any place a non-travelling American has seen or ever dreamed about. Into the eastern gate, as it were, whose pillars were the butcher shop and the crucifix store, came savants and students from the Latin quarter and the Sorbonne. The clergy was much in evidence, on account of the proximity of St. Séverin, church of the workers; St. Julien le Pauvre, church of transients; and Notre Dame, cathedral of the greedy gang who ultimately sold out the country.

At the western end, our street was guarded by the two large and prosperous cafés, the Brasserie Dalmatienne and the Café St. Michel. From that direction came the respectable middle and even upper-class white-collar and professional men, business men, from the place St. Michel and the boulevard St. Germain, and customers for such shops as Maurice's *La Vie Silencieuse*, the stamp collector's, book-lovers bearing volumes under their arms, writers blinking in the sun as they looked for No. 30, the publisher's headquarters, and twenty-franc patients for Dr. Clouet and the dentist, Dr. Roux. The neighbourhood shops had staples and perishables for neighbourhood needs, and the quarters of recreation and supply that belonged to all Paris (like Les Halles and the zoological and botanical display in Le Jardin des Plantes) were used by inhabitants of our street and were really a part of it. The public transport system served it from the western end, the Métro station being not twenty-five feet from the corner; the railway station a hundred feet further on. Several lines of tramcars passed through the *place*, and buses radiating in all directions had their terminal in the place St. André des Arts, in front of Noël's taxidermist's shop.

When the Oustric bank scandal (the first rumble of the Stavisky affair to follow) could not be kept out of the papers, no matter who owned them, several prominent politicians, including members of the Chamber and the Bank of France, a Cabinet Minister and an Under-Secretary were involved and could not squirm out from under. As usual, when anything sinister happens, his enemies tried to pin everything on Caillaux, who cleared himself promptly.

The faces round the Caveau bar, when news like this was read, sometimes aloud, more often over a drinking companion's shoulder, showed mild disgust which deepened into resentment. Thérèse and the chestnut man called the absconders and crooks foul names; Monsieur Henri and Madame Berthelot dropped their eyes and turned away. Frémont and Pissy worked harder to get government employees into the union, but the opposition against them was forming on all sides because there were Socialists and were beginning to be reviled by the Communists on their left and the Radical Socialists led by Daladier on their right.

Early in 1931, the jackal Pierre Laval got himself elected Prime Minister, after much chicanery and some hedging by the peace-maker Aristide Briand. On January 26, 1931, Briand stated publicly that he would not serve with Laval, for Briand was honest though weak. On January 27th, Briand grew a little less honest and much weaker, and by his co-operation made it possible for Laval to worm his way into the No. 1 position. Included in that cabinet of lilies was Tardieu, who a week or two before had been ousted because of the Oustric affair.

Daladier, in the Chamber, assailed Maginot for asking military appropriations which were, in Daladier's opinion, 'too high.' Coincidentally a huge loan was granted to Rumania. Also the Verdun forts were restored. A hen with her head cut off could not have behaved more erratically than the French Government did.

All the foregoing news items were discussed and added to the encircling gloom. But what really shook the rue de la Huchette was Alfonso's fall in Spain and the proclamation of the Spanish Republic. The reader has seen how certain minerals, dull in colour to the naked eye, will glow with intense reds, purples, greens, blues and yellows when violet rays are turned on them. A similar transformation takes place in the aspect of a population when the announcement of a historical event is made. Political enmities which had been smouldering burst into flame. And ideological affinities that had been scarcely apparent unite men and women who had ignored or avoided one another.

The Navet stormed and stamped with rage, denouncing the Spanish patriots as jailbirds and cut-throats. Even a likeable roué like Monsieur de Malancourt turned pale and shook his head sadly. He definitely did not believe in a people's reign. He was smart enough not to expect a monarchy to return to France, but he preferred to have one handy across the border in Spain, and not a land where the terrible Reds would swarm like locusts in preparation for world conquest.

Monsieur Panaché blamed the Spanish uprising on the Jews, and when reminded that Jews had been chased out of Spain six hundred years before, he redoubled his accusations, declaring that the Jews outside Spain had manœuvred the revolution in order to extend their hunting grounds.

Of course, our three Communists, Milka, Stefan and Pierre Vautier, were overjoyed. They did not consider that the Spanish Socialists were really revolutionaries, but assumed that they soon would be liquidated and replaced by proletarian leaders who would surely spring up.

Our Radical-Socialists, Monsieur Monge, Monsieur Noël and the Satyr, being good fellows, were one hundred per cent for the liberated Spaniards, although their party was, as usual, on the fence.

The Socialists, Monsieur Frémont, the chestnut man, Monsieur Pissy, and Odette and Jean of the dairy shop, were heart and soul for freedom. In *Le Panier Fleuri*, Consuela, the Spanish girl who dressed daily as a bride, was loaned money by her fellow workers to hurry back to Madrid to breathe the free air again.

There was rejoicing for the Spaniards in every little bar along our street that evening. André, the coalman, his blue-eyed Alice and his little son stayed up until long after midnight, with their friends around them, drinking applejack in moderation, and talking, heads nodding thoughtfully, eyes shining happily, of things that Americans are taught to love in the primary grades of school: no taxation without representation, no cruel and unusual punishments, the separation of Church and State, free speech, universal suffrage, and the right of eminent domain. The proprietors of the Café St. Michel were reactionary, but the customers at the bar were working men, and when they talked that night about a republic, for once Madame Trévise did not contradict them sharply and inject some warning wisdom of her own.

I wish I could have seen the face of Sara, the soft-eyed Jewess, at the Hôtel Normandie that night. For not only the *garçon*, Louis, was humming and whistling as he worked, but Guy, Sara's husband, actually took off his coat and helped his wife with the work, smiling on her affectionately from time to time. Happiness is beautiful.

The date was April 14, 1931. That April 14th has passed away and with it the memory of other more and less important days. July 14th (Bastille Day) has passed away. So have days honoured in Poland, Czecholsovakia, Holland, Belgium, Norway, Greece and almost everywhere else on this earth. Little is left intact.

If only that tiny thoroughfare, the rue de la Huchette, a few hundred yards in length, could be resurrected, there would be enough of France alive today to stir a spark of hope in the hearts of men. If we could call back from degradation and disaster that small army of citizens and foreigners; the shops, the apartments; the beds, stoves, meals and draperies; the soap and olive oil; the wine, the bread, the piety and wit; the crimes and sacrifices; the knowledge, ignorance, love and hate; the indifference and the prejudice; if those faces could smile, those hands gesticulate, those dripping taps make music through the night; if those priests could walk, hands behind their backs clasping prayer-books, under the trees of St. Julien le Pauvre; if the girls at *Le Panier Fleuri* could once again say, '*Avec plaisir, Monsieur*'; if Frémont the postman could tinker with rusty latches; if the chestnut man could roar a song of the Loire; if l'Hibou could sleep on the grille over the Métro; if Sara could chew her pencil as she totted up accounts; or if Dorlan could bind books and Monge sell horsemeat and the cops loaf in the station; if only death were not the ultimate relief and birth the worst disaster — in short, if fate or history or progress or God could have spared the rue de la Huchette, from it another France might grow.

PART TWO

The Post-War Thirties

22

EXCERPTS FROM A SERIES OF LETTERS

[Received by the author in Madrid, Alicante, Barcelona, Palma de Majorca and Santa Eulalia, Ibiza, Spain, from residents of the rue de la Huchette, Paris, France — July, 1931, to November, 1934.]

This period was my longest absence from the rue de la Huchette in the course of the past eighteen years. So from the time of the Spanish revolution that unseated Alfonso until just after the United States had recognized the sixteen-year-old revolution in Russia I had to depend for news of my friends in Paris on their own talent for letter writing and what I could read between the lines of the corrupt and scattered French press. On the island of Ibiza I received the Paris papers two or three weeks late, but I had plenty of leisure in which to read them and assimilate their contents.

A city one loves exists at no matter what distance, and its symphony is sometimes heard more clearly when one is away, as the music of an orchestra is more lucid to an audience than it sounds to the performers on the stage. Had I been in another *European* country, the local events might have confused me and blurred my understanding of the Parisian scene. But France was decaying Europe and Spain was an awakening new world. The Pyrenees and not the Straits of Gibraltar form the real boundary between the continents. The short journey from Biarritz to Burgos this very day takes one back across the gulf of about six centuries.

Paris, 17 July, 1931

Cher ami,

My hour of escape at noon from this dingy barrack is not what it was before you deserted us, or rather, found it necessary to exercise your sharp curiosity in fresh fields. You were right and I would do the same if I could. Instead I look forward to a report from you of what you have found in Spain and to talking with you hours on end when you return. You will pardon me for telling you how much I have missed you, especially in the noon hour when you were gallant enough to share my table and so many of my doubts. Before you appeared, I had accustomed myself to eating alone, but never could I enjoy it. There is something in the taste of food that requires joint appreciation. One is impelled to glance across the table, and since you went away I have done that so often that my eyes must have worn some varnish from the empty chair.

The only gossip I can relay to you is a development that troubles

Monsieur Henri, although, saint that he is, he does not complain. A young boxer, formerly champion of Yugoslavia, I believe, has come to our hotel — in Room No. 6, where I used to be before I moved upstairs to escape the sound of blows and cries. He has become attentive, for what motive I cannot say, to Madame Berthe, our widow who looks daily more like a Botticelli madonna. His name is Daniel. He is handsome, gay, neat and smartly dressed, and he speaks French with an accent that makes it almost too emphatic.

Our French language, which you have almost succeeded in Americanizing — you know that I adore your accent and the way in which you find expressive words and phrases incorrectly — should not always be used at the summit of exactness. It is capable of nuances, of hints and suggestions, of subtle implications. Monsieur Daniel employs none of the aforesaid.

[Note: The Berthe to whom my correspondent refers is the widow of Jacques, Henri Julliard's brother, who formerly shared with Henri the ownership of the Hôtel du Caveau. She was then about forty years old and always dressed in black, which set off her somewhat Italian style of — not beauty but comeliness. Since Jacques' sudden death, Madame Berthe had tended her bar, while Monsieur Henri slept in the afternoons, and otherwise made herself useful around the hotel of which she was half-owner.]

The change in our madonna without child is astonishing. Each day she looks younger, like a wilted plant being revived with water. This is not an illusion; it is an actual physical change. The lines in her face are disappearing; her figure, in the same black dress, is more supple. Madame Julien has done wonders with her hair, which is still black and not grey. She smiles at customers, talks aloud to Maggie [the troublesome terrier]. Georges [the *garçon*] smiles knowingly and a little maliciously all day long and waves his moustaches when Berthe and Daniel come into view.

How will it end? Who can say? How will anything end, or will anything end? Certainly not the prefecture, where large and small we berate the foreigners more churlishly each day. The Navet is in such a rage about foreign loans the Government has made that the other day he struck poor Jeanne on one of her useless ears. Of course they are ornamental. Luckily. Her Socialist Lothario has quit her, to take some minor post in the Midi, I believe. So the day after her conjugal beating she took up with a Turk, a painter, if I am not mistaken.

Somehow — forgive me for being chauvinistic — I cannot visualize a Turk with palette and brushes. Probably because when I was young I loved madly a tall Turkish illusionist. I think of Turks perpetually bashing in silk hats or tearing coloured cloth into ribbons, threading needles and swallowing them, and never doing anything banal. Would that it were so, and that some Turk would speak to me and rush me to a transient hotel. I am past that age, and never enjoyed a clandestine situation. That is not a boast, *cher Heliot*, but a regret.

Perhaps it is better just to sit obscurely in corners and smile inwardly. Anyway, I never received a box on the ear. When I heard about Jeanne's, I tried one gently to see how it would feel. I confess that I didn't like it.

The Navet's fat son, I understand from *la petite Hyacinthe* who knows everything, far too much, advised his mother to quit The Navet. 'I know you have put up with him on my account and it hurts me,' he said. 'Leave him so I may show my loathing openly and take your side in court.'

At the risk of losing my position, I am reading in secret these days *L'Humanité*, to help me imagine what you are seeing down in Spain. It would be too much to hope that all the glowing accounts *L'Humanité* prints of the revolution in Madrid are true, but they err on the side of my heart, and that is always agreeable.

Spare me a moment when you can, if only for a postcard.

Your more or less faded friend (*Votre amie, plus ou moins fanée*)

Hortense Berthelot

Paris, 3 August, 1931

Cher Américain,

I have just returned from a long walk and still feel quarrelsome, so I am avoiding Milka, who always gets the best of every argument. What set me off is the Matisse exhibition which I visited for the third and last time today. The effect on each occasion has been to make me faintly ill with uncertainty. To what purpose those long walls covered with odalisques only slightly lop-sided and all in terms of pink and blue, with also some green and yellow, and eyes of such dark grey they look like holes burned in a baby's blanket?

That is unjust, I know. When I paused in front of any one of them, I said to myself, 'A superb colourist, a gentle facile composer who will do no one any harm.' There are many paintings by Matisse that I should like to own, if I had an apartment — but then, what should I put in it for furniture? The chairs and sofas in the gallery are Louis XIV, clashing weirdly with the pinks and blues because of the pale lavender and gold. You will not credit the statement, but on the opening evening (to which your *New York Times* sent McBride all the way across the sea, not to bury the artist but to praise him) the ceremony was opened and accompanied with music. Modern music? No, indeed. Ancient music. And the bourgeois fools (*poires*) noticed nothing incongruous.

I honestly believed I had changed when I dedicated myself to the logic and decency of our party programme. I wonder. I would have relished Matisse if I could have seen his works alone, or with you, the only American with taste and humour. You would deny that if you were present and I should have to retract, as usual. Either I do not go far enough in my judgments, or I go too far. That is why I thrive in the party. Such questions are decided for me. The wisdom of St. Karl is old, and I am young; the doctrine of Lenin and Milka is reinforced and rigid, and I am flexible.

Apropos of art and doctrine, I find it hard to accept the idea that painting I have loved is all useless and anti-social and should be replaced by propaganda. Am I incorrigible? In the Independent Show this year, one of the worst ever, I stood in front of a canvas quite ably painted and depicting a dead workman in a village gutter being nibbled on by swine. The red was red, and mud quite worthy of a pupil of Courbet. The composition answered to the rules of dynamic symmetry, derived, I believe, from the proportions of the Pantheon. I was moved to indignation, not with the Cossack who murdered the deceased worker, or because of the cowardice of the other workers who fled and left their dead upon the field. I felt an irrepressible hostility toward the painter and whoever had convinced him that photographic representation of ignoble incidents in colour and illusory three-dimensional form is good art, however well executed, or good propaganda either. Seldom does a worker visit the *Salon des Indépendants*, and how right they all are. But should one of our wage slaves stray into the Grand Palais and see the painting in question, the lesson he would derive, in all probability, is that the capitalist police are still too powerful to be successfully crossed and that proletarian solidarity is as yet far over the horizon.

You are discreet as well as sympathetic, and will not think me disloyal to the principles I have embraced in all sincerity if I confess to you my lack of clarity. My intense French sense of proportion (how I detest it!) and my grasp of reality, which has been strengthened by my unwholesome excursion into sur-reality, reminds me softly and persistently from time to time that my comrades, so few of them French, are ahead of actualities. I mean to say that they see the kind of progress they know would be just, and which Marx foresaw in advance of its materialization. Probably they are sound in this eagerness to anticipate developments. The progress must come, or else we are lost, and humanity cannot be lost. Or can it? Shaw, the Irishman, points out that a thing must be imagined before it can be made, but that does not mean that imagining a thing is making it.

I was not a good member of the vile ruling class of my country. Evidently I was wrong in thinking of country, and not in terms of strata of society. I was a fizzle as a soldier and an engineer. In the realm of art I floundered and ranted like a gander. Shall I be more worthy as a member of the party rank and file?

Please tell me frankly.

Yours for the revolution,
Pierre (Vautier)

P.S. In my state of uncertainty I do not even know when I am finished with a letter. I started to tell you of my long walk, which I hoped would numb and exhaust me to a greater degree than it has. The only suitable day for walking in Paris is the first of May, when taxi drivers take a holiday and the streets are not dangerous. Next best is any day in August, when our stupid bourgeoisie flocks out into the country to suffer sunburn, insect bites and hives. So many shops are closed and customers are absent that walking in what quarters are left in which one sees none of your tourists — thank God there are fewer of these parasites each year — is almost a pleasure.

EXCERPTS FROM LETTERS

You want news of our mutual friends. At least half of them are away. The only ones remaining are the whores, the serfs and the few Parisians who have no relatives outside the city gates. It may be hotter in Madrid than it is here, but the atmosphere could not be more oppressive. Milka is anxious to go to Spain, lacking only the funds, the pretext, the passport and visa, the invitation and the means of livelihood when she should arrive. I hope the new government, made up mostly of middle-class drips (*fripouilles*) with a sprinkling of professors, will forbid Republican Spaniards from visiting France. Should a Spanish patriot see what we have come to, after a century of capitalistic L.E.F. (Liberty, Equality, Fraternity), he would clamour for the sour-smelling Alfonso and his gaga queen again.

Is it true that when the people took over the royal palace not one book except the breviary was found and that the royal *salaud* used a scooped-out horse's hoof for an inkwell?

P.

Undated

Cher confidant,

I am writing to you, not at Mama's desk but in front of her triple mirror, which is kinder to me than to her. As yet I have nothing of my own. Mama is away with D. for the afternoon. Since grandfather came to live with us, by force of necessity she goes with D. to a small hotel in the rue Papillon, leaving me to soothe the Judge when he taps on the floor with his cane. That, dear friend, is often.

You, as a man of letters [Hyacinthe never referred to me as a mere newspaper man or writer] are not wanting in visual imagination. You can project yourself into characters and situations which unfortunately I cannot share, being ignorant of English and of life. I am studying the language, however, and my first use of it, once the grammar and syntax are mastered, will be to read your works. Meanwhile, try with me to imagine what Mama must look like, blushing kittenishly as she takes off her clothes behind a screen — I trust there is one — and hiding coyly beneath the sheets until they are accidentally dislodged. D. is no Adonis, but he comes round twice each week and has done so over a period of years, as you know. That is something. Just what he gets out of it, that he could not arrange more cheaply and with a younger partner, I cannot fathom. Mama must be inept. She could not be otherwise. She has no money, and D. doesn't need it anyway. His handbags are sufficiently renowned to yield him a good income even when France is bankrupt and America has millions of unemployed. You never explained to me why there are so many.

Cher maître [untranslatable but the utmost in flattery]. You know very well that, as I write, I am glancing at my reflection between phrases, full-face, left profile, right profile, half profile, from over my own shoulder; head tilted forward, chin lowered, eyelashes raised; head leaning backward — I have a good throat — and eyes half closed. I see myself physically, a sort of animate shell, and compared with other women I am beautiful. But am I desirable in the more compelling ways? Men look at me as I pass, but they stare at my legs. I suspect that if I were desirable they would look at me in such a way that my hands would steal up to shield my breasts — such as they are — and that I would, having passed, feel their glances somewhere near my shoulder blades and not around my hips. Are my hips really right, or must I get rid of them like an American girl? I shall not. To the last, and at any cost, I shall remain French.

What I miss in my reflection is what you supply when you are near at hand. I shall never be able to tell you how much I owe to your candid and critical attitude, not spiteful and never abusive — one counsel I can always count on and always heed.

I have news for you, my — what? You are not a lover, yet, exactly, and may never be. That is as much for you to decide as for me, for if you should look at me tenderly and say: 'Hyacinthe. It is time, and I need you,' there is nothing, utterly nothing, I would withhold or deny. The news I have is for you alone, not even to be shared by Mama just now. I am a *woman*. The proof of it I find not as unpleasant or mildly disgusting as I had expected, but I do not want Mama to giggle and whisper about it or to give me advice. Whatever she should advise, I should have to discard, pretending to be obedient.

What am I and where do I come from? Surely not from Mama. I must have come through her, but practically unchanged. Of my father I know so little, except also through Mama, and therefore my information is false. How do men make daughters? What qualities of theirs can be transformed or transmuted?

You may write to me in English, for although I think I never shall be able to speak your language, I have reached the stage where your written words, so well arranged, mean more to me than your piquant French, which only expresses what you have equivalents for in French and therefore leaves much to be desired. In justice, I must add that frequently your French is more incisive and striking (*frappant*) than that of any disciple of Racine.

I have much to thank you for, but nothing more important than your having cured me of Racine. Elliot, I shudder to think what I must have been when you first knew me [at the age of six], what opinions I must have expressed that would have closed the mind of a less receptive clairvoyant. When I open Racine and mumble the metre of that spiceless abracadabra, I wonder if I am not as silly as Mama and if simply you have not poured into an empty pitcher the wine of discernment. You tell me to the contrary, not so much with words, but with light pressure of your hand or understanding glances at just the moment when they reveal unmistakably that we are seeing or hearing or feeling and sharing the same sensation.

The same satisfying contact of spirit occurs with others, a very few others, but not nearly as often as with you. What does that mean? To me it means that I am not alone, that life lies beyond my degrading *milieu*. You have taught me to feel at one with Mozart and Beethoven, Corot and Cézanne, Rimbaud and Baudelaire, Balzac and Proust, so many others that I cannot list one-tenth of them. You have made me believe that, were those sensitive men alive, they would smile at me and press my hand as *you* do in the concert hall or in the Louvre or the rue de la Boëtie.

Elliot, sometimes I am afraid.

What has existence in store for me? To what purpose am I developing? I used to be certain that I loved the Count Costa de la Montaigne and that some day he would come for me and solve everything. That is not likely, my friend. Life is not as simple as that, and I would not have it so. You know as well as I do that no man is going to see me as you and I do, that I am only an incident of your rich and eventful career [nothing to brag of, I assure the reader, especially in 1931], that no one man will be everything to me, that I must work or create. I cannot vegetate. What is happening to France? Is France recovering? Is Honegger another Berlioz? Is Gide another Proust? I'm always prattling about art, but is it indicative and prophetic or isn't it? Is Coué another Pasteur? Is Blum another Moses? At least, he speaks wonderful French, even if I cannot understand what he is driving at.

I saw la petite Yvonne [Frémont] sitting in her window yesterday. She is pale, listless, with no orientation, not chic, not clever. But she might have been as beautiful as I am, had she had the help I have had from you. Or would she, in defiance of instructions, still have looked upon François Pissy, who has pimples and a uniform now, as another Count Costa de la Montaigne, and think of life with Pissy in a damp concierge's corner as a low-priced paradise in a country that guards that heritage of Pericles and Charlemagne with Citroën and a *crétin* called Daladier?

I am uneasy. I passed *La Vie* today, another goldfish, spotted unhealthily with rusted black, was dead and M. Maurice fished it out of the tank and walked to the quai to throw it in the Seine, then finished his lunch without washing his fingers. I wish I hadn't seen the incident.

Hyacinthe

Hôtel du Caveau, Paris VIe
4 Oct. (1931)

Cher M. Paul,

I am ashamed to have waited so long to thank you for the *saucisse de vieille castille*. It was truly excellent, with a sound body and flavour of some Spanish herb not unlike *basil*. Also for that *espèce de Jerez* (manzanilla), so pale and dangerous, to wash it down. The whole experience was surprising to me, as we others are not in the habit of thinking of our neighbours across the Pyrenees as gourmets. A cousin of mine, visiting near Biarritz once, went out mackerel fishing with some Spanish Basques and was served, at the moment when he was trying to uphold our national honour by not revealing his *mal de mer*, a cold fish pie (*tarte de poisson*) about four days old. In spite of himself he promptly sprinkled the lugubrious snack with the cognac and coffee he had injudiciously taken before embarking. The result was that he cut his visit short and came back to Paris four days before his annual vacation was over. Foolishly I had formed an idea of Spanish cooking from his report. No doubt we French are libelled and misunderstood in reciprocal ways.

My delay in writing you has had other causes than negligence. Notwithstanding that the season has been the fullest since I entered the hotel business so many years ago I do not like to count them, I have been immersed in complicated bookkeeping, filling out innumerable papers, tax forms, etc., and trying to take an inventory which events have made necessary.

[Note: The veiled passage just quoted is Monsieur Henri's only reference to the fact that Berthe's approaching marriage to the young Serbian boxer was threatening him with ruin, since in order to divide the common property he would be obliged to sell the Hôtel du Caveau at a sacrifice, if he could find a buyer.]

The inventory in question reminded me that the stove and stove-pipe in the room you used to occupy belong to you. In case I should leave here, what do you want me to do with them? If you wish, I could have them transported to my house in Montmorency, unless I have to dispose of that too. Also your bicycle is in the cellar. Shall you be needing it in Spain?

Your new war minister must be a man of wit (*homme d'esprit*).

[Note: The new minister of war to whom Henri refers was Azaña, who later organized the Popular Front, at least on paper, and then deserted it and his countrymen in order to live in security near Chambery while they were slaughtered and starved. Azaña made a ruling the day he took office that civilian clerks in the war department who could not show that they had had a chair in which to sit should be stricken from the payrolls. This cut the departmental budget by a large percentage and filled the garrison towns with malcontents who started conspiring against the Republic which had refused to pay them for doing nothing, as the monarchy had cheerfully done.]

Our minister of war [Maginot] is, as you know, still draining the public funds to build a sort of Chinese wall along the border of Alsace-Lorraine and the western provinces. Young Corre has been sent there because he speaks German, although his technical training is by no means finished. His mother was so saddened by this that she was confined to her bed three days. The poor women! While their sons are of military age, they are always afraid of war.

Julliard

EXCERPTS FROM LETTERS

Undated

Cher camarade,

[Note. In case Mr. dies or the F.B.I. care to make an issue of this salutation, I wish to swear, on my honour as an American-born citizen of American-born parentage, as a war veteran and member (not paid up to date) of the American Legion and the titular head of an American family, that I am not, never was and am not likely to be affiliated with the Communist Party or any organization whatsoever that advocates or has advocated or is likely to advocate the violent overthrow of any government the United States has had yet, except the British rule in the time of the Colonies. Of this I would have disapproved, very probably, had I been born soon enough. I did not relish Harding or Coolidge or Hoover, but I was willing to let nature take its course. Milka's use of the word *camarade*, a word which was freely used as a term of respect and affection in our war between the States, was intended as a compliment, and a mild rebuke because I was not of the fold.]

I saw with indignation in the news-reel last night the parade of murderers through the streets of Madrid and the deceived populace cheering and waving from the kerbstones, trees and the windows and steps of near-by buildings. If you were in that crowd, as you must have been, I'm sure you did not applaud the Foreign Legion, remembering how they slaughtered honest men, women and children at Barcelona.

Your so-called revolution, which is turning out not to be a revolution at all, is a deep disappointment. That old *fumiste* (windbag) Zamora! He would not be too intelligent even for the Cabinet in France. Somehow he reminds me of Briand, only he is better educated and not so gay with the women, because of his two sisters who are some kind of nuns, are they not?

I had heard from you indirectly through Comrade Vautier, who is brave and conscientious but handicapped to a staggering degree by his *haute bourgeoise* education. He is a sensitive young man, too sensitive perhaps for what lies ahead. I assigned him to help draw some posters, and after trying all night long, poor Pierre ran a fever of 104 degrees during forty-eight hours. In Zagreb it would be unheard of to take affairs of art so much to heart.

Is there a chance for me in Spain, Comrade Paul? Perhaps I am foolish to want to visit Madrid and see another country, and even if I could get a job my superiors might not approve. I am much needed here, they say. Still, I am blackly discouraged, not at the petty persecutions which crop out each day anew, but at the lack of progress we are making in educating the government employees. We cannot exclude them from the central union, or do otherwise than urge them to form larger and more powerful organizations. But men who are so basely underpaid, and who may be read into the army and shot as traitors if they try to strike, are difficult material. All tasks worthwhile are hard, I suppose.

Did Pierre tell you that I passed my finals in history and economics? I know it is foolish, or seems foolish, to attend classes at the capitalist Sorbonne, but in order to elude the police and remain here I have to attend lectures, and since I must attend them I feel ashamed not to pass.

Thank you for the Avila blanket. I feel that it belongs to me especially, being made of black sheep's wool streaked with red.

Yours for the real revolution,
Milka

3 November, 1931

Cher maître,

Not long ago I wrote you that I had nothing of my own. That is no longer the case. I have a lovely protection between me and the chill autumn air which this year is particularly vicious [an Avila blanket I sent her]. And every time I feel its warmth, through the family linen which before it comes to me will be so patched and frayed that I shall have to use it to cover chairs in summer, I am reminded of a subtler protection, an enveloping solicitude that shelters me, in bed or out — the love of a friend who, although distant, is closer than any other.

Elliot, my dear, what are you leaving — not for your successor but your substitute, who will be my fiancé? Surely the one little attribute, so important to most men's eyes, can mean next to nothing if it has been dissolved from within and is merely a deceptive mask.

Perhaps I burden you with too intimate confidences. It seemed to me that I detected a new tone in your last letter — it might have been nostalgia but I don't think so. The phrase you used, concerning what I told you about — my inevitable development — was not entirely clear, my understanding of written English is still inadequate. You urged me to study and to guard against 'the nervous or pyschological crises' which make me 'behave erratically and either act more like myself or less like myself, according to my mood'. The good God should have made women a little harder to influence, or else much easier, but doubtless he knows best.

For my satisfaction I tried to read a suggestion of jealousy into your admonitions. Sometimes I am sure that you want me to wait for you to be the first, which I gladly will do if you ask me to — providing you do not stay in Spain too long.

Yours tentatively,
Hyacinthe

I lie. Yesterday I saw the Count Costa de La Montaigne on his slim sorrel horse, in uniform, and I am *sure* I do not love him as I did. Concerning you I am sure of nothing whatsoever.

EXCERPTS FROM LETTERS

17 rue de la Huchette,
Paris 6^e,
2 Jan, 1932

Monsieur Paul Heliot,
   29 Calle de Velasquez,
      Madrid, Espagne.

It was considerate of you to think of me on New Year's Day. Little Daisy did not get her card until the day after the rest of us received ours and when we made fun of her she cried. Later when the postman brought hers, she was so happy that we all had to treat her and she got tipsy and had to be put to bed. Mariette did not scold her, because it happened on your account, I suppose. Mariette's husband gave her a radio which she has brought to the *boîte* (joint). Armandine plays it all the time, having little else to do. But then, we all grow old.

Mireille

(Mlle. Marie Verneuil)
P.S. In case I move I will send you my new address.

Date blurred

Cher M. Heliot,

Seeing Monsieur Stoff [Leland Stowe, then of the *New York Herald Tribune* and a frequent visitor at the Caveau bar] reminded me of you the other day and now a pretext has arisen for me to ask a little of your valuable time, or is time not so valuable in Spain? I hope not. Spain must be a happy land.

In one of the *bouqins* [little book, no doubt a magazine like the *Scientific American*) Georges [the Serbian *garçon*] found when he cleaned out your room, I have tardily noticed an article about my own profession and it has deeply interested me. It seems that in America, where well enough is never let alone, a new method of 'mounting' animals has been in use some time. According to the illustrations, the results are excellent, far beyond anything we can achieve here by means of stuffing. Madame Franz [wife of Ralph Franz of the *Herald Tribune* who then was news editor of the *Chicago Tribune* in Paris] was kind enough to explain the text to me, but the information is not complete enough to allow me to try the American method without instruction.

I applied at the central school of taxidermy and was shown the door by an angry old fathead who cursed me and all the Americas for disturbing his afternoon nap.

Can you refer me to anyone in America who could conduct a course in this modern taxidermy in French, for which I will gladly pay within my means, which sink lower and lower.

Noël

A NARROW STREET

13 February, 1932

Cher M. Paul,

I remember that today is your birthday, as who wouldn't who took part in that *soulographie presque historique* (almost historical binge) that marked it last year in the cellar.

Your compatriot who plays the mandolin like His Majesty the Devil [Fulton Grant, formerly of the *New York Herald*] had lunch at my table today and was very entertaining. How is it that when an American undertakes to play a mandolin he is not content with merely strumming out a few tunes but will not rest until he can do the Czardas de Monte at full speed without missing a note? I shall never forget that performance, although how M. Grant could have found the strings or you could have balanced on that piano stool after what you both had to drink, I can never understand. Americans are a race apart. Of that I am convinced. Or do they send only their hardiest specimens to the rue de la Huchette?

Excuse my cramped handwriting as I have finally contracted a kind of neuritis or rheumatism because of the dampness and draughts at the prefecture. I am the last one in our department — that is, I held out longer than any of the others. Old Madame Lefarge fairly cackles with satisfaction. She detests me because I can keep my temper and, on their second visit, the foreigners wait in line or ask for me, rather than be reviled by her. She is an ideal public servant, having all the minor ailments possible, a fiendish disposition, short stature and a healthy dislike for mankind. The thing about her is that she is impartial. She hates her own sister quite as bitterly as the most abject illiterate Italian labourer who applies for a renewal of his identity card on the day after Monsieur Mussolini has taken over the Mediterranean — verbally, it goes without saying. Unfortunately for the wayfaring Italian, he does not know that, and thinks Lefarge detests him personally and without provocation.

In my last letter I gave you incorrect information about Jeanne, The Navet's wife. It was not a Turk with whom she consoled herself after his husband had slapped her ear because of our loan to Rumania. *L'Absalom*, backed by Mlle. Nadia, insists the chap is a Persian. Also that he wants Jeanne to go with him, to Bagdad I suppose, and marry him in Persian style. The son is not opposed to this, but he wants his mother first to get a divorce and an accounting from The Navet, who, the boy is sure, has misused and appropriated funds which, according to the marriage contract, should have been kept intact for Jeanne. Poor woman. I'm afraid she won't go, or that if she does she will be homesick and find it hard to adopt the Persian customs. I've no idea what they are, but surely they are different from ours.

Your story about the Prado I have relayed to the faithful here.

Hortense Berthelot

[Note: The story to which Madame Berthelot refers concerns an American couple, middle-aged and Middle-Western, on the steps of the national museum in Madrid, where the French paintings, not very good examples, are on display in the basement. The American woman, guide book in hand, said to her husband: 'We haven't seen the French school downstairs.'

'To hell with cooking, my feet are tired,' was her husband's reply.]

The following card was written at Georges' dictation by Daniel, the Serbian boxer who was wooing Madame Berthe at the Caveau. That Georges, who could never read or write, would ask this service of Daniel convinced me that the latter was strictly *pukka* and a real *sahib*, as the British would say. From then on I felt easier about the romance which was causing Monsieur Henri so much inconvenience and the fear of financial ruin.

Undated

Cher Mister Paul,

Thanks for the white shirt and *faux-col* (white collar) I found under the bed. Amuse yourself well.

Respectfully,
Georges

23

TO BE READ ON AN ISLAND

The common people of France knew little about high finance. Neither do the people of the Blue Ridge mountains of Virginia, the pavements of New York or those called the salt of the earth or the toilers of the sea. Each slightly out-of-date newspaper I received in Spain in late 1931 and 1932 made it clear that plain French citizens could not understand why, with one hand, the Government was piling up a tremendous deficit and, with the other, was shovelling out loans to Poland, Rumania, Germany, Hungary and Monarchist Spain.

While I was actually in Paris, I thought of the city and of France in terms of my acquaintances and neighbours and friends. What happened to them also happened to me. When one is in another country, among different friends, one must depend upon what can be read in and between the lines of letters and newspapers. The report that political rows were breaking out in all parts of Paris was only an indication of what was seething between the surface on the rue de la Huchette and every other street and avenue and country lane in France. As usual, when anything happened at all, some 'Reds' were arrested, about one hundred on February 5th. Twenty citizens were injured in Montparnasse in a clash between Royalists and Socialists. In the chamber it was voted that members should not be permitted to bring in canes, for fear they would be used as weapons. The entire neighbourhood along the quai, across the wide bridge and in the place de la Concorde across the river was filled with manifestants who shouted and cat-called. Two thousand of them were arrested by the police and the so-called *Garde Républicaine*. But merely throwing two thousand indignant citizens into jail for a few hours apiece and breaking a few of their heads did little or nothing to soothe the unrest. The damage had been done. The handwriting on the wall was becoming more legible every day.

In far-off Spain, separated not so much by the Pyrenees as by centuries, I could evoke the city of light and oncoming darkness. The last time I see Paris will be the day I die. The city was inexhaustible, and so is its memory. I can stand in dazzling sunshine and experience an eclipse all my own, with Paris in dim blue lights and shrieking sirens between me and the sun and the landscape. I can recall the first moment I realized there was moonlight on the dingy old Gare St. Lazare and the surrounding streets and buildings. Before the débâcle, when street lamps were alight, soft pink and old gold, their reflection in the night sky dimmed the moon.

The same moon shone over Ibiza, in the days when life there was wonderful and free, and letters from my friends in Paris lent moonlight to my thoughts of them and of my little street and what we were all coming to.

17 June, 1932

Cher Monsieur Paul,

The Abbé Lugan is much upset because on his return from Canada he finds numerous letters from one of his former parishioners now living in Troyes, asking frantically for some papers concerning the pedigree of a certain hunting dog. You are, I think, involved. A month ago I gave the Abbé your address, and now I find that you are not captivating Madrid, as I had supposed, but are in the Balearic Islands. *Formidable!*

The Abbé is away again, but is coming back Monday, according to his letter. He writes that he sent you a letter to the calle Velasquez which has not been returned, and still he has no word from you. The Trojan (*Troyen*) is out of his mind. It seems that in 1929, about three years ago, he forwarded M. l'Abbé the pedigree of a setter named Pompier, by Debureau out of Zuleika, with the request that the Abbé have these records authenticated at some sort of canine prefecture in the boulevard Haussmann. The Abbé insists that he gave the papers to you and that you agreed to attend to the matter and forward them to Troyes. According to the dog fancier from Troyes, these records cannot be replaced and without them the setter called Pompier might just as well be Daladier.

Knowing your habits, Monsieur Paul, and remembering that you lost important manuscripts of your own on more than one occasion, I suspect your having retained dog papers three years, in as many different lands, is about as likely as that Jesus Christ will appear on earth again next 14th of July. I promised M. Lugan, however, to add my supplication to his own, in order to authenticate the dog Pompier, pacify the citizen of Troyes and vindicate our good friend of the cloth who, in spite of his dingy robes, is not a bad fellow.

I am writing this not from the hotel, which I have sold to a good chap (*brave type*) from Chatillon-sur-Seine, but from my house in Montmorency, where I spend much time in the garden. It is a long time since I tried gardening, and most of the herbs and vegetables will not grow according to the illustrations on the packages of seeds. I have one pumpkin vine, however, so healthy that I have built a platform in the crotch of a small pear tree on which rests the pumpkin, just high enough to perplex the few folks who pass by outside the wall. Marie has been ailing since we left the Caveau. She misses the draughts and dampness, and the lack of sun and fresh air. Luckily she is able to sleep most of the time. She sends you her regards.

Berthe, as you know, is married and has bought a restaurant in the rue de la Harpe. Her husband, whom you do not know, will not allow her to work there, or even to act as cashier. He is *tout à fait sérieux* and had not yet deceived her, as far as you and I are aware.

Sometimes I wish he would take over this pesky garden and let me manage the restaurant. We would both do better that way — but when are things disposed ideally?

Thanks for the postcards showing the Balearic women in their native costume. I trust you find them reasonable. No doubt you do or you wouldn't stay.

Julliard

The Abbé Alphonse Lugan was a Breton, and they, if such a thing is possible, are more stubborn than Basques. He had acted as confessor many times in his long years of service, and in the name of the Father, Son and Holy Ghost had forgiven sins which must have outweighed the losing of the set of dog papers. Nevertheless he could not quite forgive me for having misplaced the pedigree of Pompier, who remained unauthenticated to the end of the Third Republic. I saw Abbé Lugan many times afterward, and he was always polite, but a little too polite, considering the fairly intimate relationship we had maintained over a period of years.

I know that if I should see him now, while he is working day and night to help and console his people, his immense sorrow would have dissolved the little grudge he held against me. His hollow eyes would sparkle as he lowered his heavy eyebrows in mock severity. Would he now repeat, morning and evening, his simple prayer: 'Let me be neither rich nor poor'? Even that would be asking too much of any Deity now presiding over France.

5 September, 1932
7 rue de la Huchette, Paris VIe

Cher ami,

You will notice that I have progressed along our street from No. 5 to No. 7. Existence is not the same without Monsieur Julliard away, but I have grown accustomed to it, and at my age one makes as few changes as possible. No use competing with Nature.

The Hôtel du Caveau is much changed, under the proprietorship of M. and Mme. Amance from the Haute-Marne. Or rather should I say, Mme.

and M.? The latter is an easy-going countryman for whom Chatillon (sur Seine) was too large a metropolis and to whom Paris will always be an enemy. He lurks behind the bar, smoking his vile pipe and squinting out from time to time to see if the sun is still shining. It seldom is this summer.

Thérèse is gone, and with her the distinction of the Caveau cuisine. Mme. Amance, a real shrew, would not trust her to do the morning marketing and complained about the quantity of wine she drank from the store left by Monsieur Henri. Thérèse chased her from the kitchen, using as a threat the small paraffin stove which, as she waved it through the air, flared up and burned her hand. Mme. Amance was screaming for the police, who naturally paid no attention, as it was near the time for changing shifts. Luckily the stove landed in the middle of the street, right side up and still burning. Georges, the only witness present, calmly retrieved it while the two women were reviling each other, the honours going to Thérèse, I am glad to say.

Georges will stay at the hotel in the soothing belief, so characteristically Slavic, that the Amances will surely fail in business and that Monsieur Henri will be obliged to return when they are unable to make their payments. I had not thought of that possibility, but since Georges expressed it I have been unable to put it from my mind. Perhaps that is why I moved only as far as next door, above the Taitbouts, who grow more owl-like each day.

No one knows how I detest living alone, and preparing my own breakfast. The coffee at the Hôtel Normandie is not to my liking and the Café St. Michel is too far. Someone is opening a new café, with a blinking henna light, across the rue des Deux Ponts. Once or twice I have tried to enter, but the place is newly varnished, with a clientele entirely strange to me. I was always timid and unadventurous, and what little courage I had was used up in 1917 and 1918. Does that seem ages ago to you? Probably not, since you have done so many things and seen so many places.

As to the clientele at the Caveau, that has shifted, too. Mme. Amance, as you may well imagine, is of Tardieu's party (the old one called humorously 'Left' republican). Milka, Stefan and young Vautier have crossed over to the Hôtel Normandie, where Sara and Louis have moved in a cot into their room to supplement the narrow three-quarter bed. We all have lunch and dinner *chez* Daniel, in the rue de la Harpe.

Our Radical-Socialist trio have moved their patronage to the Café St. Michel, where they sit for hours each evening in the small side room and are increasingly disgusted with Daladier. Monsieur Frémont practically made over my little room here, with a door latch in American style that slides over and bars it securely while I am inside. I have a gas jet over which I can boil coffee and the girl from Gillotte's delivers my *croissant* in time so that I can arrive punctually at the prefecture.

Now that I think over my life, and I have plenty of time, it seems like a weed that was bent but not quite severed when I married Berthelot. My three sisters, especially Anne who was older, were envious of me. But how many times have I wished it were she whom my husband had chosen? Not that he treated me unkindly. He was gentle but preoccupied and inattentive, or perhaps I was difficult to approach. Who knows? It has always troubled me that when I received his papers and the Croix de Guerre with two palms I thought of him lying in his grave as he had lain on his side of our bed, no more or less remote. Soon after, when I found myself alone, I realized how much he had done to shelter me from practical affairs and how excellent he was, in negative ways. It is all very well to say that love and marriage are not necessarily interdependent, but I would have liked to experience what is written and talked about incessantly. The two Alsatians who roost above us on the fifth floor and minister to the colonel have a more valid claim to spinsterhood than I have, and yet I feel more like them than I do like Jeanne with her Persian, who seems to adore her, or Mlle. Nadia, who still is alluring to Monsieur de Malancourt.

There was a time when I wanted to grow old as fast as possible, to hasten the day when I should not have to practise a charitable deception, which, in passing, fooled no one, least of all poor Berthelot. Now that I find myself perspiring and shivering by turns and expect to dry up like a herring and become as crotchety as old Mme. Lafarge, I am dismayed. I feel like one of those sad-faced preoccupied children who, riding the merry-go-round in the Luxembourg Gardens, discover only when the mechanism is slowing down that there were brass rings to be grabbed for another free ride. I shall not descend sobbing from my carved wooden horse, but lately I have become more aware of the principle of death and see it all around me. I notice that leaves are wilting in the gutters and will turn in the autumn, that the window sash is decaying, that an ageing water-bug moves stiffly and finds it hard to scurry out of sight when the hall light is switched on (and responds).

In writing of Frémont, I neglected to say that he, too, has left the Caveau bar. That leaves the field to The Navet, who is admired as only *he* likes to be admired, by Madame Amance; the specimen from the Samaritaine; Gion and his martyred mistress from the music shop; and the eternal Georges. All the aforementioned except Georges are moderate in everything but meanness and talk, both of which have no price attached, so the bar is losing money. So is the restaurant, and half the rooms are unoccupied. They have closed the dungeons downstairs, using only the wine cellar. Georges has to snatch his drinks unobserved and seems to be more clever than Mme. Amance, watchful as she is, for Saturday he tried to cut his throat again, in company with the poor Greek (Mary), who was dragged to the station and kept in the cell overnight. Perhaps it is best that she got bronchitis and will have a week of care, such as it is, in the Hôtel Dieu.

You, my friend, are on your little coral beach, in the sun and sea air, surrounded by the gentle people you describe with such affection, and the creatures of your own imagination. What would it be like to be free from routine and squalor, to have *your* energy and zest for life? I am not covetous, in the sense that I would take your good fortune from you. I shouldn't know what to do with it, most likely, if I had it. But, dear friend, I would like to try.

Hortense Berthelot

P.S. It has taken me the better part of a week to write this, and two days more to decide that it should be posted, it is so much like a lament.

14 October, 1932

Cher M. Paul,

Thank you so much for the radio [my wedding present to Madame Berthe and Daniel] which I enjoy each afternoon and evening. My husband wishes also to extend his thanks and is sorry he didn't meet you, as so many of his customers speak of you.

We have taken the apartment formerly occupied by M. and Mme. Corre, who have retired at last and live in the rue du Bac. The son and his wife did not want it, as young Corre has modern ideas.

I want *you* to know, Monsieur Paul, that I am very content.

Berthe Petrovitch (formerly Julliard)

[Note: In a letter from Mrs. Ralph Franz she told me that Berthe and her young Serbian boxer, Daniel, were deeply in love; that Berthe looked ten years younger and even more angelic, and that Daniel, who worked like a trooper from early morning until the bar closed at night, would not permit his wife to raise her hand. At first, Berthe tried to discard her mourning and to buy brightly coloured clothes. Daniel had preferred that Berthe remain exactly as she was. Also he had the firm conviction that modern women who tried to look half their age were inferior to the old school who matured gracefully.]

Paris, 11 December, 1932
18 rue de la Huchette

Cher Américain,

Sunday, while I was walking along the quai Voltaire for a reason I will disclose later, I was seized with an irresistible desire to enter the Louvre and make the stations of the Cross as we used to do.

[Note: 'The stations of the cross' means a number of French paintings we like to see in chronological order, a tour of several miles through the galleries of the Louvre. The masterpieces were: 'Rebecca' by Poussin; 'Seaport at Sunset' of Claude Lorrain, with the sun low in the sky and flooding the sea, masts, spars and buildings; Watteau's 'Embarkation to Cythera', and then his 'Gilles' which we like much better; Corot's 'Woman with Pearl'; Fragonard's 'Inspiration'; Courbet's 'Burial at Ornans'; Daumier's 'Washerwoman'; Ingres' 'Portrait of Mme. Rivière'; David's portrait of his mother and father; Chardin's crayon self-portrait, and his still life, 'The Copper Fountain'; Delacroix' 'Death of Sardanapalus'; the fresco portrait of a woman painted for practice on his studio wall by Mottez and later transferred to the Louvre; Manet's 'Olympia'; Monet's 'Bridge at Argenteuil'; Renoir's 'Woman Combing Her Hair'; Van Gogh's 'The Gypsies'; Pissarro's 'Red Roofs'; Gaugin's 'Landscape at Arles';

Sisley's 'Bateau à l'Écluse de Bougival'; Toulouse-Lautrec's 'Jane Avril Dancing'; and Cézanne's 'Home of the Hanged'.

I had never been in that palace of eternal twilight on Sunday before, when it is filled with Sunday Frenchmen and yokels from the provinces who could not have been less comfortable in church or on a witness stand.

[Note: A 'Sunday Frenchman' was one who had no regular work, being untrained and incapable of getting a job. He lived from a small inheritance, conservatively invested, and was allowed to occupy a room and eat meagrely in the home of some relative. For this he paid, the amount of his contributions and the service he received being subjects of continual bickering. On Sunday when the other menfolk were at home there was no room for him around the house, so he frequented the museums, the public parks and the quais along the Seine — whatever cost little or nothing. This kept him out of the cafés, where he would be likely to unbalance his diminutive budget.]

I had read, in some silly book that Maurice had picked up, of how Watteau was a poet and created a dream world of his own that transcended reality. Having always held other ideas about Watteau, I went straight to the vaunted (*fameux*) 'Embarkation'. There was no dream world at all. Watteau, as I had always believed, painted exactly what he had seen and was familiar to him, namely, the foliage of the Luxembourg Gardens and backstage of the Opéra Comique where he spent the other half of his time.

Two Frenchmen, both bourgeois and smug, but trying to be properly awed, were staring at the painting.

'What poetry! What soul!' said one of them, looking nervously at the other. Having seen a Watteau he felt that he had to say something to somebody, the most common error encountered in galleries. The other fellow was more honest.

'For me it's just macaroni,' he said.

Even you cannot deny, for all your admiration of Watteau, that his brush strokes have many of the qualities of cooked vermicelli. I began to like art lover No. 2.

No. 1 was indignant and started to remonstrate, but in repeating the word 'macaroni' he began thinking about macaroni, glanced at his watch, saw that it was nearly lunchtime, and hastily excused himself without further defence of poetry or art.

Questions of art have long since ceased to stir me. I like to look at good paintings but I try to attach no importance to them, unless, like the 'Interment' (Courbet), they contain some peasant or industrial workers, preferably both. What started me out was another problem which will haunt me longer, I am afraid. I mean bedbugs.

There is no use dissembling. In the Hôtel Normandie, in practically every room, there are bedbugs. They troop along the ceilings and walls, hide themselves between the sheets, and feed on the clients who are hardier than I am. Not that they do not feed on me, but I cannot seem to ignore them.

Milka says that bedbugs have been forced on the proletariat. It seems to me as if the bedbugs prefer the underfed, underpaid and unfortunate. She and Stefan can sleep among them, and even snore. Fortunately, however, she does not disapprove of my efforts to get rid of them. She believes that the proletariat should chase them back to the oppressors or, if that is impracticable, may take the time to kill them, and sprinkle paraffin and powder to discourage them. Being occupied with important matters, she leaves insects entirely to me. So does Stefan, who has little or nothing to do, having bungled an assignment or two and got himself into mild disgrace. My skin is streaked and raw from scratching; my clothes are infested. Only this morning I found a bedbug on my tie, and wept in the street, entering a pissoir so that nobody would notice and stare. The pissoir stench has killed my appetite. So I am writing to you.

That is not intended in a derogatory sense, my friend. You are sane, and many times I wish you were here to listen to my muddled ravings. I have lost much sleep, but no determination. I believe, and I shall see the thing through. Oh, to hell with these heroics!

Pierre

Extract from three letters received from Hyacinthe Goujon in 1933
(January to July)

Cher voyageur,

As you know, the Judge has been volunteering information and giving me 'instruction' ever since I reached the age when I could listen respectfully. He has had his second stroke, poor Grandfather, and is, to all intents and purposes, already dead. Watching by his bedside in the night I began to review, as best I could, the advice and counsel he has uttered in the last twelve years. Perhaps I was tired, or exasperated with him because in so many respects he resembles Mama, but out of the infinity of talk which has issued in a rhythmic stream from his lips since I can remember, only one instance came to my mind in which what he told me proved useful. I don't think the Judge is more foolish or inconsequential than most of our public men, or our private ones either, allowing for brilliant exceptions. My conclusion, subject always to your revision, is that what men or women say has a very indirect relation to what they think, and what they think is again many spheres removed from what they are. You told me once, infidel that you are, in order to explain away some manifestation of the supernatural, that we have many undeveloped senses. I wish we had unexplored organs to supplement our feeble brains.

The Judge's gem of information, which he tossed off as gossip, making me promise not to tell anyone, had to do with Vladimir de Pachmann who has recently died. I wept, and you know that I do not often indulge in that low-priced relief, when I read that the grand old poet of the piano, one of the few besides your incredible Percy Grainger who seemed to have understood

Chopin, had gone to his reward at the age of eighty-five. Monsieur de Pachmann once paid me a tribute, or rather, an attention, that was so precious and individual that I think it removed the last barrier between me and the 'feeling' of music. Now that he is dead, and the Judge is paralysed, it will do no harm to stretch my oath of secrecy in a matter that soon will be retailed to the public, and, like linen in a bargain counter, will be rumpled and soiled.

In an issue of *Figaro*, Grandfather noticed a small advertisement (with, of course, the accompanying complimentary notice as a part of the *quid pro quo*) to the effect that de Pachmann, after an absence of fifty years from the Paris concert stage, was about to play a recital for charity on the salle Gaveau. Fifty years! Half a century, my friend! Why, only sixty years ago, Franz Liszt was alive, and de Pachmann could have been listening at his side.

Why the Judge had suddenly taken an interest in matters of art, which had made no noticeable impression on him previously, fascinated me. I had formed the habit of appearing to listen without taking in what he said, so that he had spoken several sentences before I became aware that he was talking of de Pachmann's one romance. Romance had always been ignored by the Judge, or had neglected him, in so far as I know. Still, he knew about de Pachmann because the drama involved a colleague, or member of the bar with whom Grandfather was on intimate terms. This is what he told me. That de Pachmann in all his long career had had only one pupil, a French girl, now living in Paris (as an aged woman) who had such pianistic genius and such an appeal to the master that he took time from his own practice and performance to develop her. He would entrust her to no one else. Of course he was in love with her. No one can ever convince me that a man and a woman can share, day by day, what is magic and the breath of life to them, without the kind of harmony that would create a deep and fervent love. Sometimes the art would outlast the passion, and occasionally the respect. Of what importance is duration?

De Pachmann and the pupil were married, and then began to lose the harmony and counterpoint in that ghastly endurance contest which must be, at once, a rivalry and a hash made from the remnants of initial raptures. One reads of men who love once, and never afterwards. Apparently de Pachmann was one of these phenomena. They parted; de Pachmann swore he would never again set foot in Paris, and after a couple of years the pupil married a respectable lawyer (who later became famous), gave up the piano, and ploughed through heavier courses after having eaten her dessert and sipped her liqueur.

I began to hate that woman.

At first Mama was unwilling to spend the necessary amount so that I could hear that recital. She has refused me almost as many things as her father has told me, but in the three or four instances where refusal would have meant that I never would have forgiven her, and would have borne an implacable hatred all the rest of my life, she has yielded from instinct. She has instincts, although most of them are unsound.

Elliot! You will understand! I cannot even try to write how I felt in the salle Gaveau. Mama and I were among the first to enter, and I examined breathlessly each woman's face who came in afterward. At last I saw *her* and her lawyer husband, distinguished in appearance I must confess, and looking uneasy and protective as men do when they know they are in the presence of something more important to a woman than ever they could be. She was small, chicly dressed, if a woman of seventy can be so described.

Forgive me if I do not try to write you in detail about the programme. That will be reserved for me to tell you, close by your side and vibrating with your kind receptivity. Naturally, it was all Chopin, excepting a little Brahms. Out of it, one gem will never be lost in my memory, the nocturne in F minor. He played the E-minor sonata, with all the fervour of Paderewski plus delicacy, accuracy, breadth and power. Just before the cavalry movement I thought how much indebted Chopin was to de Pachmann for being understood; how much de Pachmann was indebted to me for listening so intently, and how much I was indebted to you for having shown me what my ears and nerves and mind are for. During the finale, the presto, I didn't think at all, as hooves were pounding over me, no stupid onomatopœia but the spiritual impact.

But the nocturne. He did not play it, he evoked it. One did not hear a thump and twang but suddenly the music was around one in the room. Time was suspended as it grew and flowered, and then, like all our dearest hopes, dispersed like a drip of wine in a lake of obscurity. I was not fully conscious the rest of the evening, until . . . That wonderful old man — now dead — with the back of his coat slit under him. What died when de Pachmann ceased breathing? Not that smug detestable woman who had been inadequate, doubtless ranting about her own career, as if a woman could have a more sacred career than to sustain a genius.

After the recital, another instance in which Mama did not dare refuse me, I went *alone* — that is without Mama — and stood in the line before his dressing-room and inch by inch moved nearer. I have forgotten to tell you the most touching incident. My heart is thumping as I write and the blood is rushing to the front of my brain to confuse me. After the nocturne, not hearing the applause, de Pachmann stood looking at his hands as if they were miracles that did not belong to him.

'You've done well tonight, my hands,' he said, and waited as if he expected them to answer.

That, dear Elliot, was not fanciful. It was exact, as his sonata of Chopin was exact and not blurred with the pedal. Notwithstanding all his heart and understanding, his hands might have played him false, and not done precisely everything that he wanted from them. Every artist must have disappointments like that.

When I came face to face with him, in the dressing-room and extended my hand, my eyes on his, he must have felt what the moment was meaning to me. I am sure that he must always have been kind as well as difficult, and I am thankful that in a lifetime of tribute and gratitude and appreciation he realized what my silence and vertigo meant. What he did was to take my hand, and to the consternation of his manager, an offensive little man, and the throng of admirers, he led me into a small room near by and locked the door. There was a piano, a bench and one piano chair. Through the door and the walls I could hear mild clamouring outside. He paid no attention. With amazing vigour, considering that he was eighty years old, he pushed the bench away from the piano and indicated with a gesture of that inspired left hand that I was to sit there. The piano chair he placed in front of the keyboard.

'Which? For you?' he asked.

'The nocturne,' I said, surprised that my voice was audible.

He had played three nocturnes that evening, but he knew which one I meant, and he rose from his chair to clasp me in his arms and kiss me on the cheek. Then he played the F minor, as exquisitely as before and even more personally. He had forgotten his former wife and pupil and her stuffed shirt of a husband (*vieux fumiste*).

Today he is dead, or rather yesterday, for I have written long past midnight.

Hyacinthe

There is no one listening to music in France today as little Hyacinthe did, and Poland, which was being crushed when Chopin wrote his passionate protests, is the scene of brutality and misery and suffering, the news of which would have overwhelmed the composer entirely.

The following passage is from a letter addressed '*Cher fainéant* (dear lazy one) because, on account of winter rains, I had been remiss in writing.

. . . I was allowed today to have an ice in any café within reason, which I was to choose, in company with Cousin Dagobert.

[Note: Her cousin Émile she called Dagobert because he was absent-minded, if not gaga, and often tried to put his right arm in his left coat-sleeve. In the French children's song *Le Roi Dagobert* the king gets his trousers on backwards and is chided by the good St. Eloi.]

I had intended to drag poor Émile to the rue St. Sulpice, one of your discoveries, and where the pastry and ice cream cannot be surpassed even at Rumpelmayer's for ten times — or at least twice — the price. Your American use of exaggeration for emphasis leads me, who have contracted it from you, too far at times. On descending into the street, however, I found that all the shops were on strike, except mercifuly a few cafés. Some matter of taxes.

Your Spaniards are magnificent when it comes to taxes, if you were not deceiving me when you wrote that they pay their governmental expenses indirectly, by conducting huge lotteries in which a few win large sums and everybody has a sporting chance at whatever minute percentage.

What I wanted to say was that I chose the Café St. Michel, which I have passed thousands of times, and have entertained and stimulated with the view of my legs — which I hope you will find are improving — since I was eight years old. Émile was relieved because along with the other shopkeepers and *commerçants* the ladies of joy from *Le Panier Fleuri* had joined the strikers. Their impressario, Madame Mariette herself, whom I understood wields the blacksnake whip in an illusion or tableau which is part of the entertainment, and four of the 'girls' were on the terrace in street clothes. They appeared ill at ease, the girls, but not Madame Mariette, who always looks self-possessed. Their costumes were not in fashion; in fact, they seemed to be a mixture of several outmoded fashions. They had no skill in out-of-door make-up, and to my surprise seemed utterly without coquetry.

Elliot, I looked them over more carefully than any man for ten or twenty francs had ever done, I am sure. The tall slim one [it must have been Mireille] had plenty of spirit, if a rather meagre physique, and exchanged banter with the men that would have put to shame the chatter that goes on in Mama's little club where she learned about *frissons*. A wide-eyed little blonde looked exactly like the cover of *La Vie Parisienne*. Hitherto I had thought the popular artists draw caricatures on magazines covers. Now I understand it is impossible. [Daisy must have inspired this.]

On that subject alone you have been unkindly reticent. Elliot, I know you could smuggle me into one of those establishments, not in our quarter, it goes without saying, where, protected by you, I could see for myself what really takes place. No one will tell me. I have come dangerously near inquiring from men I should not give any hold upon me. If my curiosity gets the better of me and I get into trouble, it will be chargeable to you.

Thank God I shall not be reduced to extremes in finding pleasure. With me, I am certain, it is always near the surface, perhaps too ready for the keenest enjoyment. Shall I gain control with practice? Shall I ever have practice? Or anything at all? Even prostitutes can strike, with their neighbours. What have I, or Mama, or the Judge, whose second stroke did not, as the doctor had predicted, finish him? Please. I'm not heartless. I tremble with sympathy when he seems to be suffering, which is seldom. It is when he does nothing at all except defecate and breathe that I am impatient. It seems purposeless and undignified.

Hyacinthe

Elliot,

I am crushed and disappointed. I did not win the grand prize in the lottery. As if that in itself were not enough of a blow to my vanity, and to undermine what little faith I had in my destiny — I didn't win any prize at all, not even one of the contemptuous ten thousand which enable one to get one's money back, minus tax, I believe.

My ticket is crisp and unsoiled, so freshly printed, with the number 364825. I slept, or more often lay with my eyes open in the darkness . . . and I prayed to God sincerely — I know you cannot comprehend this — to send me a sign. In René Clair's wonderful film, the star actress got the million. I asked God if she were more beautiful or more intelligent than I am, or will be when I have reached her age, which must be considerable. All the stories, books and plays dealing with lotteries have given me the prize, since in order to get it I was willing to identify myself with an inferior heroine.

This whole affair has left me desolate — but really desolate. Having asked for a sign, I cannot ignore the one which was sent me — a blank, an insult, a rebuke.

My ticket, of course, was not a whole ticket, but only one-tenth. A whole one would have cost 100 francs and never have I had 100 francs — never, Elliot. Monsieur de Malancourt, who, next to you, is the nicest man on earth, brings large sums of money purposely when he comes to see Nadia, increasingly seldom — ah, God, time and men. De Malancourt likes to encounter me on the stairway, and I frequently permit him to do so, for, if he only knew it, the meeting excites me as much as or more than it does him. Then he lets me hold and handle a few thousand-franc bills. He has offered to let me keep some of them — not as a gift or a proposition — because he knows I would enjoy dreaming over them and would return them when the fancy had spent itself. This, Elliot, I have not quite dared to do.

If any other man had made similar gestures, both you and I would know what was behind them. I assure you — I swear to you, Elliot — de Malancourt is acting in the friendliest spirit. He has confined our flirtation to the realms of wit and does not pinch, paw, or stare, or make insidious dirty remarks to test how much I know or would stand for. In short, he is a gentleman, with the *politesse française* of which you have spoken sarcastically, and with reason. I wish there were more like de Malancourt and that France were not pocked with ruined and inadequate types of men of family, the kind Grandfather mostly knew and who have been immortalized in de Montherlant's faithful writing.

All roads lead straight to me, as you have often remarked. When I write of de Montherlant and his faded bachelors or of Proust and his Odette, I wonder — do not smile — if I shall ever be the subject. . . . You are the only writer I know, and doubtless profound and brilliant, but who could write about me in English? Elliot, I am old enough now [sixteen]. Will you promise to introduce me to some French writers you know, so I will not be lost to posterity, even if I am unimportant in my own generation? Who shall they be? Not G. He loathes women. Even if he didn't, I would find him stale and unsatisfactory. Not Léon-Paul Fargue, because he has a mistress who not only must be superb in bed but does the most artistic — I mean, actually composed — embroidery.

Céline? Decidedly no. He writes of the depraved middle and lower classes and uses taxi-driver's language. I know how chauffeurs would describe me, having overheard their remarks in the place St. Michel for the past eight years, whenever I appeared. Their voices carry, and my ears are tuned especially for whatever is said concerning me. Please do not think I have a disparaging thought for the historic *Voyage* [*Journey to the End of the Night*, Céline's masterpiece].

Shall I confide whom I would like to sit, or even lie for? Philippe Soupault. His story about Nijinksy and the tree has haunted me, and his picture, even in the vile ink of the *Semaine Littéraire*, looks handsome. If you will not have what so many men would die for — I shall offer it freely to Soupault, who, if he is the Frenchman I think he is, will not hesitate or quibble. Then he will write it all, if he recovers.

Hyacinthe

24

LESS BRIGHTNESS EVERY YEAR

On the island of Ibiza my small group of French friends followed with me the increasingly corrupt offerings of the Paris press and exchanged bits of news from their letters. Among them was Drieu la Rochelle, whose *Young European* had disturbed Father Panarioux and the others at the Caveau bar.

Nor must I forget a sailor named Jean, who later in a desperate year stood alone on the deck of a destroyer, speeding through a storm, while everyone about him was all washed up. I mentioned Jean because he was French Catalan, and tough as nails, and fought for Spain willingly and died futilely for France.

We read about Japan's refusal to withdraw from Manchuria, of Great Britain's prompt embargo on arms for *China and* Japan.

Daladier had formed a cabinet consisting entirely of Radical Socialists, and Blum, always given to gestures when there was little risk or no risk attached, left the Socialist Party because its other leaders helped Daladier for whatever they could get in return.

The Little Entente, consisting of Czechoslovakia, Yugoslavia, Rumania and Poland, was formed (by France) and agreed (with France) that there should be no revision of the treaty of Versailles. To counteract Mussolini's threats, the French Navy held manœuvres off Corsica, and Daladier visited that historic island to assure the Corsicans (who, after all, are practically pure Italian) that their mother-country, France, would never let them down. This was agreeable to the Corsicans, since any able-bodied man among them could always get a job in the Paris police force, as the Irish do in Boston and New York.

A new batch of taxes stirred up riots in the Madeleine quarter and on the very steps of that famous Catholic church with the outward form of a Greek pagan temple. The uneasy deputies had a cement blockhouse built at the approach to the Chamber, just in time for the Stavisky affair.

Stavisky was the director of the municipal pawnship (Mont-de Piété) in Bayonne, near the border of Spain. In France there were no private pawnshops, with three golden balls suspended over the doorways and windows filled with old clothes, musical instruments, watches and jewellery and other objects of comparatively little value. Any French citizen or foreigner with his papers in order, and any woman with the written consent of her husband or male head of the family, could take to the municipal loan office movable and non-perishable articles of value. These would be appraised by experts who always kept on the safe side, and a fixed percentage of their cautiously estimated value would be loaned the pawner, who was given a ticket which must be returned when the pledge was redeemed or else revalidated periodically.

In America, pawnshops are used by the poor or the temporarily needy student or reveller who wants to borrow ten dollars, or less. Not so in France. Every municipality, excepting small villages, had its official Mont-de-Piété, and the sky was the limit. The loan office had behind it the Bank de France and the credit of the Third Republic. An astonishing percentage of pledges was never redeemed, for the larger the loan the harder it was to raise the money later. The sum received had nearly always been spent or earmarked in advance, for fur coats, abortions, gambling debts, petty blackmail, etc.

Stavisky, whose name is now notorious the world over and heads the Pantheon of swindlers, was a talented financier and only lacked capital and credit. These he obtained in an ingenious way. He used the valuables which had been deposited with him and otherwise would have lain fallow, as it were, as security for large private loans on his own account. The bankers and brother financiers in question had an idea where the stuff came from but did not ask embarrassing questions, since the supply was larger the harder the times. Stavisky paid high rates of interest promptly, and if some client called at the Bayonne pawnshop for a diamond that was in re-hock, Stavisky redeemed it from the banker.

With the money Stavisky borrowed he floated several companies and sold stock, pyramiding one concern upon the other until he had a finger in practically every financial pie in France. If the pawned articles in Bayonne proved inadequate to sustain his expanding affairs, Stavisky drew upon similar pledges in the hands of some pals in Orléans and elsewhere, until the financial machinery of the Third Republic was spinning like a clock with its mainspring off the peg.

Late in 1933, *L'Œuvre*, a comparatively liberal Paris newspaper which developed such talents as those of Geneviève Tabouis and Georges de la Fouchardière (the former liberal and anti-fascist to the core, the latter a reactionary who detested Americans and America but had such wit that one forgave him everything), began to print accusations almost daily against the hitherto unknown Stavisky. According to *L'Œuvre*, Stavisky was not only a crook in his own right but had corrupted nearly all the officials of the Third Republic.

Since no one paid any attention at first, *L'Œuvre* gained confidence in itself and made larger and better accusations. Just before Christmas, Stavisky and a few of his associates threatened to sue the newspaper for libel, but the suits were never filed. This gave *L'Œuvres* still more confidence, and the sluggish public began to scent the No. 1 scandal of the century. If everyone involved in stock transactions in the United States in the year 1928 had been acting in a way he knew was punishable by law, although it seemed at first glance to be doing no one any harm, the situation would have been in some ways comparable to the Stavisky affair, which had roots and tendrils in nearly every business establishment or prosperous French home.

Chautemps was Premier in January, 1934, the year of the Stavisky shake-up. Public clamour following the long campaign of *L'Œuvre* forced the Prime Minister to take some action. Chautemps ordered the police to bring in Stavisky, but Stavisky had disappeared. Debate broke out in the Chamber. One does not have to say 'heated', since French deputies could scarcely discuss the weather or sing 'Sur le pont d'Avignon' in that epoch without getting into fist fights. The Minister of Commerce, M. Dalimier, was accused of being a Stavisky accomplice, but Premier Chautemps stood by him and let him keep his job for a day or two. Naturally, the Prime Minister was in with Stavisky too.

Comparatively few men in French public life slept soundly between January 5th, the day the official inquiry started, and January 8th, when Stavisky was found dead in a villa near Chamonix. It goes without saying that the coroner's verdict was 'suicide', and that the mystery of how and by whose hand Stavisky died has never been cleared up. That must not be held against the *Sûrété Générale*. Any working detective who got too close to the facts would have committed the same kind of 'suicide' that Stavisky did; that is, he would have known too much to live.

On the same historic day Monsieur Garat, the mayor of Bayonne, was arrested. Scandals and disclosures followed in rapid succession, and French official integrity cracked up like the surface of a mudhole in the heat of the sun.

Dalimier, since Chautemps could no longer protect him, resigned. Deputies and Paris editors were forced to admit that their campaigns and newspapers, respectively, had been financed by Stavisky. M. Georges Bonnet, who was soon to be Ambassador to the United States, called undue attention to himself unwisely by protesting his innocence too much. Everyone in Paris knew that if Bonnet was not guilty, it was because no smart man like Stavisky would trust him as far as he could kick a steam-roller. That did not prevent him from making an impression on our State Department and in Washington society.

Some daring French detective produced Stavisky's cheque-book. Its contents revealed clearly that the self-righteous M. Tardieu, darling of big industry and respectability, had been paid large sums from the Stavisky trough. Even Fabre, head of the Comédie Française, had been well subsidized, so that Stavisky could have his favourite actress. The Minister of Agriculture was involved. Attorney-General Pressard was caught in the act of sabotaging the investigations. There were a few tardy suicides among the deputies. A former Cabinet Minister, Renault, was mobbed by his fellow-lawyers in open court. Judges, keepers of gambling houses, financiers and minor politicians fell like nine-pins. Among the innocent bystanders to suffer was Mlle. Jeanne Chautemps, niece of the Premier. She upheld the family self-respect by killing herself.

Perhaps the most far-reaching disclosure in the Stavisky affair was the fact that the super-pawnbroker of Bayonne had been financing the Radical-Socialist party (again I must remind the reader that the party was neither radical nor socialist but opportunist-centre). Whether or not M. Daladier knew about it depends on how well he was informed about his own party affairs. Anyway, when the smoke cleared away, the patriot Daladier was appointed Prime Minister to succeed Chautemps, now thoroughly in disgrace.

Will the most ardent advocate of law and order blame the citizens of Paris if I add that this appointment was more than they could bear? They rioted. The lower-middle-class merchants and shopkeepers had been impoverished by taxes, the proceeds of which had been squandered; the nation had been manœuvred into bankruptcy; parliamentary wrangling and graft had become the order of the day. Even such traditional enemies as the Royalist *Croix de Feu* and the Communists joined hands against the police, the unfortunate symbol of corrupt authority.

On February 6th the first major riot occurred and some shots were fired which, like other historic shots, were heard around the world. Only in this instance, with the aid of modern press and radio, the sound waves made the world circuit in record time. Seventeen Parisians died instantly and five more lingeringly when the police fired into the mob.

Daladier resigned. The same day, national censorship was clamped down and newspapers became skeletons of their former inadequate selves. The National Federation of Labour called a general strike, which was blamed on the Communists. In Herriot's city of Lyons, rioting occurred. War veterans joined the indignant citizens, standing side by side with Royalists and Communists against the so-called government.

Old Papa Doumergue, who could not recognize the national anthem when it was played, was called upon to save France. He formed a cabinet consisting of six former Prime Ministers and got a promise of co-operation from every party excepting the Socialists (who were just left of the Radical-Socialists in the fantail of parliamentary opinion).

To quiet the rioters, Doumergue announced that their 'leaders' would not be arrested. The Comédie Française came through handsomely in the programme of national unity by taking off the boards a play called *Coriolanus* which makes light of parliamentary procedure, and substituting, I swear to you, reader, Molière's *Malade Imaginaire*. Seventy-five per cent. of the French workers answered the general strike call as a 'warning to fascists.' In Rome Mussolini made a speech pointing out that the French riots were an argument for fascist discipline.

France was still breathing, but vultures were wheeling in a lead-coloured sky.

I received in the next mail this short note from Pierre Vautier:

Cher ami,
Three nights I have passed in the streets to no purpose. I was not killed, so it's just as well that I wasn't wounded.
Vive la France!

Pierre

In another letter, two weeks later, he told me that Milka had been stepped on by a horse and afterwards had been clubbed by a hysterical policeman. Messieurs Monge, Noël and the Satyr left Daladier's party and joined the Socialists. Pissy announced at the Café St. Michel that henceforth he was a Communist, then tried to make good through the regular channels. He knew very dimly about Marx, Lenin and Stalin, but, to him, the air seemed less foul toward the left, so stalwartly he shuffled over. Frémont got drunk and lost a full day's pay.

Police Commissioner Chiappe, one of the ringleaders of Pétain's Cagoulards, the hooded order conspiring for a fascist dictatorship, was ousted on February 2nd.

The Stavisky scandal and the ensuing riots were high spots, or low spots, of 1934. However, other news events leaked out through the strictest peacetime censorship suffered by the Third French or any other republic (unless one includes the U.S.S.R.).

Whenever an article in the newspapers touched on American interests, I was called upon to explain. Sometimes it was harder than others. When a statement from Moscow charged that the United States and England were selling huge quantities of war materials to Japan, which had become the world's foremost purchaser (with money) of arms and ammunitions, I could only say that industrialists were the same the whole world over and that it was a bleeding shame.

Hitler signed a ten-year non-aggression pact with Poland, using the best German ink.

The French Government caused three-minute propaganda films to be shown in all movie theatres, to bolster the public morale. In a letter from Mme. Berthelot she told me that Monsieur Monge, after hearing the Marseillaise played badly in so many cinemas, had written a letter to Doumergue offering to conduct a free school for union musicians in which they would be instructed to play the stirring national anthem intelligently. He received an answer from a secretary that the matter would be referred to the appropriate department. Two weeks later M. Monge received an unannounced visit from two officers of the Sûreté Générale, who searched his small room and horse-butcher shop for Russian propaganda.

The Royalist youth organization (*Croix de Feu*) came out in favour of a 'corporate' state.

Doumergue's plan for saving France had one main feature in common with all previous plans for saving France, by no matter what Premier. It decreed a salary cut and reduction in personnel in public offices and institutions, including postal and railway workers. Strikes broke out; meetings of protest were held. More riots occurred in Paris suburbs. The lower-middle-class *Intransigeant* placed the blame for the disorders squarely on the narrow sloping shoulders of Leon Trotsky, for a change.

The Radical-Socialist party had been thoroughly discredited by the Stavisky exposure and its numerical strength was diminished. Herriot had replaced Daladier as its titular head.

In the international field, events were moving faster. The disarmament conference at Geneva, with representatives from ten nations, agreed on a blanket arms embargo plan *contingent on acceptance by Japan*. Japan turned it down.

With great pomp and oratory, Mussolini received Hitler in Venice for their first get-together, on June 15, 1934. A couple of weeks later Hitler, buoyed up by promises of solidarity from his brother dictator, ordered the blood purge which knocked off Röhm, Von Schleicher, and others among his former pals.

Steadily, since the Stavisky scandal, the Socialist Party had been gaining at the expense of the centre, and in July the Communists joined the Socialists in a 'united front' against fascism. The bankers and industrialists, whose sharpest tool was Bonnet, were thoroughly aroused and started sniping in all quarters, not in favour of fascism, but *against its enemies*. In the controlled press, 'united front' adherents henceforth were referred to as Communists or 'Reds'.

In 1934, following the assassination of the King of Yugoslavia in Marseilles, a Cabinet shake-up made a place for the wily Laval. The *Berliner Tageblatt* became lyrical over the appointment and foresaw untold benefits in Franco-German relations. In Paris, Monsieur Herriot, not so well pleased, walked out of Doumergue's coalition, and Flandin, to make confusion more confounded and for ironic climax, was boosted to the leadership of the 'democratic alliance'.

Political parties, in the interest of clarity, should not have names but numbers, like football players on the field.

25

OF HOSPITALITY

The night train from Barcelona, via Cerbere and Perpignan, arrived in Paris about nine o'clock in the morning. That did not prevent me from waking about four o'clock and dressing in my lower berth as noiselessly as possible. I had had an experience the night before when the train stopped at Narbonne that prompted me to avoid disturbing my travelling companion by raising the window shade.

The express was crowded that trip and all the way from the Catalan capital across the border into France I had felt lucky because I had a compartment all to myself. At Narbonne, I was awakened by voices just outside. One of them, that of the conductor, was hushed and apologetic. The other, that of a Frenchwoman who sounded vigorous if not young, was raised in protest, and must have been harsh and uncompromising under the best of circumstances.

'This is the only upper,' the conductor said, and I felt sure he must have said it to the same party many times before.

'Impossible!' said the woman. 'How much extra for a lower?'

'I assure you there is no lower unoccupied.'

'I shall not accept this one,' the woman said, and there was just enough of a pause to indicate that the conductor was shrugging his shoulders. If she wanted to stand in the draughty corridor all night, it was her own affair.

'But, Monsieur. There's a man inside,' the woman continued.

'*Ça ne fait rien, madame. C'est un Anglais*,' the conductor reassured her.

I didn't relish being tagged as an Englishman just then, having tangled with a rather foul collection of them in Spain, men and their peevish angular wives who had had some kind of gravy under the Hapsburg monarchy with a British queen. The members of that faction spoke of republicans in scathing terms George III could not have topped.

Furthermore, I didn't know how to take the conductor's well-meant remark, whether to feel that a Sir Galahad quality showed through my gruff exterior and had aroused the Frenchman's awe and admiration, or whether he thought of Anglo-Saxons as an inferior and unenterprising race from whom women in distress had little or nothing to fear. Anyway, the woman decided to risk my company and at dawn was sleeping soundly when I wrestled into my clothes.

My eyes smarted and my skin was rough with cinders. The water in the first-class gentlemen's lavatory was not running or even dripping from the tap. Cold air blew down my neck and up my sleeves and trousers' legs. I was shivering. My teeth were chattering. There was no prospect of breakfast or even coffee for hours to come. Nevertheless I tingled and caught my breath with excitement as the unseen but familiar landscape of France rushed past me in the darkness and mist. By the time dawn tinged the eastern sky, I could make out the shapes of long files of trees, with white streaks of road, plaster houses with red-tiled roofs, giant haystacks, and walled gardens in which the Brussels sprouts were still standing.

When we reached the Paris suburbs I strained my eyes so as not to miss a sign or building. Commuters were flocking to the depots to take the local trains; shutters were being hoisted; the cobbled streets were stirring with desultory traffic. Sleepy chambermaids, servants, factory men and women, white-collar workers, bakers' boys and dairy girls were going drowsily about their business. Cafés were filled with customers who huddled around the counters for their meagre breakfast of coffee and crescent rolls. I felt ghostly and at the same time, conspicuous. All those people were dear to me, and I was alien to them. I could have jumped from the train to shake hands with them all, but knew that had I done so I should have been dismissed as an eccentric. I was elated, and at the same time blackly depressed. Everywhere I looked I detected a dogged air, a slowing up of reflexes, a sullenness of demeanour that was new to me in France. Daily I had been reading of France's trials and humiliations, the cupidity of her leaders, the futility of the people's protests, the arrogance of France's enemies, the imbecility of her allies. Still I was shocked when I saw the results, as one recoils and tries to hide one's dismay when encountering a friend who has been ill or has been stricken with some staggering misfortune.

There was no one to meet me in the Gare Orléans, since no one knew I was coming. Had the Hôtel du Caveau not passed from the hands of Henri Julliard, I should have hurried there without hesitation. As things were, I was not at ease, and proceeded cautiously. I checked my hand luggage in the parcel room and took a taxi to the place St. Michel, and with every click of the meter and jolt over unrepaired streets my heart beat faster. I was empty-handed, inconspicuous, unkempt from the journey, and with no plans for the morning.

I thought of the bats that zigzagged back and forth in the rue de la Huchette at dusk and dawn and wondered if they flew perpetually, like souls condemned to restlessness and torment, without respite or repose. It was too late in the day to see them, but still I imagined that they must be there, hiding beneath some window ledge or eave. Of the men, the women and the children I did not dare to think before I was sure that they were safely where they should be.

The taxi pulled up in front of the restaurant Rouzier, on the opposite side of the *place* from my street. I got out and paid the driver and was standing on the kerb, undecided as he drove away. Then I saw the drudge, Eugénie, with the slate-coloured hair. She was standing in the rear of the terrace of the Café St. Michel and wheeled quickly as no doubt the sharp voice of Madame Trévise called her back to her duties. I crossed over to the international news stand; the proprietor reached for *L'Œuvre* and handed it to me absent-mindedly as I drew alongside. I was startled, then relieved. He had recognized me, but had not realized that I had been away. But when I paid him the former price of the paper he reminded me that now the bandits charged 50 centimes. Evidently many of his customers, from force of habit, made the same mistake.

When I walked a few paces towards the Seine and paused in front of the booth of the chestnut man, I was brought up short again. My friend from the Loire was absent, but the price tags on the turquoise green Portugaises and the flat grey Marrennes of incomparable flavour would have caused a traffic jam a few years before. I hadn't been in Paris half a day before it was clear to me that the rich had become richer and the poor much poorer, as a result of the recent events.

That morning I entered my street from the western, or St. Michel gate. The militant concierge of No. 32 was muttering curses as she tried to erase a violent political slogan that had been chalked on the wall. The publishing house at No. 30 looked as if it were closed, with the same dusty books stacked in the front windows. Whoever read such books (*The Attitude of the Faithful toward Immodesty*, *The Truth about the Church in Spain*, etc., etc.) I have always been at a loss to understand.

Maurice had gone with his bucket to the Seine to draw water for his exotic fishes, who, according to Maurice, found river water more to their liking than that from Paris taps.

Only Bernice was in the music shop at that hour. She always got up early, swept the place, and dusted the shelves and instruments before she prepared Gion's breakfast and called him from his morning sleep. In my absence, a friendship had sprung up between the pale Bernice and the equally subdued mistress of Panaché. The two men, who liked each other in so far as they could like any member of the human race, had forbidden their respective girls to speak to each other beyond 'Good morning' or 'Good evening', fearing that if Bernice and Louise compared notes they might find common grounds for complaint.

M. Dominique was at his littered desk, squinting through a jeweller's single eyeglass at a stamp, so I got past No. 24 unnoticed. The cleaner and dyer, Madame Joli, who looked like a Lesbian and called her little husband *Mon Trésor*, nodded absent-mindedly. I had seen her infrequently, so she had not missed me.

The day being Monday, Julien and Mme. Julien had not raised the shutters of the barber shop. Monday morning was the only time during the week they could seem to get together in bed, and that was possible only because Julien took his usual morning walk in the markets, then returned, undressed and crawled back about the time his handsome wife was awakening.

On the other side of the street I caught a glimpse of young Mme. Corre, the pale homesick girl from Burgundy, in the grocery store.

The blue-eyed Alice, wife of André the coalman, was busy serving teamsters at the bar. The tailor, Saint-Aulaire, was deep in *L'Action Française* and its tirade on the menace of Communism.

Abreast of the window of No. 18, the Hôtel Normandie, I caught the eye of Sara, the Jewess, as she glanced up from her ledger. A flash of recognition stirred highlights in her warm brown eyes. Her face, while preserving its essential sadness, relaxed into a welcoming smile.

'Monsieur Paul!' she said, extending her hand.

'Madame Sara!' I replied.

As she reached for the bottle of cognac and two tiny glasses, I felt suddenly at home. It was seldom, unless pressed by a drunken client, that Sara clinked glasses with anyone. We did not say much about Spain, where the enemies of the Republic were in clover once again (without the King and Queen and hemophiliac princes, with assorted relics of their royal parentage one hundred per cent. non-Spanish). To a hard-working woman with soft eyes and neat shoulders who has seen only a ghetto, a munitions factory, a mayor's office (to be married) and a third-class hotel with bedbugs and modern comfort, it is hard to be lucid about distant lands. But I sensed as we chatted and drank that Sara was happier than she had been for many years, and soon afterwards, when Guy came in, buttoning his trousers, his hair tousled from sleep, he kissed his wife on the cheek as she poured him a glass of cognac to join our little feast.

Through all the years Guy had overworked and neglected Sara, he had focused his better qualities on one humanitarian hobby. He was a rabid anti-anti-semite, a baiter of Jew-baiters. The recent news of German pogroms had inflamed Guy to such a point that he had seen, however tardily, that his Jewish wife was an angel and, as such, should be comforted and cherished. On that November morning, Guy entered definitely into my friendship. Love marches on.

Before I knew it, I was surrounded by Milka; Pierre; Georges, the Caveau *garçon*; Monge; Frémont (who had the day off); the pimp, Robert; and Madame Absalom. At noon there miraculously appeared in the small and already overcrowded café, Hortense (a little grey); Noël, looking gaunter than ever; Lanier, the *gueule cassée*; officer Flammarion from the *Poste de Police*; Mary the Greek (who was still lovelier than Mona Lisa but pitifully in need of clothes); and timid Jean, the Socialist butter-and-eggs man. Someone had gone across to No. 5 (I never got beyond No. 18 that first day) for Léonard's accordion, which they took without ceremony from his room for me to play. And the day was filled with music, and somehow most of us missed our lunch but ate onion soup and sausage with sauerkraut in mid-afternoon. I cannot say just how it happened that I took time off for a dance or two at the Bal St. Séverin, and to teach Robert, my brother musician (I disclaim his other profession) how to play *España Cani* and a Spanish sailor's song called *No Te Vayas*. Naturally, we could not slight Madame Mariette and Mireille, not to mention Armandine and little Daisy, who could not leave their place of business.

There was little work peformed or business transacted in the rue de la Huchette that day, but money changed hands in a healthy, hearty way, each paying according to his ability and receiving according to his needs. I awoke the next morning in one of the first-floor front rooms of the Hôtel Normandie (there were only two) which ordinarily was reserved for couples in a hurry. So my eyes, growing accustomed to the thin light, rested on a bland white *bidet*, and an area of wallpaper figured with either jellyfish or chrysanthemums. Pierre, in writing me of bedbugs, had indulged in understatement. I did not complain about them, since Sara refused to accept a franc for the night's lodging or my transportation on the shoulders of Guy from the back room up the stairs and into bed.

Louis, the one-armed *garçon*, who had sung *Zoum La La, Auprès de ma Blonde, Les Montagnards, Aubreville, Mon Lazare,* and other French songs and ballads, had passed out two hours before I did. Neither he nor anyone else seemed to find it strange that I had come all the way from Spain without baggage. Louis travelled lightly himself, when he travelled at all. When he offered to buy me a shirt, however, I remembered my suitcase, typewriter, and canvas overseas bag at the Gare d'Orléans and sent him to retrieve them.

My problem was to get dressed without allowing my head to tip too far forward, and find lodgings before he got back. I didn't think the bedbugs could get into my suitcase or typewriter unless I opened them, but the duffle bag was pregnable. Georges, the Serb, had convinced me that the Caveau, without M. Julliard, was out of the question. Some woman and her grown son who was studying the violin were in my room with my stove.

In No. 8, an attic room was vacant next to that of the Satyr. I rented it and as I unpacked my stuff, in full view through the open window, I could see the two Alsatian old maids across in No. 7, peering through the lace curtains and nodding busily to each other. I shall never forget these two old maids, of whom I had thought with ridicule over a period of years. As a matter of fact, when I first went to the rue de la Huchette in 1923, Elvira and Roberta were not very old maids. They kept too much to themselves, fearing otherwise that their tyrant, the Colonel, would discharge them.

On the day after my return, we all took it easy. I walked with Pierre Vautier all the way to Notre Dame de Lorette, near which there is a national museum left to France by Gustave Moreau. The museum is filled with Moreau's own works, the least said about which the better, except for some portfolios of animal drawings. The curator or director was Georges Rouault, one of the most gifted modern French painters, who drew a small salary for guarding the worthless junk of Moreau in order to eat while painting splendid works of his own. Roualt was a master of *gouaches*, a kind of water-colour, into which he instilled a vigour the medium had not known before his time. He worked in the museum, since no one ever visited the place except by accident or to see him.

As Pierre and I walked, we talked about Laval and Flandin.

Flandin was the most outspoken Nazi among French politicians, one who loathed a working man to such a point that he turned pale whenever he saw one. When Papa Doumergue, the last duffer in France who should have been selected to save it when the people rioted against Stavisky and Daladier, tumbled off his perch on the issue of a budget to be balanced largely from the lower brackets of government employees, Flandin was chosen Prime Minister. That was a kind of political accident that frequently occurs in democracies. The French politicians of the Right were afraid a Left Leader would get in, and started talking for social justice and against monopolies. The leaders of the left, especially Blum and Daladier, were afraid of one another.

From whatever causes, Flandin got in just in time to have Pétain reinstated 'permanently' as a member of the Superior Council of National Defence. Modernity, personified by a brilliant officer named Charles de Gaulle, was buried. Promptly, aboard the fastest train, Laval was sent to confer with Mussolini and give him all aid and comfort in his plans to invade Abyssinia. If Stavisky had lived, this might not have happened, since the

Bayonne financier had put up the funds for Haile Selassie's resistance.

Laval admired Mussolini with all his heart, and Il Duce got him into the good graces of Hitler. On the visit in question, Laval promised a slice of French territory in Africa and a share in the French railway from Abyssinia to French Somaliland.

In a similar spirit, Flandin and Laval sent a French trade commission to do business with the Japs in Manchukuo. Meanwhile the army put its dead hand on de Gaulle and his fellow-exponents of mobile warfare, as against sitting behind the Maginot line until Hitler thought of the bright idea of walking round the end.

26

THE HEART TO RESOLVE

Victor Hugo, on the barricades when the Second French Republic was being scotched by the ancestors of the same industrialists and bankers (with figureheads out in front to distract the populace with a false show of government), remarked that he could only take part in battle half way. His conscience would permit him to expose himself to death but not to kill his enemies. So he was out there unarmed.

As I walked that day in 1934 across the city we both loved with Pierre Vautier he was in a somewhat analagous predicament.

'I can go along with my comrades in despising all the fakers and their chicanery,' he said. 'I can accept the logic of Marxian socialism. Why can I not confuse hope with reality?'

One of Pierre's duties as a Communist had been to conduct noon-day meetings in factory yards and near-by cafés. He was no longer the bewildered boy of twenty who had been struck by his father with an umbrella, but an earnest man of thirty-one. He spoke in public well but dispassionately, in an even tone of voice, giving excellent reasons for what he asked the workers to do but without conviction that any great number of his hearers were responding. The men he was trying to help and to organize, with little success, were suffering injustices and were being herded to slaughter and slavery. This he understood. Meanwhile, Laval and Sir Samuel Hoare, in the name of the class which was born tightly organized and had the funds, arms and ammunition, were building up Mussolini and giving away Abyssinia. The futility of it all was consuming Pierre, like a loathsome disease he had innocently contracted. He had been weak in many ways, but his intellect burned steadily, like a night-lamp in the sick-room of his soul. He craved gestures of protest as an addict longs for drugs, knowing they would not cure him or uplift society.

At dinner that night, we talked with Milka, who ordered and ate what she needed, nothing more nor less, and moved in her incisive sphere of revolutionary practicalities, as surely and cheerfully as ever. She would no more have thought of glancing to one side at doubts or hesitations than a racing driver would have taken his eyes from the road on a bend to sneer at hostile rooters in the crowd. The girl I had known as a student was a drably dressed woman of thirty-five, more constant than fanatic, and very much alive. Her father had been a revolutionist in Zagreb, in constant danger of the police. He had been a goldsmith by trade and must have been practical, like Milka, because he had chosen his profession deliberately as being best suited to his political activities. Goldsmiths were highly paid; so he had to work only a few hours a week to live and maintain his family. The rest of his time was for the workers of the world.

When Milka was seventeen years old, and handsome in her candid way, her father sent her to a dentist. There were no dentists who were also revolutionaries in Zagreb then, so he had to patronize a reactionary one who had an excellent reputation. The dentist took a fancy to Milka and one day, after the dental treatment was over, he made her a clear proposition. Either she was to be his mistress or he would denounce her father to the dread police. She had to make her first big decision and, like St. Mary of Egypt, she came to the conclusion that her body was not of sufficient importance to keep intact at the cost of her father's torture and subsequent death.

I could imagine Milka going about her distasteful duties with contempt she could conceal only because of the obtuseness of her blackmailer. But after three years the dentist tired of her, anyway, or found a more alluring young patient; so he denounced both the father and Milka. The father was arrested, and died without divulging the names of his comrades, in spite of the fact that a wooden wedge was driven with a mallet slowly into his rectum, he being given a chance to rat after every stroke of the hammer. Milka escaped, and without money or friends, somehow, got into France. From Chambery she was able to contact her father's co-revolutionists whose lives he had saved while splitting slowly up the middle, and they got her enrolled at the Sorbonne and sent her a meagre allowance with which to carry on the family tradition.

She had never told me, until that evening *chez* Daniel, in the shadow of the former home of Madame de Staël, about her antecedents and the way in which she had stood where the brook and river meet with feet more reluctant than our kindly Longfellow ever dreamed of. Even then she did not take off her drab blouse and show me what Pierre must have noticed but had never mentioned: an ugly seared area under her smooth left arm where police had placed a red-hot coal and kept it there until it had been extinguished by her blood. And not until much later did I learn that, having been arrested when her father was, she had been obliged to purchase her safety by consorting with a plain-clothes man whose uncle had influence in the court of old Franz Josef, who was then Milka's sovereign and protector and defender of the faith.

So, if the reader finds it hard to understand why, starving and rotting under the grandstand of that Paris stadium converted by Premier Daladier, and later used by Reynaud and Hitler as a concentration camp, Milka, now forty-two years old, is looked on as a rock in a weary land by fellow prisoners she keeps from despair by the force of her spirit, having lost, of the 135 pounds she carried in there, exactly fifty pounds, he must concede, at least, that she came up the hard way and is a chip off the old block.*

I had a chance that same evening to size up Madame Berthe's young husband, who was presentable and energetic, well-liked in the quarter and whole-heartedly in love. In the midst of the meal I saw Berthe enter, still in black but radiant, and pause in the doorway to smile as Daniel kissed her respectfully on one soft cheek, then the other. As Hortense had written me, her wrinkles had disappeared, all except the becoming crow's feet at the corners of her eyes. I hastened to her, and Daniel beamed as I too kissed her cheeks and told her how glad I was that someone was happy and that she was the one who had been chosen.

I am sure it was because she was so engrossed with her first real passion that she did not seem depressed on account of what her Indian summer idyll had meant to Monsieur Henri. Henri had been willing, when he saw how things were going between the handsome young boxer and his infatuated sister-in-law, to continue running the Hôtel du Caveau with Daniel as a partner. This, Daniel was not willing to do. With the arrogance of youth, he thought of Monsieur Henri as quaint and old-fashioned because he was lax about bill-collecting and hesitated to raise prices in proportion to the fall of the franc. Instead of the traditional French menu, dear to the heart of Henri Julliard, and consisting of *hors d'œuvre*, soup, fish, meat, vegetables, salad, cheese, dessert and coffee, Daniel served a more modern meal, in Dalmatian style, with meat, mashed potatoes and sweet and sour cabbage on the same plate, requiring fewer dishes to be washed, less help to be paid, and yielding a comparable amount of nourishment in a briefer space of time.

Neither Daniel nor Berthe was worrying about Abyssinia, or even France. They were wrapped up in their profitable restaurant business, which was succeeding beyond their hopes, and in each other. It is true that Berthe found the hours long, between six in the morning when Daniel went to market and two in the morning when he came home eagerly and with plenty of what it took, after closing the bar. Of course, he slept four hours in the afternoon, leaving the establishment in charge of the cashier, the pious Mme. Claire whom Monsieur Henri and the American reporter had rehabilitated. Claire had turned out to be a first-rate *commerçante* and, after the American had left her to work in Detroit, she had entered on a liaison with the neighbourhood physician, Dr. Alphonse Clouet. They planned to get married years later, when they could afford to buy a place in the country and raise rabbits and poultry, in preparation for which the unbusy doctor had littered his private office with pamphlets about trap-nests, weasel-proof warrens, and a kind of 'American home' that had been shown at the Colonial exhibition and was portable, economical, easy to set up, and could be

*Milka Petrovna died of dysentery on September 12, 1941.

shipped compactly, F.O.B. Le Havre, for only 50,000 francs. The doctor had about 4,000 in French Government bonds, and Claire was saving twenty-five a day from her thirty-franc salary, since Daniel furnished her board and the doctor had a large double bed.

So while Flandin, Laval, Bonnet and the others were selling the country out from under them, a lot of French men and women were making plans for a future which resembled other futures of which they had known.

When I returned to my attic room at No. 8 about three in the morning, l'Alouette (the Lark), as the statuesque concierge was called, having pressed the button controlling the door latch to let me in, opened her door and, standing unembarrassed in her beige flannel nightgown, bare feet on the tiles, handed me with a sly sleepy smile a letter smelling enticingly of musk or some rare perfume. The Lark was so called because she sang, in a lusty and rather metallic soprano, arias from *La Bohème*, *Louise*, *La Tosca* and *La Traviata*, while performing her duties as janitress and guardian of the gate. The neighbours and tenants could set their clocks at ten a.m. when the Lark started singing, that being the hour when she considered that whoever was not already stirring had forfeited his right to quiet in the home.

I knew, with a sinking of the heart, that the letter was from Hyacinthe, whom the Lark envied and admired, envied because of her youth and normal size (the Lark was five feet eleven in her bare feet) and her excellent diction. The Lark had never been able to lose her Marseilles accent, even when singing in Italian. A quick reading of the message, however, set me at ease again, and made me ashamed for having feared, if only for a moment, that Hyacinthe would prove untactful or demanding. The letter is typical of the finest French tolerance and understanding, with an undertone of banter and a play of wit, a reproach so gentle as to be acceptable without resentment, and enough protective vanity to save the face of all parties concerned.

'Elliot,' the letter began, 'I understand very well that because with you safely at a distance I revealed myself so completely, you have not wished to startle me by claiming abruptly the familarity to which I have made you feel entitled. That is delicate of you, and endears you to me all the more. At first I was hurt when I heard you were back and even saw you pass my window without a glance upward — no doubt because you were afraid of breaking your chivalrous resolution.

'I reasoned thus: You could not be heedless or cruel. Nothing I had written could have offended you. Then your aloofness must be deliberate. Suddenly the truth broke through the clouds of my obtuseness. You were *waiting for a sign from me*. A cruder man would have rushed up the stairs, risking to find me unprepared. A vainer one would have embraced me overbearingly, as if he already owned me. You — the Frenchman who pretends to be an American, even to the point of improving on our vocabulary at the expense of pronunciation — were perfect.

'But come now, quickly. Please! Tomorrow morning. Not in this stupid barracks, it goes without saying, where Mama spills daily more powder as her blood-pressure makes her face more russet and autumnal. In the Café de la Régence, inside, against the southern wall, no later than half-past nine.

'Your devoted
'Hyacinthe'

I doubt if ever a man was pardoned more subtly for having got boiled and, as a result, having slighted a dear friend.

Some tourists will remember the Café de la Régence in the rue St. Honoré, not far from the Comédie Française, the Hôtel du Louvre and the Palais Royal (in which the expatriate who wrote 'Home Sweet Home' lived in 1840). There was a table in the centre at which Napoleon had played chess, and chess champions from all quarters of the world frequented the Régence. The terrace afforded a good view of the Opéra, at the end of the broad busy avenue, at just about the right distance to keep between a music lover and that degenerate institution in France, after World War I. Between the terrace and the inner café where a trio of musicians (violin, 'cello and piano) played at dinner-time (the food was good if not excellent) selections like the 'Bacarolle' from *The Tales of Hoffmann*, Nevin's 'Narcissus', Dvoràk's 'Humoresque' and Saint Saëns' 'My Heart at Thy Sweet Voice'. The Régence was not a political café, and the memento of Napoleon did not bring too many tourists. It was a favourite rendezvous for men like Monsieur de Malancourt, or who wanted to be like him, and the women of their temporary choice. Usually a French *bon vivant* invited his light of love to the Régence *before* the seduction, so the couples to be seen there were attentive, from the male angle, and coy or reserved on the part of the female.

At late breakfast-time, however, there were a few English and Americans, on account of a house speciality called '*œuf au cheval*', which consisted of an egg on a layer of Gruyère cheese on a slice of *pain mie* (something like American bread, but not much) neatly toasted in a hot oven until the white of the egg was cooked firm, the yolk still soft and fluid, and the cheese partly melted. Hyacinthe adored eggs on horseback and watching her enjoy herself is one of the lost pleasures I mourn from the bottom of my heart.

I had first taken Hyacinthe to the Café de la Régence when she was almost fourteen, because her mother kept her in black most of the time out of respect for distant relatives who seemed to know just when to die, in turn, in order to prevent Hyacinthe from wearing the colours she loved and understood. Not that she was not ravishing in black, so pale and demure, with those haunting hazel eyes and curved lashes, not too long. But black does not compose well with pastel colours; so I selected for Hyacinthe the best cafés where the chairs or benches would supply her black clothes and white skin with a strong intermediary red, ultra-marine, gold or corn-yellow, and sometimes royal purple or violet. Oh yes, and in the Café de Rohan, so safe and select if one knew which room to patronize, a Veronese green that brought out the warm highlights in her eyes and, reflected in her throat, and her dainty capable hands, lent her an eerie quality she liked now and then to exercise.

Make of it what you will, Hyacinthe loved her shapely body and wanted not even its reflections wasted, not a curve or a surface, not a single fine-spun wisp of hair, or a gesture of a crooked finger, or a swish of silken knee. Behind her smooth forehead, and revealed by her hazel eyes, was a mind that baulked at nothing, that was more sensitive than a seismograph and most supple and resistant than a Toledo blade.

She was perfume and morning and rest and atmosphere and sky, and she honoured me with her friendship because, a stranger from a distant land, I wandered into the little street where she, too, was a stranger. She gave me her confidence because, with a zest for life like hers, and so much she had to share, it was imperative to extend it to someone, and no one else was available.

On the morning of which I write she was just turned seventeen. She had left home early in order to pray at the shrine of the Virgin in the Madeleine. I doubt if the Virgin was accustomed to commune with suppliants as highly intelligent, or who asked her for guidance with more sincerity.

'I know it annoys you, Elliot, when you are reminded that I cling to a form of worship which seems to you quite empty and illogical,' she said, after I had ordered our hearty breakfast. The perfume she had selected that morning was Molyneux No. 5, which is not obtrusive in the aroma of food. Her gloves were of black suède, as were her high-heeled narrow shoes. She sat on the bench beside me at precisely the right distance, so that I could feel dimly her warmth and not be hampered in my movements.

'When you need rest from yourself and the turning of your restless mind, you get drunk, my friend. Religion is my repose, and it comforts me. I know the Church has strayed far from the thoughts of Jesus and the humble, who must have been more attractive in pastoral lands and ancient times than we find them today. The fact remains, I am a Catholic and it comforts me.'

'I am almost converted,' I said, not sarcastically. 'I wish you would send some of your tolerant French clergy to Spain, armed with flit guns.'

Hyacinthe looked at me closely. 'Elliot. What has hurt you so?' she asked.

She knew that had everything been well, I should not have introduced an acid note into our reunion.

'Things are going very badly down there,' I said, meaning Spain.

'The Church has often been corrupt and its priests have been bestial and greedy. Worse, they have been short-sighted. It is not the impurity of Her human agents one worships, but Her spiritual perfection,' said Hyacinthe.

'Perfection is the ultimate. Why not worship it plain?'

'It needs to be dramatized,' she said.

That brought us to the subject nearest to her mind. She had decided on a career, from which neither her family nor all the archbishops, nor rebuffs of any kind would dissuade her.

'The cinema,' she said, 'while manufactured in quantity by the Americans' (she spoke of Americans sometimes to me as if I were French or Siamese), 'is produced with style and significance in France. The medium is characteristically French. Molière himself wrote cinema before the day of the camera. American pictures are like American food, wasteful and rich in material, haphazard and boorish in conception. Why, Elliot, the exceptions, the first-rate films you have produced' (I had become American again because the remark was complimentary) 'provide the most devastating criticism of the run of the mill, for illiterates who know the alphabet and arithmetic, but never literature or algebra.

'The German films are strong, sometimes, but they have no sense of tempo or of timing. You remember the one we saw at the Ursulines in which the switch-tender's daughter was betrayed and everybody died — but everybody. Where was the crescendo of seduction, the presto of rage, the adagio of disappointment? No. The whole piece was a dogged persistent largo.

'The English cannot make pictures because as a race they are incurably frivolous, and think the middle ground conceals truth as a tropical island has hidden treasure buried some distance from the shore. When they portray love, they talk about lust or kippered herring, and chase each other across lawns where the girl, had she not tripped over a croquet wicket, might never had known that the cold exterior of the rather bony hero, who talks as if he had a hot potato in his mouth, covered a rather decent income and a willingness to be married in a church that is neither Catholic nor Protestant, but on the fence, like everything English.'

The *œufs au cheval* had been placed in front of us but were still too hot to taste. So she continued. I would not have stopped her for the world.

'One reason for the superiority of French films,' she said, 'aside from the Gallic instinct for ensemble and synchronization, for atmosphere and restraint, is the acceptance by our public of middle-aged heroes. Hollywood sends out on the screen either callow youths who not only have not lived long enough to learn what acting means, but have not seen or felt enough to interpret a script; or men with four or five children and three wives — only one at a time, perhaps — who play opposite *cocottes* cast as gentle young ladies or college graduates with breeding who have to try to act like hard-boiled creatures of the slums. In either case, one leaves the theatre before the show is finished, to spare oneself the sight of a heroine who is going to suffer a calf-like honeymoon with a fresh young bungler or, worse, is going to have to learn about love from a settled middle-aged party who needs the tricks of a professional to arouse him at all.'

There was nothing I could say in rebuttal, except that our photography was tops.

'Your Carnegie Institute, or some philanthropic institution, should ship it over here,' she said, 'without your producers or censorship.'

Her plan of campaign took my breath away, as familiar as I was with her determination and ruthless realistic approach. She knew, she said, that in order to get quickly to the top she would have to become the mistress of some influential producer or director or both, or if not, some backer or male star who could stand in her way. But since she was a virgin, and could offer this rare attraction as bait, when most of the actresses could not compete on those terms, if any one of them could (her words), she believed she was justified in proceeding, as follows:

The system was unjust, the men who took advantage of it were unchivalrous and mean. Therefore she was within her rights in duping them. A hymen was too great a price for anyone to demand merely for a chance to be an extra. So she was going to select her man or men who could do the most towards getting her to stardom, promise them the prize when she should reach the goal, which with her physique, brains and talent could not be long in achievement, and then, when the moment came to deliver, she, having established herself, would laugh in his or their faces.

'I believe you can do it, Hyacinthe,' I said.

'If you will be patient and help me,' she answered, and I thought when she looked straight into my eyes that I saw in hers an infinite sadness.

27

ONE BITTER PILL DESERVES ANOTHER

Not even the reactionaries in the rue de la Huchette came out openly in defence of Laval's blessing to Mussolini's Abyssinian campaign or the League of Nations' abject attitude in the face of Japan and Fascist Italy who mocked and defied the hypocrites of Geneva. From one end of the street to the other, my decent and well-meaning friends were ashamed of what their Government was doing, and worried not only about the ethics involved but also the practical consequences.

'What can one do?' asked Madame Berthelot, as we lunched that day. My appetite had not been sharpened by what Hyacinthe had told me at breakfast, but I kept the engagement. It would be hard for me to say for which of those two women, so disparate in age and temperament and natural gifts and talent for companionship, I had the deepest affection.

In spite of my desire to be of service, I could suggest nothing that Hortense could do to stop Laval and Mussolini, short of assassination. Neither of us would have objected to that, but neither of us had the necessary zeal to attempt it either.

'We are as helpless to control our Government as we are to change the weather,' she said. That was literally true. No matter how many Frenchmen voted, or how they voted, the same predatory combination ran the country for the benefit of large employers and speculators on a colossal scale. Voters in a so-called democracy may depose tyrants or crooks in isolated cases but they cannot give birth, full grown like Minerva, to honest and experienced statesmen to take their places.

Those of us who were familiar with France between the two world wars knew that there was continual agitation among Frenchmen for a restoration of the monarchy supported by a dictatorship. In that way the co-operation of the monarchists and their social influence was secured in a manœuvre which was really intended to break the rising power of labour and reduce the general standard of living in order to keep the workers helpless and the police all-powerful. Even Lyautey, one of the most unscrupulous colonial administrators who has in modern times been given sway over a subject population, was mentioned as the possible iron man of France before he died in 1934. In January, 1935, a Paris newspaper conducted a poll to choose a most likely dictator, and Pétain won, hands down, so by the time he wrote his first proclamation in 1940 and started it, 'We, ———,' in the style of the Bourbon kings, the idea of governing France by absolute decree was not new to him. Of course, he had not counted on having the decrees he signed dictated by a German Führer, or at least O.K.'d when their hearts beat exactly as one.

A letter from Pierre Vautier which I received in Mexico City in April of that year (1935) contained sidelights on Pétain's growing influence and the way in which the army was being prepared, not to defend the country, but for police work in reducing parliamentary control and as a bulwark against organized labour. While Pierre had not enjoyed his year at St. Cyr, he had not left his brains behind when he entered, and, in spite of his distaste for military studies and engineering, he had learned to keep track of the score.

Paris, 16 April, 1935

Cher voyageur,

Milka, who is too busy to write you just now, asks me to thank you for the Mexican embroidery. As you know — you seem to notice everything — our red Jeanne d'Arc (without army and with the 'voices' safely written down) has not, in her passion for reform, lost her Slavic taste for bright colours. She is having your material made into a blouse by one of the Croatian comrades in the rue de Serpent and plans to wear it a day or two after you return, knowing that the first two days will be spent in drunkenness and music and that any new clothes would be stained with cognac or otherwise ruined.

Today, when she was holding the embroidery across her shoulders, to help her guess what it would look like when the comrade seamstress got through, I stepped up behind her and saw in the small cracked mirror that I was definitely getting bald. In the first few days I knew you, even then I thought of you as old enough to be a colonel, which would by now have put you so far in your dotage that you would be eligible for our general staff. The machinations and absurdities of those *vieux crétins* (it rhymes with Pétain) are beginning to take form.

You have read, no doubt, how Laval, who had befouled us in Africa and the Mediterranean and prefers Il Duce to young Eden — both are gallows-meat; so are Laval and Flandin. Anyway, Laval, before his conference with Mussolini to celebrate the New Year, dissolved the league opposing conscription. That was one of the little signs, of course, that the term of conscription was to be lengthened, and the money ground out of the workers in prices and the small shopkeepers in taxes was to be spent on more soldiers instead of modern arms. That suits old Pétain to a T, also Gamelin and Weygand, and Chiappe (the Paris police commissioner) who is part of the same dirty gang.

When a few weeks ago the students of the technical schools staged a strike, it was blamed on the Party, as a matter of routine. Actually we had nothing to do with it, or it would have been better organized. I have read so much lately, in the books Milka hands out to me, of how people rise up and protest spontaneously and afterwards prove to have been perspicacious and sound that I was intrigued with the students' demonstration. What was behind it was simple enough. A few young patriots, backward in their studies, resented the fact that they had to compete with Germans, Italians and examples of God-knows-what Central European races. Our engineering schools have been filled up with foreigners, practically all of whom are potential enemies in war. The least amount of thought by our Paris editors would have convinced them that Communists are not whooping it up for any *national* movement. I have noticed, as little as I am permitted to know of Party affairs, that we are blamed mostly for what we have no hand in, and our most telling coups pass unnoticed altogether. Perhaps, after all, it is good strategy to be systematically misunderstood.

There has been an agitation for a longer term of military service ever since the Left started gaining in the elections. It is not against Mussolini or Hitler, who eventually will destroy us unless Russia steps in. They are building highly mechanized and mobile armies, as one of my old professors said 'like navies on land'. The mobility of such forces enables them to avoid great risks, as well as to strike quick and telling blows before an enemy is ready. Who cannot see that the war will depend on tanks and airplanes? Instead we are piling up more soldiers to be fed, while they learn squads right and left and infect servant girls, or vice versa.

Colonel P. (the Colonel is still alive) got drunk in a Café one evening when I was at St. Cyr and talked quite freely about Gamelin, who has been promoted to chief of staff. Gamelin is fifty per cent. like Cæsar and Napoleon, according to P. Those great generals of the past made quick, clear decisions and carried them out with dispatch. Gamelin will say yes to anything half-way reasonable, but that is as far as the matter ever goes. Weygand, of course, still thinks the year is 1917 and that Americans will be superfluous in the new 1918. He has been retired to an honorary position where he will have more time for church politics.

Pétain thinks he is the Saviour, and he has behind him all the Cagoulards and too many of the army officers. Milka insists the rank and file, or ordinary soldiers, will not obey right-wing traitors but only revolutionaries of the Left. If you ask me, in confidence, I think the privates will chuck them both into the nearest river or well. Our famous poilu thinks mostly of girls he can lay and the pinard (red wine) allowance, and of the day when he can put away his badly fitting uniform and take injections in the family W.C. without a sentry looking on. If he can be made class-conscious, and can remember what it means, we are saved. I expect a sure remedy for baldness to come sooner.

I saw Bertrand (Brun) the other day, because I was wearing the scarf you forgot to pack and he mistook me for someone else from behind. He almost fainted. Then, when he saw I was unmoved, he told me, out of spite, that he and Breton are supporting Trotsky. Aragon is with us; so is Jean-Richard Bloc. You'll agree that we have the best of the bargain.

When you get back to the United States, send me a consignment of faith, which seems to come so easily to your countrymen. By the way, I saw one of your lady Evangelists the other night. She was being shown the sins of Paris in the Oubliette Rouge.*

Pierre

It is a striking coincidence that Laval, who got into office in January, 1935, just in time to give Mussolini the all-clear signal for his adventure in Africa, wormed his way back into the trough precisely at the moment to let down the English, who for once were ready to act and to put Il Duce in his place. Their strongest argument, their fleet, was already in the Mediterranean with a large force of submarines so that a British undersea craft was within striking distance of every Italian warship. Laval spiked all this, in the name of France, notwithstanding the fact that all up and down streets like the rue de la Huchette the voters and their wives were indignant and ashamed, and behind any kind of leader would have given their last drop of blood or the money they had saved to stop Mussolini's arrogant strutting for ever.

Mussolini sounded off on May 7th, warning the 'Powers' not to interfere in his theft of Abyssinia. The only powers in question were England, France, the United States and Russia.

The farce in the League of Nations is familiar to everyone who can remember back that far. The Negus made a dignified speech; the League appointed an undignified committee. Mussolini gassed and bombed the Abyssinians; Laval stuck by him. In order to save its face, the League voted sanctions, omitting the only one that would have stopped the campaign, namely, an embargo on petrol. The United States Department of State could not see its way clear to persuade American dealers not to sell fuel. So what could the British and French dealers do? Laval got together with his moral equal and social superior, Sir Samuel Hoare, who still is around somewhere behind Churchill, and they gave away the Abyssinians and their territory.

---

*The Oubliette Rouge was a small tourist-trap near St. Julien-le-pauvre, where bawdy songs were sung in French and the drinks were watered to such an extent that temperance was automatically accomplished. It was about as wicked as a Greenwich Village tea-room, and the prices were about as high, in relation to the value received. I will not disclose which of our female preachers was steered into the Oubliette Rouge, when plenty of dives with bona-fide sins were within a stone's throw, but she was one with a certain charm and an unofficial relish for life on this earth and deserved a better sample of sin.

In Concord, Massachusetts, in June, I received the following note from Hyacinthe:

Cher maître,
Hurry back, for I need you worse than ever. Elliot, I can no longer ignore what is known as politics, although I scarcely understand the meaning of the word. These pronouncements and conferences of names — it is hard for me to think of them as men — are poisoning the atmosphere. I take up the newspaper — no longer *L'Action Française*, but any newspaper; I choose them at random. Something terrible is happening and, ignorant as I am, I tremble for our beautiful France.

Elliot, are we or are we not in danger? Have we not been insulted and imposed upon? Who should act?

Last night I bought all the papers and, after reading column after column, confused and contradictory and utterly untruthful, I began to cry. And I couldn't stop; so today my eyes are still swollen. Perhaps my headache resulted from breathing that unhealthy odour of ink. I thought I should never get the smudges off my fingers.

I try to be calm. After all, the Italians can't do anything worse to Africans than I have heard Cousin Émile tell me about the government of Lyautey. That is not the point. Africa, to me, exists in the paintings of Rousseau (the *Douanier*), an ordered jungle somewhat flat, each leaf and frond in place, with monkeys in full-face, never profile, for inhabitants. How disgusting that is! How abominable for French families to treat their daughters to such an education! I attended the most exclusive school in Paris, and Mama, whom I have ill-naturedly disparaged and whom I might to try to love if I didn't have to see and hear her every hour of every day, spent more than she could spare so that I might be equipped for life.

Look at me, or, rather, examine my equipment. Looking at me is deceptive. I am beautiful, and sometimes I believe my eyes have in their depths the mysteries of existence. My grammar and syntax are impeccable. My taste is fairly sure. In the eighteenth or the nineteenth century I should have made my mark. What can I know today? No one cares for society any more, the *haute monde*, I mean. Intelligent men and women are trying to blunt and not develop their wit and understanding.

These politicians have become important, and I cannot grasp what they mean. Please come. I know from what you have said that you despise them. So do I, without being able to define my grounds. That doesn't mean that we can shut our eyes to their threat to us and our enjoyments.

I *will* succeed. I *will* become somebody or something. If, to do it, I must vote, I will vote. Forgive me, I am becoming hysterical.

Hyacinthe

Hyacinthe's sensitive awareness of danger and the crumbling of the only society she had been taught to recognize was symptomatic. Everywhere one went, after Japan's aggression was topped by Mussolini's defiance of all so-called democratic governments, men and women who had got along well hitherto without knowing a plebiscite from an alderman were beginning to read what they could find on international affairs and to talk a modern Mother Goose in which the words 'Communism' and 'Fascism' fitted into all the rhymes.

When I found myself again in the rue de la Huchette, my friends were trying to forget the recent humiliation to which they had, in common with the rest of the French, been subjected by the double play, Laval to Hoare to Mussolini.

'Now he's got the poor negroes (*les pauvres nègres*), let him be quiet for a while,' said Madame Absalom, apropos of Il Duce.

Monsieur Noël and his cronies felt about the same way. They had disapproved of the treachery and the abject attitude in the face of Mussolini's empty threats, but once it was over they wanted to settle down in peace again, and take up life where it had been flowing steadily, so they thought, before World War I. Like victims of blackmail who make the first few payments on the promise that they will be left unmolested for ever afterwards, my French friends hedged and dissimulated. What else could they do, except revolt? And the army, equipped for police duty against unarmed civilians, but not for modern war, had machine-guns, tear-gas bombs and authority to coerce and murder in the name of the law.

Opinions differed as to the willingness of soldiers in the ranks to shoot, gas or bayonet French workmen. There was no doubt that the high officers and most of the low ones (liberals having been carefully weeded out) would carry out the wishes of the large employers if they could. The Navet; Madame Durand, the florist; the tailor, Monsieur Saint-Aulaire; and Madame Absalom expected a military *coup d'état*, but each for different reasons.

The Navet believed in absolute authority vested in an individual approved by the clerical and capitalistic clique with which he had for years curried favour.

Madame Durand, under a law favoured by the Socialists, had been forced to pay the balance of a week's wages to the lame Jacqueline when she had fired her on the spur of the moment. A firm hand in government, she believed, would not countenance an outrage like that, which encouraged worthless girls to be lazy and impudent.

In case Pétain and Weygand and their disciples took over and dissolved Parliament, Monsieur Saint-Aulaire would get all the business he could handle, making new uniforms, and expected the high officers who already had patronized him to recommend him, perhaps, to a brigadier-general, if not the marshal himself. He visualized himself standing on a balcony in the rue de Rivoli and watching Pétain ride by at the head of a column, on a snow-white horse, wearing a uniform of horizon blue which fitted so perfectly that it received a cheer from the crowd, a uniform by Saint-Aulaire. No French dictator would wear khaki, of that Saint-Aulaire was sure.

Madame Absalom thought the army would disperse and subdue the workmen, not because she stood to gain in that event.

'The *salauds* always get the best of things in the end,' she said to me.

I did not smile. Already I was beginning to wonder.

The group that gathered in the Caveau bar before the Julliards were forced to sell now patronized the Café St. Michel, which had a larger bar, of which they appropriated the end near the rue de la Huchette. There was not so much argument as there had been in former years, since the reactionary members had stuck with Madame Amance in No. 5, and only the former Radical Socialists — now just plain Socialists — the former Socialists — some of whom had moved over to the Left and called themselves Communists — and the old-line Communists remained.

Monsieur Henri, when he came back to the quarter to collect payments from the Amances, who were never able to pay in full and frequently had to pass up payments altogether, had one glass of brandy with his successors at the Caveau, as a matter of politeness, then called at the Café St. Michel. The women who were politically conscious all adhered to the Left contingent. Mme. Berthelot seldom left her room after dark, but Mariette left the Caveau cold and took her midnight recess with her former companions, ignoring the dark looks she received from Mme. Trévise, who suspected that her husband strayed down to *Le Panier Fleuri* on occasion and entered the small side door in the rue Zacharie.

When Mme. Trévise said as much to Madame Absalom, another fellow-traveller with the Left group, the old woman cackled knowingly.

'Between you and me,' she said, 'the men are all alike. And who can blame them?'

When I entered the street from the rue des Deux Ponts in 1936, on my way from New York to Spain, the old carpenter was sitting in the middle of his shop filing a saw with utter disregard of the hideous sounds he was producing. I noticed that the place was nearly empty and not littered with new work redolent of the fragrance of lumber and sawdust. The one apprentice he had retained when No. 2 was dismissed in 1929 had left to take a job in the Schneider ammunition factories near Rouen, and the old carpenter had not replaced him. There was less and less demand for the services of a good but slow cabinet maker.

It was impossible for me to pass the Hôtel du Caveau. When I entered, the café was empty, except for a stranger (M. Amance) behind the bar who spoke to me politely. I snatched a quick drink and hurried away. At the other end of the street I received another shock, for standing in front of the grocery store at No. 27, looking very dignified and self-conscious in a brand-new linen duster, was Monsieur Noël.

The gravity of his face deterred me from asking why he was working in young Corre's grocery instead of stuffing cats and dogs. I shook hands, as if nothing was changed, and was on the point of suggesting that he step across to the Café St. Michel for a snifter when it occurred to me that Étienne Corre might be a strict employer. He had been a schoolboy in a smock when first I had known him in 1923.

The small group at the bar, dominated by the alert Mme. Trévise, was not thinking of Noël just then. Like Frenchmen the length and breadth of the land, they were talking about Hitler, who had sent his troops all the way to the Rhine, in defiance of France. Mme. Trévise and Lanier, whose face had been seared and twisted in World War I, were blaming the English, Mr Baldwin in particular, who had refused to back up their French Allies in military action to oust the German forces from the thirty-kilometre neutral zone. The Satyr, the horse butcher and Monsieur Pissy, who because of his union activities had been given night duty in the Gare St. Lazare and had not learned to sleep in the daytime, were denouncing Pierre Laval. Laval had let down England when Eden wanted to keep Italy out of Abyssinia.

'It was a dirty Englishman [Sir Samuel Hoare] who gave Abyssinia to the macaronis,' Mme. Trévise insisted.

'Laval made him do it,' Pissy said.

From the small back room came a weary voice I recognized as that of Pierre Vautier.

'They're both pisspots,' he said, and let his head sink down again on his arms, which rested on the table.

'At least, pisspots are useful,' said the gloomy Satyr.

I heard from both Frémont, the postman, and The Navet that day, and from many other sources throughout Paris, that Gamelin, the new Chief of Staff, had wanted to attack the German forces at once, with all the military strength of France, with or without the backing of the Cliveden set in England. Had this course of action been followed, the rising power of Hitler could easily have been overthrown.

It is interesting to note that on January 22nd, just before Hitler took over the Rhineland in March, Laval got out from under and left Sarraut, a colourless stop-gap, holding the bag against the outburst of popular indignation. Laval stepped aside just in time to avoid being the target of the huge Leftist demonstrations in February of that crucial year, and in March the Chamber adjourned until after the elections, when the Popular Front swept the country and Léon Blum took charge, or, rather, took office as Prime Minister.

In the rue de la Huchette, I found many of my friends who agreed with Gamelin that the Germans should be subdued right then and there before it was too late. I did not find a man or woman among them who believed for a moment that this would be done. They knew the politicians were against it, because they were fighting their own war against labour, and for once the going was hard. The French bankers were afraid to oppose Downing Street because London controlled the franc and might devalue it, in reprisal, if the French did not behave.

The families who had sons in the army were in a special category, having their own flesh and blood directly at stake. Pissy and young Pissy were eager to go, but they had no property. Madame Corre, who held her age so well through trying years, began to fade at the prospects of Étienne having to abandon the business his father left him and the education, including travel in Italy, England and Germany in order to acquire languages, they had given him at a sacrifice. Étienne himself, while anxious to get rid of the grocery business, did not want to waste any more years in the army, having served his eighteen months. He wanted to become an export broker and was trying to establish himself in that line. That was why Noël, whose taxidermist trade was at a standstill, had been hired as assistant, to help young Madame Corre, the homesick girl from Dijon, in the no-longer thriving Épicerie Danton, from which the beans in trays, pride of Corre the elder, and the spices of Arabia had gone like the snows of yesteryear. A breath of old France had gone with them.

As soon as the group in the Café St. Michel found out that I had crossed on the *Normandie*, they set aside politics for a while. The *Normandie* was the pride, not only of the French marine, but of all the French, from the poorest to the most influential and prosperous. Shop girls, delivery boys, Sisters of Charity, clerks, even the pathetic old Taitbouts, would pore over columns in the newspapers and cheap magazines, or listen to descriptions on the radio whenever the *Normandie* was mentioned. Hyacinthe, who already, at 19, was attracting attention by her work on the screen and who had become the local celebrity, eclipsing even Monsieur de Malancourt, had dozens of folders and pamphlets and saved clippings about the great ship that was to rule the ocean, not with force but with elegance, and put the British and the Germans to shame.

'We French have done so little lately that the *Normandie* has become the symbol of our race. As long as we can be predominant in comfort and taste, and match the speed of the Americans, we are not lost,' she said.

I did not have the heart to tell them that my trip on the *Normandie*, because of the frightful vibration caused by her powerful engines, had been my all-time low in Atlantic crossings. The liner was taken out of service for six months, following that maiden voyage and return, and the French engineers succeeded in correcting what was wrong with the original design, so that after 1936 the *Normandie* fulfilled the dreams and hopes that the French had placed on the ship in advance.

28

OF PROPERTY AND FRATERNITY

The songs of the Loire which formerly issued from the Caveau, roared by l'Oursin (the oyster and chestnut man), came nightly from the little bar of André, the coalman, after the split in our street between adherents of the Right and Left when Monsieur Henri sold his hotel. That meant that the blue-eyed Alice was obliged to stay up each night until closing time, 2 a.m., or later. André, of course, with his day's work ahead, had to go to bed right after supper.

L'Oursin got his nickname, meaning 'little bear' or 'sea urchin', because in season he sold those cheap and prickly delicacies. The name fitted him perfectly, much better than Léon Saliel, which appeared on his identity card. He came from a fishing village not far from Perpignan, and years of good eating and drinking, combined with the open air, had given him a globular figure from which hair grew stiffly in profusion. The wine and cognac he had drunk, interspersed with applejack and *marc*, had given his voice a bucolic timbre, and his powerful lungs lent it volume and carrying power. He never spoke or sang in an ordinary tone, but always histrionically, as if he were ringmaster of a circus introducing his own act.

Each morning he scrubbed himself from the waist up with something like saddle soap, only stronger, and once a week he borrowed a bar towel from the *patronne* of the Café de la Gare and went to the public bath near the Cluny. But oyster shells are muddy and roasted chestnuts sooty. Also his beard, blue-black and stiff, grew so fast it showed an hour after he had shaved. He wore a turtle-neck sweater, inside coarse baggy corduroy trousers which were held up by a wide blue sash. On rainy days he wore sabots. If the sun shone, he wore leather brogues. Socks he considered effete and useless.

I do not wish to give the impression that l'Oursin was brutish or unmusical, or that mingled with the badinage he shouted was not a lot of common-sense. His bulk was forbidding, his costume utilitarian and his means of livelihood was not conducive to fastidiousness. In fact, he looked about as black as the coalman did, except when he lumbered from the bath. His walk made it plain that in his youth he had gone to sea.

The discerning women liked him; the others were mildly afraid of him for no reason whatever except his epic masculinity. Madeleine, the proprietress of the Café de la Gare, kept him roaring with her shrewish tongue when he was attending to his business. Blue-eyed Alice, the coalman's wife, leaned against the bar and simply watched him with an understanding smile, and let him rave. She was the kind of woman who liked to please a man, and understood his needs; so in spite of her drowsiness she was reluctant to send him out into the cold when two o'clock came. L'Oursin was seventy years old and looked fifty. She was forty and looked thirty-five. If he drank too much (for him) after midnight, when they had the bar to themselves, she would gently dissuade him. On rare occasions when she was afraid he would fall in the street if left to his own devices, she accompanied him to his door on the quai a block away. A disrespectful thought of Alice never once crossed his mind. She was the wife of his good friend, André, a man like himself.

Way back in the early 1920s, l'Oursin had seen from an expression on The Navet's face that the latter was afraid of him, and while he had never followed up the advantage, it lurked in his mind. When he chanced to pass The Navet he would take up his full share of the pavement, with perhaps a little to spare. In the evening at the Caveau he would shout down The Navet's opinions if he felt in an expansive mood. Along with the *garçon*, Georges, he had taken a healthy dislike for The Navet's satellites, Monsieurs Gion and the floor-walker, Panaché.

One night, just before the Popular Front election in 1936, when class feeling was high and campaign talks were violent, Alice had such a severe migraine that l'Oursin, although well along in drink, insisted that she close her small bar and go to bed.

'*Alors, fiche le camp, grosse fainéante,*' 'Come on, get to blazes out of here, lazybones,' was the way he put it.

The Normandie bar was filled with Jews who had fled from Germany, and while l'Oursin was by no means an anti-Semite, he disliked hearing a foreign language to which he could not reply. The rooms in Sara's hotel, in those days, were mostly occupied by refugees sent her by her rich uncle in the Temple quarter. The uncle had paid for their transport, in many instances, and kept them afloat while they tried to adjust themselves to Paris and find a way to keep alive on their own initiative. This was hard because the French, feeling the pinch of unemployment, would not give foreigners permission to work and taxed them heavily if they tried to do business.

Passing up the Normandie, l'Oursin saw that the only light was in the Caveau. So he headed that way. Gathered round the bar were The Navet, M. Gion, M. Panaché, and the neighbourhood dentist, Dr. Roux. As the chestnut man barged in there was a sudden hush in the conversation, which had been carried on in confidential whispers, and the conservative quartet looked away with distaste and murmured when l'Oursin bellowed lustily:

'*Bonsoir, Messieurs.*'

Only Georges, the Serb, looked pleased and stroked his wide moustaches.

The Navet and his cronies hoped that the chestnut man would swallow a quick one and beat it, which might have been l'Oursin's first intention had he not seen so clearly that the Right was eager to be rid of him. Anyway, he spread himself over a generous section of the zinc, lighted a particularly vile cigarette and asked for a shot of red. Georges grinned and poured out a large tumblerful of low-grade Pinard. No one spoke for as long as a minute. The Navet tried to look unconcerned. He would have liked to leave the place, but in front of his satellites, especially the dentist who had good connections, he could not afford to appear timid or undignified. Then l'Oursin started talking to Georges. The parties of the Left, he said, at last had got together. They would win the election and start a house-cleaning in the Ministries. Almost anybody, even in the lousy prefecture, might find himself out of a job, the chestnut man said.

Then he spread out a little farther, jostling Panaché ever so slightly, begged his pardon with elaborate politeness, and treated the company to another heavy silence, broken only by the ticking of the wooden Swiss clock. Sweat began to show on The Navet's forehead. The dentist paid for his unfinished drink and, after shaking hands with The Navet, made his getaway.

L'Oursin resumed his talk about the Popular Front, and what Blum would do when he got the Premiership, with the working men behind him. He wouldn't break his promises like that *salaud* Tardieu.

The Navet could stand it no longer. The veins on his forehead stood out, and he swelled like a pouter pigeon.

'Monsieur, you exaggerate,' he said, turning to confront the chestnut man, who broke into such a roar of laughter that the watchdog in the carpenter shop next door started barking.

The chestnut man paid not the slightest attention.

'Blum is a gentleman,' he continued, pretending not to notice the effect of his words. 'He'll put through the forty-hour week — (louder) *the forty-hour week*, and a law to protect the unions, so the dirty skunks can't fire the committees. The minimum wage . . .'

'Do you know what that will cost? Twelve per cent, monsieur,' said The Navet, white with rage.

'Who'll have to pay?' l'Oursin asked, but directly of Georges, who shyly disclaimed any knowledge.

'Monsieur!' piped The Navet. He was hopping like a snapdragon and waving his arms, but the chestnut man remained as if unaware of his existence.

'You don't know who'll have to pay?' l'Oursin demanded of Georges.

Georges sweetly shook his head and wiped his moustaches.

'We'd better go,' Panaché said in an undertone to Gion.

L'Oursin began describing the employers and bankers who'd pay the extra twelve per cent and take fifteen per cent out of the public like the stinking bastards they were.

'Stay,' said The Navet to his two supporters. 'This place is public.'

'Exactly,' said l'Oursin, glad that The Navet had played right into his hand. 'This place is not only for measly little pencil-stiffs and cuckolds . . .'

Georges could contain himself no longer. He tried not to look at The Navet when he burst out laughing, but somehow he made his effort too conspicuous. Everyone knew that Panaché and Gion kept their girls in such a state of submission and spied on them so carefully that they could not possibly have cheated. The Navet had been hit in his most sensitive spot. He had laid traps for Jeanne, beaten and bruised her, given her the third degree for hours on end, and not a shred of tangible evidence had he been able to find. Yet he was aware that somehow she had got the best of him, and that the neighbours knew what he could only surmise.

That night was an active one in No. 32. The Navet had burst into his apartment in a maniacial state, not noisily, but with silent venom. Without taking time to remove his coat and hat, he had rushed to the bedroom, switched on the light, torn the bedclothes off his wife as she lay sound asleep and accused her as she opened her eyes. He had caught her at last, he said, and knew everything.

'Don't talk so loud, Eugène will hear,' Jeanne said.

'You admit you've been a whore,' said The Navet, burning with incredulous satisfaction and triumphant rage.

'I've never accepted money,' Jeanne said, coolly.

The Navet lost all reason. Grasping a large blue vase, he shattered it on the floor. He began to throw Jeanne's toilet articles at her, perfume atomizer, box of powder, lipstick, mirror. The latter made a gash above her eye.

'Tell me his name,' shouted The Navet.

'*Penses-tu*,' said Jeanne. (Imagine!)

He began to yell and rave, advancing with a trunk strap on which was a heavy metal buckle. Jeanne screamed. Windows were flung open, upstairs, across the street. The footsteps of Officer Masson echoed hurriedly in the street below. From the pavement l'Oursin was shouting:

'Sure. You'll beat up a woman. Come down here. I'll show you. I'll fix you up for Tardieu!'

'What's up?' cackled Madame Absalom.

'The Navet thinks he's *cocu*,' roared the chestnut man.

'Who doesn't?' asked the shrewd old woman, reaching for a shawl.

'Less noise. Chiappe'll hear you,' said Officer Masson, addressing himself to l'Oursin and Madame Absalom and disregarding the diminishing sounds from The Navet's apartment. The chestnut man lowered his voice to a whisper; Madame Absalom merely chuckled; and the neighbours whose heads were protruding from various windows talked less and listened harder as the commotion abruptly ceased with a scream and a thud.

What had happened did not leak out until the following day, through the sensitive grapevine of the servants. Eugène, the fat son, who had always sided with his mother against The Navet, had picked up the crockery umbrella stand in the hallway, the only weapon that came to his hand, and floored his father from behind as the latter was lashing Jeanne with the strap and buckle.

'After all, he's his father,' said Madame Durand, the florist, who, being virtuous although a hard employer, sided with The Navet because she detested pretty women and feared the Popular Front. Alice, the coalman's wife, blamed herself for l'Oursin's drunken exhibition of himself and took him to task quite severely. She had heard much talk around her little bar of how the Left, when Blum got in, was going to help the working men. She knew all too well how badly the working men needed help. Nevertheless, she was timidly conservative and afraid of reform; so she kept her huge and gentle husband out of all political movements and wished she could do the same for l'Oursin, Monsieur Frémont, Pissy and the rest of her radical customers. Since Pissy had turned Communist, Alice served him with the same ready smile, but chided him when he spoke against the Church which she attended perfunctorily, although she sent little André to the public school.

In The Navet's home, matters had reached a stalemate. Dr. Clouet had taken a few stitches in the back of his scalp and, as long as the adhesive showed, The Navet went to and from the prefecture via the place St. Michel instead of walking the length of our street night and morning. Eugène, who believed he was now his father's match in strength, started taking boxing lessons secretly in order to improve his chances when the combat came. Jeanne, who was welted but not badly hurt, continued to meet her Persian at the Café Cluny two blocks away. Of course, the difference was that The Navet had positive knowledge of what he had long suspected, and still could not find the name of the man who had dishonoured him. That he did not throw Jeanne out into the street convinced everybody in the neighbourhood that he had, as Eugène contended, misappropriated funds from Jeanne's dowry and could not replace them in case of a showdown.

The chestnut man lapsed into ordinary correct behaviour for a while, the conservatives were not molested as they gathered nightly in the Hôtel du Caveau. The Socialists held forth in the Café St. Michel; the Jewish refugees scurried in and out of the Hôtel Normandie; and because Milka, the local leader, had her dinner with Stefan and Pierre Vautier *chez* Daniel, just round the corner in the rue de la Harpe, visiting Communists from other quarters began to think of the little Dalmatian restaurant as a safe and comfortable rendezvous. Neither Daniel, an athlete and business man, nor Madame Berthe, his demure wife in black, was alarmed at this, since Milka's friends always paid their bills, were seldom drunk or noisy, and formed a steady nucleus for their growing clientele. There was still a friendly and neighbourly feeling in the rue de la Huchette, but class alignments became more sharply defined. It was as if a hand of cards that had been dealt at random had been sorted into suits.

It took the elections of April 26th, the overwhelming Left victory that provoked fascists everywhere to turn against a democracy they can no longer dominate and control, to draw the class lines sharper.

The Popular Front consisted (reading from left to right) of Communists, Socialists and the misnamed Radical-Socialists. These parties got 381 seats in the Chamber, as against 237 for the Right. They were pledged to a programme of social reform. Léon Blum, a well-to-do Jewish æsthete and scholar, with prosperous business interests on the side, became Prime Minister and formed a Cabinet of Socialists and Radical-Socialists (led by Herriot and Daladier, whose Stavisky connections seemed to have been pardoned or forgotten by his party and the public). The Communists promised to support Blum but would not join his cabinet until they had a chance to see him in action. Their numerical strength in the Chamber had risen from 10 to 72.

Blum had been converted to Socialism by Jean Jaurès, and with him had founded *L'Humanité*, the Socialist organ that had become Communist in the middle twenties. His elegant French was admired by Hyacinthe and Mme. Berthelot. It was less effective with factory hands or railway employees, but the workers respected him and cheered him without following in detail what he said.

One evening just after Blum's occupation of the Hôtel Matignon (the Premier's headquarters), the Satyr failed to come home, and the next morning the papers were filled with violently coloured accounts of the first sit-down strikes. In scanning the list of factories, department stores and mines affected, I noticed the name of the restaurant in the Bois de Boulogne where the Satyr was assistant chef.

That same morning in the concierge's lodge at No. 11, a bitter argument took place between M. and Mme. Frémont who ordinarily were affectionate and in accord. The pale blonde Yvonne, dressed neatly for work and handbag in hand, stood by to wait tearfully for the outcome.

'You can do as you please and lose your job and go to prison,' Mathilde Frémont said to her husband. 'My daughter shall stay at home today.'

'No daughter of mine will desert her fellow-workers,' said Frémont, and, turning to Yvonne, said: 'Go — and stay until it's over.'

Madame Frémont tried to clutch at Yvonne's sleeve; Frémont, more brusquely than he had intended, jerked her arm away. His face suffused with anger, he repeated to his daughter: 'Go.'

Sobbing helplessly, Madame Frémont sank down on the bed. The postman glanced at her with pity a moment, shrugged his shoulders, picked up his uniform cap and started down the street.

Yvonne had just recently got a job as salesgirl in the Galeries Lafayette, which enabled her to dress more attractively and help increase her own dowry, which in 1936 had reached the sum of 6,000 francs (£48). She had heard some of the other girls say there was to be a sit-down strike that day and had asked her parents what to do.

The sit-down strikes, although none of them occurred in the rue de la Huchette, and only the Satyr and the gentle Yvonne were directly involved as participants shocked every inhabitant. While the movement spread and the Government, bewildered, was unable to decide how to act, everyone in our street took sides, with increasing tenseness and excitement and flaring animosities. The right of property had been attacked and was now being officially defended, with blood and iron and discharge slips and broken heads and funerals. That the sit-down strikers were acting in an orderly fashion and had been careful not to destroy or steal seemed to make the concerted demonstrations more ominous. At first the Communists were accused of organizing the movement, until it spread so far and had so many adherents that the Red baiters could no longer admit the Reds had so much power.

The Navet and his group were yelling for martial law and an overthrow of Blum by the army of the Right. On one point, the street was unanimous. The strikes were illegal. The strike sympathizers, in the minority, smiled and said 'What of it?' whenever this argument was advanced as conclusive.

In the rue de la Huchette, the men and women who came out frankly in support of the 'sit-downs' were: Henri Julliard; Georges, the *garçon*; Thérèse, former cook; Hortense Berthelot; Léonard, the accordion player; Milka, Stefan and Pierre, in a block; Noël, Monge and the Satyr (who sat and struck); Madame Absalom, who relished novelty and illegality; Odette and Jean, in the dairy shop; and Colette, the delivery girl; Frémont (not his wife); Officer Masson; Madame Mariette, Mireille, Suzie and little Daisy, of *Le Panier Fleuri*; Sara, Guy, Louis the one-armed *garçon*, the dog, Mocha, and all the refugees in the Hôtel Normandie; Mme. Julien, the barber's wife (but not the barber); Maurice of *La Vie Silencieuse*; Pissy, the railroad employee; Nadia, the beautiful model; Hyacinthe, the beautiful young actress; the roaring chestnut man, and l'Hibou, the tramp.

Since the same sharp alignment held intact through the crises that followed, and persists even today under invasion and persecution, I am listing the members of the other faction, omitting only the listless and indifferent and sub-normal who were capable of no affiliation and who had no tangible opinions.

The Navet was the most vociferous; Father Desmonde and Father Panarioux were more influential. Other Rightists follow; M. and Madame Trévise and the drudge, Eugénie; M. de Malancourt; Judge Lenoir and Anne Goujon; Dr. Clouet; Dr. Roux; M. and Mme. Corre, both elder and younger; the religious publisher; Alice, the coalman's wife; Gion of the music shop, and Bernice; M. and Madame Durand, the florists; the tailor, M. Saint-Aulaire; Mme. Joli, cleaner and dyer; M. and Mme. and young Jacques Luneville, of the dry-goods shop; M. Dominique, the stamp man; Julien, the barber; M. and Mme. Gillotte, the bakers; Mme. Spook (Mrs. Root), the Englishwoman; Officer Benoist; M. and Mme. Lanier, of the *clandestin*; Mme. Frémont; Dorlan, the bookbinder; the aged Taitbouts; the Alsatian old maids and the retired Colonel at No.7; Mme. Claire, at the Caveau; Marie Julliard; Daniel and Berthe Petrovich; the floor-walker Panaché; the delicatessen proprietor; Villières, the paint dealer; the old cabinet maker at No. 3; M. Salmon, the butcher; and M. Luttenschlager, who sold church supplies.

29

OF 'NON-INTERVENTION'

There comes vividly to my memory an evening in November. My friends in France were gathered around me in the Caveau bar to hear about my friends in Spain, who, fighting gallantly, were already doomed to destruction. We were still in the compass of that most terrible of all years, 1936. It was not so discouraging that Fascists in every land were scheming and battling for Fascism. What else could be expected? What dealt our pre-war world its mortal blow was the supine cowardice and hypocrisy of so-called democrats who played into their hands and sealed the death-warrants of countless innocent millions.

France might have recovered from Manchukuo and Abyssinia, the Stavisky scandals and the sit-down strikes and Hitler in the German Rhineland. From the treachery called non-intervention, forced on the weeping Blum and willing Delbos by Baldwin-Chamberlain-Halifax-Simon, neither France nor liberty could raise their heads or staunch the flow of life's blood from their hearts.

In October, Italian troops, airplanes, tanks, artillery and ammunition were being rushed to the support of Franco, and German technicians, materials and supplies were freely at the Rebels' disposal. The ruling clique of England had already made its choice and was keeping France and the United States in line. The elected government of Spain and the republican Spaniards were to be sacrificed to the monarchists, mediæval Catholic hierarchy, landowners, rich manufacturers, generals (there were 257 of them and 21,000 army officers), Italian Fascists, Moorish mercenaries and Hitler-heiling Germans.

The excuse was 'Communism', which did not then exist in Spain, and the slogan was 'War must be prevented from spreading at any cost.' That the cost was the annihilation of free men and innocent women in a rising republic, the surrounding of 'Republican' France on all sides by Fascist armies and governments (Germany, Belgium, Italy and Spain), the opportunity for the dictators to train their armies, try out and perfect their equipment in the field and experiment on the helpless civilian population (as at Guernica), and the despair of workers everywhere, did not deter the Cliveden group, assisted by their semblables in France, including Bonnet, Delbos, Laval and Pétain.

How far from the chancelleries of Washington and of Europe was the rue de la Huchette! How much better informed were my friends in the shops and cafés than the statesmen seemed to be! The Fascists of the St. Michel quarter wanted Franco to win in Spain; they wanted the doctrine of fascism to spread, and looked forward to its influence in France. The Republicans knew that what was happening to their brothers across the Pyrenees was going to descend on them, and who was behind it, and that Blum their hope, and the Popular Front, their duly elected bulwark against reaction, were showing the white feather.

In late 1936 French patriots like Henri Julliard, Pierre Vautier, Frémont or Noël had not given up resisting, but inwardly they could not continue hoping, as did Hortense Berthelot, the steadfast Milka, Mariette, Maurice, the budding Hyacinthe or the roaring chestnut man.

In 1936 the night was falling fast and as yet there are no streaks of dawn, no cleavage, no clarity, no consecration.

I had escaped from Ibiza a few hours before the Italians came, on a German mine-layer, *Die Falke*. This I managed by representing myself and my wife as neutrals, along with the Spanish leader of the left, Cosmi Mari, who I said was my cook, and a German girl who passed as governess to my stepson, Peanut. The story of those years in Spain and my reportage of the early days of the war are included in my *The Life and Death of a Spanish Town*. The immediate sequel, in which my fugitive party, ill-equipped with money, clothes or papers, was shunted back and forth between the world's most-powerful navies before we landed finally at Marseilles, was told, on the evening in question, at the Hôtel du Caveau.

Henri Julliard was back behind the little bar; Madame Marie was sleeping upstairs. The *garçon*, Georges, had been rewarded for his patience and was happily on the job. As Georges had predicted, the Amances had been unable to make a go of the hotel, and Monsieur Henri had been obliged to take it over. In spite of the financial loss involved, I think Henri was glad to be in his element once again.

His old customers, who had been scattered among the other cafés, all except The Navet's diehards, came straggling back, but the two inimical elements, for and against the Popular Front, did not clink glasses as in former years. The conservatives showed up right after dinner, between seven-thirty and eight o'clock, and dispersed about ten. During those hours, if Mme Berthelot, Mme. Absalom or Mary the Greek wished to linger in the restaurant, they sat quietly at the tables, pretending not to listen, no matter what they heard. This was easier for the others than for Madame Absalom, who sometimes flung a challenge at The Navet, who haughtily continued what he was saying, without a glance round.

About eleven, after the Rightists were safely out of the way, the chestnut man, Frémont, Noël, Monge, the Satyr, and often Milka and her two faithful comrades, Stefan and Pierre, would drift into the Caveau and the session would begin. Father Panarioux, although an anti-Marxist, got through playing the organ at St. Séverin, where he had many talented pupils, about the time Mariette of *Le Panier Fleuri* took her nightly recess. More than once I have seen them approach the entrance simultaneously, from opposite directions, and do a kind of hesitation dance at the doorway, each insisting that the other should take precedence, although for different reasons.

'You both wear skirts. So what's the difference?' cackled Mme. Absalom on one such occasion, and the chestnut man led the roar of laughter in which the priest benignly joined.

The situation in France was so similar to that in Spain that my friends reacted to events there as if they were seeing themselves in a dream. Against them was the same line-up, the enemies of the democratic ideal.

(a) the military clique who were fascist-minded.
(b) the bankers, large employers and landlords.
(c) the reactionary Catholic clergy.
(d) Italy, Germany, Portugal and Japan.
(e) a vengeful subject race in Africa.
(f) a deposed aristocracy.

The Spanish military rebels were not as powerful as the corresponding group in France. They struck because they had more support from abroad and a more helpless opposition. Relatively, the Spanish capitalists were as strong as the industrialists and financiers of France. The Spanish clergy had never been put in its place, as had the French. Neither had the Spanish aristocrats. The Germans and the Italians did not want France to be Fascist and therefore better organized for resistance. The time had not come to wipe France out entirely. Spain was the logical first step in European conquest, sealing the Mediterranean and threatening the Channel, opening the road to Africa.

By the time I reached Paris from Spain in November, the Republican element in the rue de la Huchette was in profound discouragement. Franco's failure to seize power as he and the dictators had planned was not considered a defeat, and every acre of territory his Moors overran was chalked up as a victory. That Madrid, Valencia, Alicante and Barcelona were still in the legitimate Government's hands became day by day less impressive, as Italy stepped in, then Germany, then Portugal — and then England.

The gloating satisfaction of the enemies in the street — there was no further use in pretending the existence of a 'united' France — was hard to bear, and fanned the ill-feeling that was transforming the formerly charming and harmonious neighbourhood into two hostile camps, one already triumphant, the other resentful and desperate.

As Franco took Toledo, continued the defence of the Alcazar, made possible simply because the Government had no artillery, and the rebels advanced nearer to Madrid, The Navet grew bolder. He smiled, waved patronizingly to Republicans along the street, and encouraged other fascists to come out of their shells and breathe more easily. The first to respond was Mme. Durand, the florist, whose customers were all entrenched against a popular regime. The girl who worked for her after she had discharged Amélie, then the lame girl Jacqueline, was crying one morning, after seeing in the paper a picture of some dead Spanish children, killed by Mussolini's intrepid bombers from Majorca. Her eyes were blurred and she made a mistake in change. The cash did not balance that night; Hélène, the tender-hearted clerk, could not make up the difference. Madame Durand dragged her, accusing her of theft loudly the while, to the police station at the corner of the rue du Chat Qui Pêche. Little Colette, the dairy girl, a friend of Hélène, tried to find out what was the matter, and Madame Durand slapped her. Colette dropped the bottle rack she was holding and dragged the screaming florist from the station, while Officer Masson hopped ineffectually around and the sergeant bellowed for order. Before she was subdued, Colette tore out a handful of Madame Durand's crisp hair and raked her cheek with fingernails. Colette was arrested, her socialist employers bailed her out and hired a socialist lawyer. The night after Madame Durand recovered damages amounting to fifty francs, her plate-glass windows were broken with paving stones at an hour when both Hélène and Colette had airtight alibis.

Had not Franco's forces been drawing closer each hour to the suburbs of Madrid, the tension in our street might have abated. As it was, the anticipation of easy victory and the prospects for a similar triumph at home goaded those who had property or privileges endangered by the Popular Front into a spontaneous show of force against their neighbours on the losing side. The inhabitants of the rue de la Huchette, for the most part narrow and egocentric in their outlook, like people everywhere who moved in restricted circles, did not realize that their line-up extended over all the continents, representing two irreconcilable ideologies about to tear the world apart in the act of devouring each other.

One evening in the course of those terrible days in November, when Madrid was hanging in the balance and free men everywhere had become Madrid, a young man entered the Caveau bar in khaki. He was not a prepossessing youth, and his suit was not exactly a uniform. He had no cartridge belt or gun, and only an ordinary cloth cap, a conspicuous plaid with a long sharp visor.

'*Mais, Antoine. Tu es tout à fait militaire!*' (But Antoine, you're rigged up like a soldier!) said Henri Julliard.

The chestnut man spilled a little of the red wine he was about to drink and set down the glass, embracing the embarrassed young man like a bear.

'*Tu vas te faire casser la gueule là-bas?*' (You're going to get your face smashed in down there?)

Young Pissy nodded. He was neither shy nor bold, and certainly not excited or emotional. What he had decided to do had been the result of two weeks' meditation while tending a machine in the Renault factory up-river.

His life did not pass through my mind in an instant, like that of a person drowning, but my first view of him returned like a flash to my mind. His father, then, as now, a railway worker stationed in the Gare St. Lazare, had been holding him over the gutter near the west end of the street, and, blinking absently at the uninspiring passers-by, Antoine had been pissing. I had seen him, a pale schoolboy for whom his mother bought one egg (1) every Wednesday and Saturday, *chez* Odette and Jean. The parents had had no eggs, being fully grown and not needing them.

Antoine, knowing I had just escaped from the fascists in Spain and how I felt about it, looked straight at me and smiled.

'When do you leave? — Excuse me,' said Milka, in a business-like way. She would have torn off her own ears and slept with Georges Bonnet for the chance Antoine was taking, but instead she jerked her own ridiculous cap down farther on one side of her forehead. The 'Excuse me' was intended to convey that she knew the orders were not to be divulged. The Blum Government had not yet posted sentries to prevent Republican Frenchmen from going to fight with the Spaniards, but no permits to travel were issued if it were known that the traveller was going somewhere the Germans and Italians might not approve of.

I beckoned to Antoine to step aside with me, not knowing what to say or how to say it. Of the men and women in that room, only I knew what he was headed for.

'You know you're likely to be bumped off?' I asked. 'Things are tough down there, and they won't get any better.'

He nodded. 'Sure,' he said.

Pierre Vautier was standing very still, erect, almost at attention. He was staring at Antoine as if he were a ghost. I could almost see the working of his mind. He had also seen Antoine, playing on the pavement with his father, who with a tray and glass could imitate a drum, who told of a horse named Senator he had ridden in the cavalry. Pierre was wondering why this lad, whose pimples were clearing and who was filling out well after a lanky, stringy youth, had thought of the right thing to do while Pierre, with all his education and culture, had missed the obvious. I saw Pierre withdraw quietly and leave by the side door, and I knew he would be with young Pissy on the train for Perpignan. Stefan was a little slower in making his decision, about ten minutes slower, since he had come to depend on Milka to tell him what to do.

There was no demonstration when the three volunteers went away. Pissy, the elder, Milka, the chestnut man, and, hobbling at my side, Madame Absalom accompanied them from the Caveau bar to a taxi in the place St. Michel. Stefan was slightly drunk, Antoine was sleepy and Pierre self-conscious.

'Cut the throats of the macaronis,' Madame Absalom said. She disliked Italians slightly more than the rest of the human race. But under her arm was a package she shoved crossly into the taxi when the men had entered and were about to be driven away. She never mentioned what was in it, but Pierre wrote me a few weeks later that Absalom's woollen muffler had served as a tourniquet.

While Madrid was making her heroic stand, Englishmen of the ruling class were helping to put non-intervention across. Only one Frenchman might have stopped it. His name was Blum, and he failed to act, or rather he acted like a craven. It is all very well to say that he might have believed he was keeping France out of war. War is bad, but it is better for self-respecting men to die while they still feel like men than to become cowards and hypocrites and the laughing-stock of an unscrupulous enemy who will make them fight or enslave them after they are demoralized.

The British leaders decided on an embargo against sending arms, planes, tanks or ammunition to 'either side' in Spain, knowing that the Republicans were represented by the legitimate Government elected by popular will and that Italy and Germany, through Portugal, were supplying and would continue to supply the rebels with everything they needed, including fully equipped units of troops and technical advisers.

The Spanish Government could get supplies only through France, even if they were sold to Spain by Russia. The British policy, in effect, was to permit Franco to obtain, without putting up cash but by mortgaging future Spain, all the arms and soldiers and food he needed, while the Republicans were to be shut off from supplies and slaughtered. Not only did the British plan this chicanery, but they forced the French to take the initiative, under pain of a double threat:

(a) a refusal to guarantee the eastern frontier on the Rhine.
(b) a devaluation of the franc, controlled by the London exchange.

In other words, an invitation to Hitler to dominate France and set up a Fascist rule, and the ruin of the Popular Front Government, which would fall if the franc collapsed.

As if this were not enough, the British coerced twenty-six other nations into signing the non-intervention pact, including Italy and Germany. The former celebrated the agreement by landing 5,000 troops in Cadiz the day after it was signed, and the latter by persuading the rebel general Mola to swing his offensive north, where the minerals and coal were that

Germany needed. Who cared about Madrid just then! Aggressors, the world over, were given *carte blanche*.

It will be hard for future generations to credit the fact that while the rue de la Huchette and the rest of the world were squaring off for a life-and-death struggle, the merchants of France and their politicians were planning a World's Fair. This was conceived originally to revive the tourist trade which had dwindled in Paris since the American depression. Shoddy exhibition buildings were erected in the Champ de Mars and complicated systems of entrances and raised passageways were built, until the quarter around the Trocadero and the place de l'Alma looked like the New York subway above ground and exposed to view. Just below the old theatre, near the main gate, the Soviet exhibit, housed in an ultra-modern building and topped with a rather bad statue holding a star aloft, faced the Nazi entry.

The fact that many needy Jews were able to get temporary employment enraged The Navet to the point that he spent most of his evenings at the Fair, counting them and making remarks they could overhear if they were not too busy. The restaurant in the Bois where the Satyr was second chef had a branch near enough to the Rumanian and Czech exhibit, so that French visitors who did not care to risk foreign food but liked foreign music could hear the gypsies play violins and timpani on one side, while refugees from Prague played Strauss waltzes on the other.

That the Fair was a failure was evident from the opening day. The only exhibit that attracted any permanent attention, or has survived, was Picasso's mural called 'Guernica', which only a few artists and labourers could understand. Only the Germans seemed enthusiastic. Of course, the French Government lowered the bars for tourist traffic and admitted anyone without question or surveillance who said he came to see the Fair. On the boulevards and avenues of the Right Bank, one heard German more frequently than French for a while, and the square-headed owl-like Nazis, all with guide books and cameras, swarmed methodically from one end of the city to the other, and took long tours through provincial France.

In those days of 1937, no one had heard the term 'fifth column' except a few Spaniards in the region of Madrid, where Franco had boasted that he would find in that city, to support the four columns of his quadruple attack, a fifth within the city limits. Nevertheless, it was the Exposition that gave the Nazis their chance to establish and organize their supporters, look over and survey the ground they were soon to occupy, and honeycomb France with spies and traitors. This may have been in the minds of the French officers and members of the Sûreté Général, but none of them protested openly. The Germans were well-behaved, and seemed to have plenty of money. As Hitler had intended, the bourgeois French were impressed and began to whisper that the Führer was, after all, looking after his own and to express quite freely the wish that France had such a man.

Not many of the German tourists wandered into the rue de la Huchette. A few of the most thorough did, however. A trio of them, all men and all cropped closely and wearing rimmed spectacles, peered into the Caveau one day when Milka was there. When one of them asked in halting French if there were any points of interest near by, Milka spoke up in good German. There was nothing worth seeing, she said. They had wandered into a slum where frequently the housewives dumped pisspots out of the windows. They had better keep their heads up as they walked back to the place St. Michel.

The three Nazis nodded gravely and thanked her. One of them scribbled a word or two in his notebook, and as they passed along the street they walked rather hurriedly, glancing uneasily toward the upper windows.

30

A DEAD MAN ON THE PAVEMENT

As the war in Spain went worse and worse, and it slowly dawned on the Republicans, even the honourable Henri Julliard and the hopeful Mme. Berthelot, that the Italian and German invasion was to be condoned by France, the enemies of the Popular Front wore an air of relief and satisfaction. My friends sank deeper in despair.

Pierre Vautier, who had just fought at Jarama, wrote me:

Cher Elliot,

It's wonderful to be surrounded by noble people for a change. As for me, I am still without faith. Even in the midst of a battle, I am haunted by the conviction that decency and unselfishness are dreams from which men are forcefully awakened or which end in oblivion.

I cannot say what my comrades felt or thought when they started out of a ditch and, rifles in hand, began to trot across a field. There were a few bare fig trees, some rocks, a rolling and desolate terrain. I saw, two hundred yards away, the flash of rifles, a machine-gun, heads and shoulders appearing and disappearing above a sandbag parapet. The enemy. I heard the whine of bullets and the sharp, insistent rat-tat-tat. St. Cyr! I had not heard a machine-gun since my miserable days in school. I began to be aware of an undertow that slowed my progress forward, a slowing down of time. Each clod of earth, tuft of grass, ping of bullet, slap of feet on turf became distinct. I found myself standing quite still, looking at the smallest almond tree I have seen, thin, helpless and awkward, like a colt. Elliot, it was in blossom. Two blossoms. The sight of them made me cry.

'Come on, *mon vieux*, they'll shoot you.' It was the voice of one of my American comrades. I roused myself, started trotting again and, as I ran, discharged my rifle. It slammed viciously against my shoulder.

'Get down, you fool,' another comrade said. He must have been French because I did not, as in the instance just preceding, remember your appalling accent. God, what a hash is one's mind!

'Get down!' This time more insistently, with a blow on my shins of a rifle barrel. It was hot. It hurt dimly, as if I had been anæsthetized in between. Before I dropped, I realized that my comrades were flat on the ground — all except me. One American was clutching his abdomen and hiccoughing blood. Another was dead. How did I know? I cannot say. It was my first sight of a corpse, but there was no mistaking that life was not in that deflated uniform. No blood.

My comrades rose again. So did I. When we got to a ditch, the one with sandbags on the parapet, we stumbled in and my rifle was discharged again; luckily it was pointing in the air.

Later, I could not say how long, I was huddled in a deserted shed which smelt of manure. In my hand was a mug of coffee. Stefan came running in. He was jubilant. A victory. We had advanced under fire, routed the enemy and taken his first line of defence. His second line he had given us free of charge. What will Milka say? How glad she will be! That was Stefan. I did not ask him if he had remembered to keep trotting, or had aimed before he fired. . . .

Elliot, three nights now I have lain awake because of the cold, and have been sure that I love Milka. Can that be possible? I don't mean that I love her solicitude and integrity. I am gnawed with regret that I have not clasped her knees and kissed her all over. Twice I dreamed of her and she became poor Mary. I beg of you, in the name of our friendship, do something for Mary. Why is it, here in Spain, I am aware of everything I have done or left undone? Was there ever such a fool?

Two days later. Antoine has been taken to Villa Paz with a bullet through his jaw. We have heard that the surgeon in an American. God, I hope so. Tell M. Pissy, if he hasn't heard already. You will know what to say. He will know how to act.

Elliot, I have slept on a concrete floor with my head on a sill and water running down my neck. I have eaten spoiled tomatoes cooked in rancid oil. I have covered with her skirt the body of a woman, ripped with a bayonet, four days dead. What I cannot stand, *mon vieux*, are the glad voices and hopeful eyes of the Spaniards and the orations of Comrade M., who prates about victory as if it were baking in some oven and had only to be removed when nicely browned. I shouted '*Merde!*' at the top of my voice — and was sent to the doctor.

Who can possibly fail to see that we are *foutus*? Not those leprous Socialists or that slimy Blum!

Pierre

I found M. Pissy with l'Oursin and André the coalman. Alice was behind the bar. Pierre was quite wrong. I did not know at all what to say.

'You have a letter from down there?' Pissy asked.

The letter was in my hand. Perhaps he saw the oddly ruled paper on which it was written.

'Yes. Your son got hit — nothing serious,' I said.

'In the belly or the legs?' Pissy asked. The faces of André and l'Oursin, stained and streaked, eyes staring dumbly, seemed suspended in the smoky atmosphere.

'It's shameful. You had no right . . .' said Alice, eyes hard, lips tight.

'Hold your tongue,' said André, gruffly. She looked up at him in astonishment.

'*Oui*,' she said, as if she were in school.

'In the legs or in the belly? It makes a difference,' said Pissy, setting down his drink because his hand was trembling.

'In the head.'

'Ah, the head. Is that letter in English?'

'No, in French.'

I folded over the page and handed it to Pissy. No one spoke. All breathed hard as he read.

'Happily the surgeon is American,' he said, and drank his applejack, wiping off his lips with the back of his hand. 'They're handy (*commodes*), those Americans.'

The news of the victory of Guadalajara reached the rue de la Huchette about eight o'clock in the evening, by radio in the Café St. Michel. Mme. Trévise, bitterly as she distrusted the Popular Front, was more contemptuous of Italians. By and large, the French loathed Italians as thoroughly as the Germans hate Jews, but not for the same reasons or from similar causes. The antipathy of the French for the 'macaronis' was not introduced by government leadership and propaganda. It was as natural as the liking for red wine. Of course, Noël, Monge and the Satyr were jubilant. They had had no victories and were quite boyish and uninhibited. Not knowing what else to do, they drank and called on their friends, up and down the street. The Republicans came out of their shells.

Frémont defiantly went to the pitcher where his savings were kept and took out ten francs, looking at Mme. Frémont in such a way that she did not dare remonstrate.

'Be careful, Papa,' said Yvonne, putting her arms round his neck.

He smiled. He still had hopes of convincing his daughter that her mother was a foolish short-sighted woman.

Madame Absalom was by that time definitely committed to the weaker side, not because she believed in socialism or popular government, but because her 'ex' was a toady of Pierre Laval, who had practically owned Clermont-Ferrand. L'Oursin was in an expansive mood and had gathered under his wing l'Hibou, the tramp, and the old woman whose name no one ever knew and who thought she sang like Yvette Guilbert. When the crowd left André's place to drop in at the Hôtel Normandie, André, who had taken one or two drinks more than usual, was moved to join his friends. Alice was worried, but made no objection. Her huge husband had shown signs of impatience with her anti-Blum opinions, and had taken the position that Blum was doing the best he could. Milka was attending one of her meetings; she seldom had fewer than three a day.

Instead of turning in at the Hôtel Normandie, which was filled with gloomy refugees, l'Oursin beckoned his followers to continue to the Caveau. It was the hour when The Navet, Gion, Salmon, Dr. Roux and Panaché had gathered for their after-dinner chat. They had not heard about Guadalajara.

Somehow the chestnut man had gained control of his group, to the point that the others were doing as he did, as if they were playing a game of follow-my-leader. He entered the Caveau with his hearty booming laugh and started singing 'Les Montagnards' at the top of his voice. I heard Noël's firm bass, the off-key voice of the drunken old woman, the whisky tenor of the tramp, Frémont, Pissy and the others carrying the air. Since the bar space was limited and occupied, l'Oursin's group lined up behind them and reached for their drinks over their shoulders. Monsieur Henri looked worried but not disapproving, and Georges, the Serbian *garçon*, beamed.

The Navet was livid with fright. Behind him, and between him and the door, was the big reckless man he had openly reviled, and l'Oursin was drunk and knew of old that The Navet was afraid of him. The situation seemed to amuse the chestnut man no end.

'*Tu es au courant, toi?*' (equivalent to 'Have you heard the news, old chap?') asked l'Oursin. The Navet pretended not to realize that the chestnut man was addressing him. He turned to leave the café, but l'Oursin was in front of him. The latter roared with laughter, spilled his drink on The Navet's bowler hat and repeated his question.

'What news?' asked Monsieur Henri, to divert l'Oursin's attention.

'The victory!' roared the chestnut man. He burst into the Marseillaise, half his companions joined raggedly. Panaché started for the side door and, in doing so, jostled Mme. Absalom. The chestnut man grabbed him by the shoulder and spun him round.

'I beg your pardon,' tardily said Panaché to Mme. Absalom. The chestnut man roared approval.

In a dim corner, seated alone at her table, Mme. Berthelot was smiling. The tableau, indeed, was ridiculous. The Navet's crowd was afraid to make a move, the Popular Front was circumspect enough but showed no signs of relenting. They edged close to the bar, increasingly careless about crowding their opponents, stepping on their well-polished shoes or staining their clothes with wine and alcohol. André, the coalman, trying to find the W.C., stumbled into the kitchen and awakened Thérèse, the cook, who had passed out in her chair. She was a forceful woman, even when half asleep, and insisted that André help her finish the bottle of Pinard on the floor beside her.

As suddenly as he had taken the notion to scare The Navet, l'Oursin decided to leave him in peace, and led his cohorts away. The following evening, however, the wife of Julien the barber told the chestnut man what The Navet had said he was going to do at the prefecture: have 'the dirty Communists' cleared out of the *quartier St. Michel*. The political rift between Julien, anti-Socialist, and his handsome wife had not then become public knowledge; so The Navet, while getting shaved, had not been over-cautious.

The chestnut man waited until eight o'clock; then he swaggered alone and cold sober to the Hôtel du Caveau, entered the bar, shoved The Navet to one side as if he were a window dummy, reached for the drink that had been in front of The Navet and was about to drink it when Dr. Roux, cane in hand, stepped up to him. L'Oursin's hearty laughter shook the bottles on the shelves. While the dentist's cane played a soft tattoo on his unheeding shoulders, l'Oursin took Dr. Roux's head under one hairy arm and forced it, face downwards, into the little sink in the middle of the bar. This was filled with dirty water. The Navet rushed out of the Caveau shouting *'Police! Au secours!'* The dentist followed, dripping, his cane broken. Gion and Panaché had vanished in the short course of the mêlée.

'Vive la France et les pommes de terre frites!' boomed the chestnut man when Officer Masson came in, followed by the Rightists. Monsieur Henri was about to explain what had happened when Hortense Berthelot stepped forward.

'This man,' she said, pointing to The Navet, 'and this one,' indicating Dr. Roux, 'attacked Monsieur l'Oursin, set on him with a cane.'

Georges smiled and nodded confirmation.

'Is that true?' asked Officer Masson of Monsieur Henri.

'Evidently,' said Henri.

The Navet began to splutter.

'I won't prefer charges,' roared the chestnut man, and reverted to the Marseillaise.

'I know where we shall get satisfaction,' The Navet said, leading the dentist away.

That was the last of the Rightists in the Hôtel du Caveau. The Navet and his friends gave all the cafés in the rue de la Huchette a wide berth and gathered nightly in the new place with neon signs across the rue des Deux Ponts. The freshly upholstered back room there became a meeting-place, not only for the local enemies of the Popular Front, but others who arrived in private cars, and whose faces were crafty and determined, sometimes exultant.

The exception was the 11th of September, 1937. I was in Madrid and received the news of the affair on my next visit to Valencia. I had seen no French newspapers for several weeks and had not opened the American papers I found waiting for me. The first communication to receive my attention was a letter from Hortense Berthelot. It had been opened by the government censors and showed signs of having been read repeatedly and with satisfaction.

Paris, 13 Sept.

Cher Voyageur,

Bloodshed at last! A corpse on the pavement in our little street!

The Navet, Julien and the dentist — the three who have become inseparable — came into the hotel last night about nine o'clock with an inspector of the Sûreté Générale. The latter was not on duty, but our *grand cocu* made it clear that his friend was armed with automatic and authority. He was looking for the chestnut man, or said he was. Instead he found Milka.

'You dirty cut-throats. You've all found your match. You thought you'd have an easy time, didn't you?' The Navet said to her. *'Monsieur, je ne vous salue pas!'* she replied.

At that moment Thérèse the cook came shouting out of the kitchen, a bottle in her hand.

'Don't talk that way to your betters,' she yelled, advancing on The Navet.

'This man is an officer,' The Navet said.

Thérèse took a deep drink of wine, then sprayed it in the face of the Sûrété Générale. The three intruders and the moistened officer retreated. The Navet brandishing his cane. He and his friends are never seen without canes, now. Georges says they have swords concealed inside.

'Don't deny you know nothing about dynamite,' The Navet said to Milka, as he closed the door behind him.

At ten o'clock, Frémont came running from the Café St. Michel. Two buildings had been blown up near the Étoile. Milka hurried out to use the telephone. I could only think of what *le cocu* had said about dynamite.

This morning *Le Martin* and, of course, the party journals of the Right accused the Communists. The buildings had been destroyed, with the loss of only one life, that of a policeman. Not only were the bombed premises empty of regular employees but the caretakers had luckily taken a short walk at the exact moment necessary to prolong their lives. One structure belonged to the Confédération du Patronat Français (Employers' Association), the other to the Associated Metal Industries.

L'Humanité attributed the incident to Rightist provocations.

After dinner, l'Oursin and his friends, Pissy, Frémont, the three ex-Radicals (Noël, Monge and the Satyr), decided, for some reason I do not know, to venture across the street and annoy The Navet in the new café. Some kind of meeting was in progress, attended not only by our neighbours, including the barber and Monsieur Saint-Aulaire, but the Prefect of the Seine. Seeing the Prefect was closeted with the Right, l'Oursin did not persist, but in re-crossing the street he encountered a gang of young men, former Croix de Feu, now some political party with another name.

'Down with Moscow!' 'Death to Communists!' they were shouting, and other remarks about the *Front Populaire* not convenient to write down. Without hesitation, l'Oursin picked up one of the students by the legs and began knocking down the others, using the first as a sort of bludgeon. In the free-for-all that resulted, involving not only Frémont, Pissy, the ageing Satyr who did yeoman service, but the barber and the new café proprietor, our own mild Georges and the musical pimp-macquereau from the Bal St. Séverin. [That was Robert.]

Because of the proximity of the Prefect, no doubt, police cars with sirens charged into the *mêlée*, our friends scattered into the rue de la Huchette, the dishevelled Right contingent formed on the pavement in front of the new café. There was much screaming and opening of windows.

When the confusion subsided, I saw, sprawled on the pavement, directly beneath my window, a young man, flat on his face. He was dead. Stabbed once, deeply in the heart. More police came on the scene; all night there was searching and scuffling of feet. Georges had been bruised but not cut, and his razor, so often wet, was dry. Julien the barber received only a black eye until he got home, where his wife split his head with some hair-curling device and expelled him for ever from her bed.

Monsieur Henri suspects that Robert did the stabbing, but no one arrested him, since he had no political affiliations. The chestnut man has served notice that no Cagoulard, as The Navet and his associates are now called, shall use the rue de la Huchette with impunity after dark. The sergeant gave him a severe talking to, but our neighbours of the Right keep very much out of sight just now. There are rumours of a plot, not by Moscovites, but financed by Michelin and some other industrialists. Lefarge [the old woman at the Prefecture] is heartily in sympathy with the Cagoulards and hints that Pétain and Weygand are in it, too. Laval and Tardieu are implicated; so is that count with the bizarre Italian name, and, of course, de la Rocque.

Milka tells me the dead student was the son of a wallpaper manufacturer. I cannot forget how he looked on our pavement.

Your devoted friend,
Hortense

P.S. (the 14th)

Lefarge is a mountain of information. It seems the Government has found an arsenal in Clermont-Ferrand and has questioned several hundred members of the new Ku Klux Klan, meanwhile afraid to detain the principals who are out on bail, or publicly denounce the hero of Verdun and his former chief of the secret service who is one of the ringleaders of the plot.

The Prime Minister is moving heaven and earth to hush up the scandal and minimize its importance. Only *Ce Soir* and *Humanité* are triumphant, and, of course, Milka, in her energetic way.

We have no more honour, no more authority.

Young Pissy has malaria. His ward was not screened. Perhaps you saw him. If so, write. His mother no longer tastes the little food she swallows.

PART THREE

The Death of a Nation

31

BETWEEN RELIEF AND SHAME

The Popular Front election, April 16 to 21, 1936, was the last held in France, as the Popular Front election in February of that same year was the last held in Spain. In France the civil war that broke out when Blum took office was not conducted with armies and explosives, but the French anti-republicans were promptly aided by foreign fascist Governments which planned to dominate them openly later, when democracy had been destroyed. The Cagoulard movement was financed largely by Italian and German funds, and Blum's Government (whether Blum or Chautemps was the Premier) was so demoralized by the farce of non-intervention in Spain that the widespread plot to overthrow the Republic was hushed up. The leaders went scot free, and the political murders the hooded conspirators had committed were not investigated.

The Right, in France, was able to take over without the formality of a general election by means of a politician named Daladier, a baker's son who went to school under Herriot and later undermined his teacher in the Radical-Socialist Party. Daladier's record, on re-examination, seems to have fitted him ideally for Munich. Briefly it is as follows:

He first became Prime Minister, to succeed Paul-Boncour's brief regime, on January 30, 1933, the same day that Hitler first became Chancellor of Germany. France already was bankrupt and disrupted, but not hopelessly. Daladier lasted until October, and showed no grasp of either the internal or general European situation. His idea was to cut salaries and increase taxes in the lower brackets. His cabinet consisted entirely of members of his own party and his policies were attacked consistently by Léon Blum. His party was supported by Stavisky funds.

In January, 1934, Daladier took over for the second term of office, just in time to order the police and military to fire on citizens who were rioting in protest of the Stavisky exposure. He lasted seven days, and in that time earned the nickname 'the murderer'. The popular outcry against him frightened him so badly that he promptly resigned, making way for Doumergue.

An outsider not familiar with French politics might have thought that Daladier was through. Not at all. He got himself elected by the Popular Front (Communists, Socialists and Radical-Socialists) when Blum, after non-intervention, resigned, a broken man, in April, 1938.

The date marks the second great victory for the Right in the French civil war, the first being the support of Franco in Spain against the Spanish Republicans. Daladier, while the rest of the world was worrying about the

Czechs, busied himself with the repeal of the labour laws and social reforms enacted under Blum and Blum-Chautemps.

'Nowhere else but in France and Mexico,' Daladier said, 'do employees work only forty hours a week.'

The Communists, Socialists and some of his own Radical-Socialists denounced Daladier for his *volte-face*, but the parties of the Right warmed up to him instantly and gave him the support he needed to remain in office. To the enemies of the Popular Front, Daladier seemed to have been transformed for their purposes by heavenly intervention. Daladier left French foreign affairs entirely to Chamberlain, whose umbrella had already become the symbol of humility and double-dealing throughout the world. If the workers would work longer hours for less money, Daladier said, France would be safe; the national defence would be adequate.

Before he put across the repeal of the Blum reforms, on the basis of which the Congress, still sitting, had been elected, Daladier (having been left out of the conference at Berchtesgaden because, as he put it, 'some other powers might have wanted to be represented if I attended') was invited to Munich, with the result which the world knows now and all but the imbeciles knew then. American movie-goers will remember, standing uneasily on the edge of the group consisting of Hitler, Mussolini, Chamberlain, Goering and others, a short unprepossessing man who looked like Napoleon, only stouter, and who seemed to be trying to maintain his dignity and keep out of everybody's way. That man was Daladier, representing the Third Republic. He signed, when the time came and when he was told, on the dotted line. What is noteworthy is that of all those present he was the only one whose country had pledged itself in writing to stand by the Czechs and defend them against aggression. Hitler had never promised to guarantee the Czechs against attack; neither had Mussolini *or* Chamberlain. The British were not committed irrevocably. Only France.

When, returning to Paris, Daladier saw the field at Le Bourget crowded with people, he thought he was going to be mobbed and was afraid, according to the story that spread through all France.

'I am torn between shame and relief,' said Léon Blum.

So were my friends in the rue de la Huchette, whose husbands and sons had been mobilized. Even to those who had not seen it or felt it directly, war is such a terrible thing that any immediate avoidance or postponement raises hopes and gratitude in their hearts. What it means to a generation which had already suffered it is many times more poignant.

The effect on Daladier of sudden popularity, in place of the contempt he had suffered because of the February riots and his taint of Stavisky, was to inflate the man. Because he had signed away the honour and safety of France, he considered himself a hero and was beginning to see himself a dictator.

How far removed are the selfish and traitorous activities of a Laval, a Bonnet or a Daladier, or the cowardice of a Blum, from their victims in a sheltered little street!

A week before Munich, Étienne Corre, son of the retired grocer, was called to the colours and sent into the Maginot Line. He was selected with other specialists, because he knew German, which was still in current use along the Alsatian frontier. His sad young wife, with the aid of Monsieur Noël, had been carrying on the business in l'Épicerie Danton for some time and trade had been falling off progressively as times got harder. When Étienne went away, his wife lost her strength and appetite, and, after she had fainted in the store, was persuaded to take to her bed.

In his apartment in the rue du Bac, old man Corre could no longer be content with pacing the floor and escorting his wife to parks and museums. So he and Gabrielle came back to the store and, in the interest of economy, were obliged to dismiss Monsieur Noël. The latter, for want of anything better to do, went back to his taxidermist's shop in the place St. André des Arts. Trade in the grocery store was at a standstill, since no one bought fancy groceries when war was just over the doorstep. Noël's twenty francs a day earned as a grocer's assistant could not be made up in his taxidermist's shop. No one brought cats or dogs to be stuffed when reservists were being summoned to the border, to face the German army which had been holding manœuvres across from the Maginot fortifications.

Throughout the years I had known the rue de la Huchette, I had seldom passed l'Épicerie Danton without stopping for a word with the Corres, especially if I had just returned from a journey. The bug-eyed old Breton, continually puffing at his short-stemmed pipe, was so wistful about distant lands, so appreciative of any travelogue I could throw his way, that his attitude made my adventures seem piquant and important, even to me. That time, although I had just disembarked from the *Normandie*, he did not ask me about New York or London or Spain.

'You're back at work,' I said.

He glanced uneasily at his wife, who was seated on the stool behind the cash drawer.

'Do you think things will arrange themselves?' he asked. 'What do you hear at the newspaper office?'

I had not been connected with a Paris newspaper for about eight years, but Corre had never been strong on chronology.

Madame Corre, of the alabaster skin, the trim well-rounded figure, the lavender perfume, white well-kept hands and curly light-brown hair, seemed to age in front of me. Her hazel eyes, undimmed since young womanhood, were dull with fright. Her lips were blue. The skin sagged around her determined jaws. Her voice was thin and shrill.

'My son is in the Maginot Line,' she said.

'*Dis donc*, it's safe down there,' grunted Corre.

A sudden gust of anger distorted her usually placid face.

'It was for that we spent our money, having him taught German. If only he had not studied that accursed language someone else might have been chosen,' she said.

'Who would have figured anything like that?' asked the old grocer, defensively.

'While I was nursing him, you were on the Somme,' she said, her voice rising. Both of them seemed to have forgotten I was still there. 'You were buried in a trench. . . .'

'Our trenches weren't much good in those days,' he said. 'The walls are of concrete in the Maginot Line, two metres of concrete reinforced with rails.'

'And what if all that crumbles? On you there were only a few shovelfuls of dirt.'

'No need to get nervous,' he said. 'Perhaps everything will arrange itself. I read, just this morning, that the Cabinet has been meeting. Perhaps we'll not bother about the Czechs, after all. Is that possible, Monsieur Paul?'

Just then it didn't seem possible, but I hadn't the heart to say so. As I proceeded down the street, I saw signs of panic and uncertainty. The publisher in No. 30 had closed his metal shutters. The windows of the flower shop at No. 23 were devoid of colour and the door was padlocked. Madame Absalom, having heard that I was back, before I got near No. 10, sent Mary the Greek to summon me to her bedside. The peppery old woman, some time between the Cagoulard exposure and Hitler's seizure of Austria, had decided not to get up any more. She had bought some second-hand clothes for poor Mary, still beautiful and tragic at forty, and installed her in the yarn shop, where the Greek madonna did the leg-work faithfully while La Absalom cackled orders through a rift in the portières that screened her bed from the front of the establishment.

What impelled Madame Absalom to give her ancient legs a permanent vacation no one ever learned. She simply announced one morning that she was going to stay in bed for the rest of her years, and she did. Even more thoroughly than formerly she kept track of the happenings in our street and neighbourhood. She kept Mary jumping and fetching from dawn until late in the evening, and often in the night. She insisted there was nothing wrong with her, except the general lassitude that had poisoned all France.

I entered her little alcove and pulled up a kitchen chair. I had no news for her, being as uncertain as the rest of the public as to when war was coming. She knew I had been predicting its outbreak all along. But Madame Absalom had a rare item for me. It seemed that Julien the barber was on the list of reservists quite likely to be called. A few evenings before, when young Corre and young Luneville had both received marching orders, Elaine, the barber's wife, had spoken her mind. She had been faithful to Julien, fool that she was, all the years they had been married, including the recent period when she would not let him come near her in bed. There would be war and Julien would be called away, of that Elaine was sure.

'The moment you are out of sight, I shall find a real man,' she said to Julien. 'I shall be his slave. He shall do with me as he likes, all the tender tricks I couldn't bear from you. Nothing that he asks will be too much, or half enough. Do you understand?'

Madame Absalom's mimicry was at its best as she sat up in bed, her wiry grey hair in a tangle, her flannel nightgown flapping as she gesticulated and turned.

'She'll be a hot piece, that one. Some poor idiot won't know what's struck him, *n'est-ce pas*? She's been saving it up for quite a while,' said the gleeful old woman. Then she added, almost wistfully, 'Now why couldn't I have thought of something like that for my "ex"? He would have bitten off his nails. He would have been beside himself. Ah, well, it's good to see *some* woman get the best of one of them.'

I could not resist dropping into the barber shop for a haircut, just to size up the situation. Julien was pale and wan; his hands were trembling. Elaine was watching him, covertly, with a mischievous glint in her eye. As she hovered at my side and smiled at me provocatively, I could see Julien adding me to the list of possible undoers. No doubt she let him think the same of every man who entered the door.

'How soon will the war commence in earnest?' Elaine asked me, in a tone quite different from that of the despairing Madame Corre.

'It can't be long,' I said. 'Will you stay in Paris? The stations already are crowded with people running to the country.'

'Not for me, the country,' she said. 'I'm not afraid.'

'And if there isn't any war?' asked Julien, trying to be defiant.

'Then I'll start an offensive of my own,' she said, and looked at me so invitingly that it would have been inhuman not to respond.

In the music shop, Gion and Bernice were taking an inventory. He also might be mobilized, in which case he intended to hold her strictly to account for each article in stock. He had agreed that she was to take out enough from the receipts to buy her food each day, within the limit of six francs. Bernice, terrified at the idea of remaining in the city alone, in the midst of gas and bombing attacks, could not count or add. She was wishing for the one kind sister in the orphanage who had shielded her, years ago, from the strict mother superior.

From Father Panarioux I learned about the drama that was taking place in the back room of the Luneville's dry goods store, *Au Beau Marocain*. The priest was haggard from incessant prayer and shared with me, his infidel friend and bridge partner, the problem he had taken to his God without satisfaction.

M. Luneville, just turned forty-four, had been an orderly to General de Castelnau, the defender of Nancy, in World War I. His son, Jacques, in 1938, was twenty-one. Mme. Luneville had urged her husband to visit his old chief, who had influence with the General Staff, and obtain for Jacques a safe place behind the lines. The boy was in the infantry. Luneville the elder had refused point-blank. All through the other war he had been taunted because he was an *embusqué*. His son was not going to suffer the same humiliation. He would fight like a man, if war had to come, said Luneville, and the boy was of the same opinion.

Both husband and wife had appealed to the priest, who, a fervent patriot himself, could come to no decision.

'Poor woman. This will undermine her faith,' he said. He did not mention that he had asked permission to become a chaplain at the front and had been told that he could not be spared from the organ.

M. and Mme. Frémont, who had never become reconciled since their bitter dispute about Yvonne and the sit-down strike, continued their struggle for the timid girl's allegiance. Mme. Frémont brought in all the newspapers of the Right, which praised Daladier for his stand against the forty-hour week and the unions, and read the editorials aloud while Frémont choked over his dinner.

'Frenchmen will have to choose between the forty-hour week and the one-hundred-hour week imposed by the enemy's cannon,' was *Figaro's* comment.

'The national defence is another term for the profits of Schneider,' said Frémont. 'Daladier will never fight Hitler, but only the workers of France.'

'Your cronies would rather fight for the Moscovites in Spain than do their duty here,' she retorted.

Without answering, Frémont strode to the pitcher on the shelf and took out another ten francs. His wife began to cry, turning to let her tears fall into the dishpan as she struggled with her growing resentment.

'Be careful, Papa,' said the gentle Yvonne as her father paused at the door.

'Drunkard!' said her mother.

'*Sotte!*' said Frémont, and slammed the door.

32

BOARDS ACROSS A DOORWAY

Daladier took advantage of his popularity just after Munich to repeal Blum's forty-hour week, as a warning to labour that French workmen must work as hard and as long, and for as low wages, as Germans and Italians did in the totalitarian countries.

'If peace is assured in our time, as Chamberlain says, why work overtime to build cannon?' asked Henri Julliard.

'Hitler and Mussolini need the cannon. We'll either sell them, at a good fat profit, or they'll come and take them free of charge,' said Milka.

Milka, however, a true revolutionist of a family of revolutionists, was privately disgusted because of a blunder made by Marcel Jouhaux, head of the C.G.T., or *Confédération Générale du Travail*, who had announced, two weeks in advance, a general strike of protest against the breaking down of labour laws. A general strike could only be an effective weapon if it came without warning. Give the capitalists, politicians, the press and the army two weeks in which to prepare, and the worker would only walk into a trap, she insisted, and all of us agreed. It proved embarrassing to Milka a little later when her party workers added a worse error to Jouhaux's original one. Jouhaux, who could have carried with him at that point the directors of the C.G.T., foresaw that he was going to lose and that Daladier would add to his power at the expense of the underpaid workers, especially the government employees. He wanted to back down and call off the strike. The Communists wouldn't let him; so Milka, having seen the situation clearly, worked hard and faithfully against her own better judgment.

It was then that I noticed the profound change that had come over Pierre. He had come back with the disfigured Antoine after Negrin, the Spanish leader, had, like the gentleman he was and is, ordered the foreign volunteers who had risked their lives for Spanish freedom to leave the country before the débâcle. Stefan had stayed, not far from Belchite, where a hand grenade, exploding prematurely, had blown off his hands and his head.

I remembered Stefan as a gay young student, hypnotized by the headstrong Milka, running her errands, understanding her moods and whims. I had never heard him disagree with her or resent her reproaches or neglect a task she had set for him. His devotion was not to her womanhood, but to her strength, which he lacked. She did not cry when Pierre brought her the news, but nodded grimly. In the months that followed I saw her more than once drop a tear in memory of her disciple and room-mate, but in each instance it was not out of regret that he was dead. She wept when, late at night, after hours of untiring work, she was confronted with some colossal stupidity, some chance remark of a non-class-conscious neighbour, a headline to mislead the geese, a poster about gas masks or a bucketful of sand. At such moments death covered itself with an alluring garment and life was endless and discouraging.

Whenever we met, Pierre was courteous but I could not fail to see that he was avoiding me. I had heard his first uncertainties. He had written me of all his doubts. His contact with the noble Spaniards had uplifted him at first, until he saw what nobility without machine-guns really meant. He had seen the bravest die and the jackals feast on their bodies. He had seen reason stabbed to death and fanaticism drink the blood. The faith and conviction that had eluded him when he was stronger he seized upon in desperation. There was no more rigid follower or defender of the party line. Like Antoine, Pierre had been disfigured, and like Stefan, he had died.

There was no trace of his battlefield passion for Milka. They spoke to each other curtly, like an officer to a soldier. They had little use for me. Each evening they dined *chez* Daniel, in company with other Communists who were as busy as they were. Two of the regulars turned out later to be agents of the Sûrété Générale.

On the eve of the general strike of November, two things were apparent. Daladier, Bonnet and the saboteurs of the Popular Front, including in our street The Navet, Saint-Aulaire, Madame Durand, who had just returned from the country after the Munich exodus, and Julien the barber — all were eager that the strike should take place. On the other hand, the noncommunist unionists were willing to make concessions and did not want to go through with the premature threat Jouhaux had made. That could only mean one thing. The Government, the Communists *and* non-communist leaders all assumed the strike would be a failure.

Why should the Communists want the strike to fail?

Because if it did, Daladier would be sure to take excessive revenge. The workers would suffer, but it would make them more resentful and therefore more revolutionary.

The workers in our street who had the most to lose, in each case a government job with nearly twenty years of seniority, were Frémont and Pissy. That they would obey the call was sure. When the unlucky day arrived, they were joined by Eugène, The Navet's son, who had a small job in a gymnasium; Hyacinthe Goujon, on her way to be a star; Elaine, the barber's wife, who threatened to walk the boulevard and offer herself to the first presentable man who spoke to her if her husband raised the shutters that day; Louis, the *garçon* at the Normandie; the girls in Lanier's laundry; and the butcher boy who worked for Salmon. Had she not been prevented by an attack of bronchitis, Hortense would have risked her job with the others. Of that number, totalling ten, M. Pissy, was a member of the Communist Party. Frémont was a Socialist. The remaining eight had no affiliations whatsoever.

Afraid of 'Communist' disorders, Gion, Madame Durand, Madame Joli, the cleaner, and Luttenschlager, purveyor of articles of piety, closed in sympathy with the workers; as did Maurice of *La Vie Silencieuse*, Monge, the horse butcher, Odette and Jean in the dairy shop, and Monsieur Henri Julliard.

I could not repress a smile as I passed old Dorlan, the bookbinder, working away on orders eight months overdue. I am sure he did not know what was happening outside. Corre came down to open his grocery, then changed his mind and spent the day in the Café St. Michel. Of the taxis usually lined up in front of the Brasserie Dalmatienne, only two put in an appearance.

The bus lines, the tramways and the Métro were unimpeded, and before noon the taxi drivers began to drift back to their places. The Tory *Petit Journal* came out as a handbill, prepared by scabs. Nearly all the newspapers were abbreviated. Still, those of the Right proclaimed the strike a failure, while *Ce Soir* and *Humanité* exaggerated its success. It was not until the next day or the day after that the news became public to the effect that in all the large factories around Paris and in the other important cities the tie-up had been almost complete, that the ports of Le Havre, Rouen, Cherbourg and Marseilles had been at a standstill and that even among the browbeaten government employees the turn-out had been impressive.

Instead of emerging triumphant, the Tories were badly frightened, and while Daladier set all the government agencies in motion to disrupt the unions and play the non-communist element against the small minority of Reds, all the resources of the large employers and war speculators were pooled in a concerted drive. Another battle in the French civil war was in full progress, and again the Germans and Italians threw their weight with their fascist brethren who were fighting the Third Republic.

The Communist Party at that time was second in numerical strength in the Chamber. That does not mean that the Reds were predominant. They were second in a list of nineteen, and all the other eighteen were lining up against them. Daladier tried to outlaw the Communists and disband the party, planning later to arrest the leaders and put them out of action.

When the butcher boy appeared for work, the day after the strike, Monsieur Salmon would not let him enter the shop and refused to pay him the two days' wages due. The boy asked the police sergeant to help him collect, and was referred to a special court for 'commercial disputes'. Madame Lanier locked out the girls for a week and then took them back at a reduction in pay. Their percentage of earnings 'upstairs' remained the same. Eugène, The Navet's son, got his job back without question, since his mother's Persian lover was one of the gymnasium's best customers.

The reason the general strike was not a complete victory for the Left, as the 1936 elections had been, was because a large percentage of the members of the C.G.T. were government employees, receiving less than a dollar a day with which to support themselves and their families. This horde of sub-human victims of a corrupt bureaucracy had been systematically demoralized. They had no security beyond the whims of their superiors, who, in turn, were beholden to secretaries who licked the boots of Cabinet Ministers. Half of the public employees in the C.G.T. were afraid to strike, and of the braver half Daladier, Bonnet and Co., visited their revenge. The Communists again had manœuvred themselves into an unpopular attitude. With justice on their side, they had jeopardized another honourable cause, lacking tact as well as a grasp of popular psychology. They were unquestionably right in holding out against the Munich fraud, and they knew the repeal of the labour laws was designed for private gain and not for national defence. Their obtuseness in forcing a losing general strike caused a split in the ranks of labour, turning non-communists against them. That was what Daladier wanted.

The general strike offered Daladier an excuse for news suppression and censorship that never was relaxed again.

When I first went to the rue de la Huchette there was little drunkenness in evidence. Mary the Greek would drink a few Dubonnets and sing, Georges would try to cut his throat, and the old woman who imitated Yvette Guilbert would sometimes fall in the gutter and be taken to the police station for the night. The wreck of the Popular Front brought so much dissension and discouragement to the little street that friendliness all but disappeared; there was no longer love and harmony in all the houses, and dirt and dissipation got the upper hand.

It was not for the purpose of reforming her that Madame Absalom befriended Mary the Greek. The old witch did not drink herself, except now and then a sip of benedictine after meals. Nevertheless, she seemed to enjoy, as a weird accompaniment to her nightly monologues on the worthlessness of man, the off-key wailing of poor Mary, who declaimed about her home and children in Detroit, shuffled the torn remnants of the papers she still retained, and mourned the days of love with Pierre who had left her for a *tapette* and a foreign *'anarchiste'*. In the daytime, Mme. Absalom made Mary toe the mark. The orderly regime of desultory work in the yarn shop, the regular meals and the comfort of a staunch protector did wonders for Mary and made her better able to stand a mild evening's debauch. Early in 1939, the two women were joined each evening by Frémont, who had been discharged from the post office on Daladier's instructions, Pissy, the railway worker, also out of work as a result of the strike, and young Pissy, who because of his record in Spain could not find employment. No middle-class employer would trust a 'Red'.

A few francs came Frémont's way because of his knack as a tinker, but none of the conservative inhabitants of the rue de la Huchette would call on him to enter their houses. Each night, following the strike, he would take ten francs from the pitcher containing the savings for Yvonne's dowry, until Mme. Frémont took what remained, 2,500 francs (£12 8s.) and fled, with her daughter, to her mother in the country. Thus Frémont lost the job of concierge of No. 11, since a man and wife are required for that semi-official post. Throughout Paris, the police department was encouraging landlords to get rid of concierges who had radical tendencies and who might shelter questionable characters. This was in preparation for the outlawing of the Communist Party, which Daladier manœuvred just after the Stalin-Hitler pact. The ambitious Premier had been working on the project since the first big hand he received when he got home from Munich.

The Spanish Republicans were being slaughtered by Franco's well-armed Moors and Mussolini's Italians, aided by German technicians and British duplicity. In the side streets of the entire world, as in the rue de la Huchette, the finest citizens were heart and soul with the champions of freedom and human dignity in Spain. Not so the landlords, manufacturers, clergymen, army officers and financiers. The London press was as hypocritical as the Paris press and the New York press. All over the world, the helpless workers were losing influence in their respective governments.

In 1923, just after Suzanne led me to the Hôtel du Caveau, Henri Julliard was fifty years of age, and I was thirty-two. In 1939, when he showed the first symptoms of Bright's disease, he was sixty-six and I was forty-eight. It was a long rough road we had travelled together, friends from the first, sometimes understanding, often misunderstanding. Yet in all that time I can remember no major issue on which we had disagreed. A remark overheard, a headline, a glimpse through the window of the dingy little bar, and I would look over at him, and he would raise his eyebrows to look across at me. Had I not been so numb with misery on account of the brutal injustices in Spain, I should have been more deeply depressed when the Hôtel du Caveau closed its door. Madame Marie, frightened and loyal, could not keep it going. She took her sick husband to their house in Montmorency where quietly, in isolation and the hope for France he never could relinquish, Henri Julliard started slowly to die, a little day by day, as shells and bombs from Italy and Germany raked the helpless bodies of Spanish patriots, as the clubs of police and the bayonets of Senegalese battered and pricked the outraged French workers, as the day came nearer when no Frenchman could raise his head, when Liberty, Equality and Fraternity were stripped from the public buildings, when the land that had been civilization's darling became the orphan of rampant violence.

The windows of No. 5 were boarded, the door was chained and padlocked. I saw my old friend ride away in the small truck his son used for delivering typewriters. Marie, hunched up like a marsh bird in the rain, was by his side. He had around his neck a woollen muffler. His luxurious Savoyard moustaches were white, not grey.

'*À bientôt*, Paul,' he said simply.

33

'UNTO THE LEAST OF THESE'

It was a grey day, sharp but not cold, with a minimum of dampness in the air. Hyacinthe, my wife Flora, and I were seated in the stuffy old Comédie Française witnessing a performance of *Le Chapeau de Paille d'Italie*. Just outside the traffic was streaming into the avenue de l'Opéra, from the swirling Palais Royal, the pont du Louvre, and the rue Faubourg St. Honoré. We did not then look away and hide our tears at the mention of those names and places but already they had taken on a quality of unreality. Most reassuring was the inside of the national theatre, which belonged to the rue de la Huchette and the other side streets as did the central markets, the museums, the grand boulevards and the parks and gardens, now bleak and cloaked with dead leaves. It was a Thursday matinée and all the subscribers were in their places, among them the wistful sad-faced woman in the first balcony box, stage left, accompanied by her watchful chaperon. Year in, year out I had seen that woman, passed close to her purposely in the corridor, inhaled her perfume, always elusive and individual, remarked her clothes of old-fashioned velvet and stiff silk. She was France, inscrutable, mysterious. So was the old critic who brought his niece on Thursdays; Jeanne and her Persian lover who sat four rows ahead; the dowager who commented aloud, but so piquantly and naïvely that one accepted her interruptions as a super-performance.

The company, as is often the case in desperate days, outdid itself in that graceful farce-comedy on the one and only French theme, the *cocu*. French women were betrayed so often that their situation was practically devoid of dramatic material. Not so the gentlemen on whom had been glued the fatal horns, the badge of ridicule and unrest. Some took it calmly, others ranted and raved. They were comical just the same.

There was something uncanny about the gaiety of that afternoon on the draughty old stage, with the national hams cavorting and the mistresses of Cabinet Ministers in period costumes holding up their end of the show. They also were accomplished actresses, in the Comédie tradition. It was as if that performance had been dropped, like an orchid on the pavement, in the midst of disaster. A few days before, the remnants of the Spanish army had crossed the border into France, the most despairing ones tearing from their families at the last momènt, and rushing back to be killed by the Fascists. A few days later, Hitler was to annex Bohemia, according to prearrangement with M. Georges Bonnet.

Always my mind dwelt on the army of Spanish children down on the Catalan border as they crossed over into France. Much that I had seen was too terrible, even for me, an observer trained in mass heartbreaks and modern frightfulness, to retain. I can only record, in passing, a certain mudhole in which starving children of patriots were croaking and peeping like frogs; a woman so weak with hunger that she could scarcely hold her baby in her arms, who went through the Spanish convention of refusing twice, insisting she was not hungry, before accepting food from me.

Just a few days later, after a performance at the Comédie, Hyacinthe and I sat silently in the Café de Rohan, across the street from the theatre.

'Was I as intelligent as your son at his age?' she asked, and then answered for herself: 'No. I was a prude, a dupe and a snob.'

'You liked Vespers at the Madeleine,' I said, because I was thinking of something else.

Only two days before I had visited a dingy dining-room in Perpignan, a little-used hall of a small cheap hotel where the proprietor was one of the understanding ones and had opened his pocketbook and his establishment to the children whom Franco and Mussolini had driven from their homes, after trying repeatedly to kill them, from the land, the sea and the air. A few, in fact, wore bloody bandages where intrepid aviators, fresh from mass, had spattered the helpless refugees with machine-gun bullets, in order to demonstrate to each other a new method of diving. Children are volatile and resistant, especially when eating after a long interval of hunger. But in one corner was a pale grave-faced little boy with hair closely cropped and large dark eyes, who was trying to eat his soup and lagged behind the others. It had been the same in every camp of refuge for children I had seen in Spain, in every dining-room, in every dormitory, in every group on the beach for a swim or in the classroom to learn the alphabet. There was always one child, wiser than the rest, less demonstrative, less hopeful, more obedient. An irreconcilable. He knew the grown-ups were trying to make it easier, and responded as best he could. With the best of goodwill, he could not sing or smile or feel in the air that the earth was the place for the likes of him.

Hyacinthe, beside me on the plush bench in the Café de Rohan, did not come at once to the subject that was preying on her mind. That was not her way. Instead she told a story that summarized Fascist venom and cruelty.

In Hyacinthe's building, No. 32, the second-floor apartment had been rented to a Spanish refugee, one of the few who were permitted by Georges Bonnet to live in Paris, since the German Embassy had registered an objection to having Republicans close by. He was a tall ascetic man with lean jaws and thin hands and eyes that were sadly humorous.

This exile had a wife and little son, and the boy had a bicycle. Hyacinthe caught the concierge of No. 32, who thought the sun rose and set in The Navet, puncturing the tyres of the bicycle of the 'dirty Spanish Red' (aged 7) with an old-fashioned hatpin.

As she was telling me about the hospitality accorded a child without a country, I suddenly understood what was on her mind.

'Hyacinthe, you should save yourself,' I said.

My remark took her completely by surprise. *'Vous dites?'* (What's that?) she asked.

'Get away from here, while you can. Go to America,' I said. 'You could succeed there.'

She sighed. I could see that she had thought the matter over and had made her decision.

'I am lost, like the rest of France,' she said. 'I have spent my life developing two qualities which seem to me the most characteristic and important. First of all, I have been French, night and day, asleep and awake. Second, I have occupied myself with my femininity.'

'You can be French in America,' I said. 'Everyone will like it. Only the boors Americanize themselves, as the worst type of Americans here imagine they have become French.'

'I'm afraid to be a foreigner,' she said. 'I have thought of them, always, as monstrosities — except, of course, you, the cosmopolitan.'

No agony or indecision was acute enough to make Hyacinthe forget to be gracious. Perhaps there were other young women in the world who were, in certain ways or by other standards, more beautiful and desirable than Hyacinthe. Not many. Unluckily her manners, her tact, her feeling for nuances, could not live after her as an example to a brusque and boorish world.

'How different it must be to be a boy!' she said. 'I find in trying so consciously to be feminine, I have failed to be human. Your Spaniards are human, from birth.'

'Don't be severe with yourself,' I said. Indeed, her humanity had grown warmer in recent years with each succeeding day. Her director, who had cast her first as a clothes-horse and light comedienne, had already corrected his error. She had an almost effortless dramatic appeal. In one rôle, I could have sworn she was Yvonne Frémont, the girl from another class and kind she had watched through two intervening windows. Later she told me she had impersonated Yvonne and that had been her first real triumph.

'We are human in America,' I said.

'You are sentimental. But human, also. Americans, of all the people of the world, are good-hearted, frank, like children. Among them, as a relic of France, I should be anachronistic. A curiosity.'

She took my hand and looked at me with devastating sadness.

'I have thought about it, hour upon hour. — Elliot, I cannot go away. I am a part of Paris, of the stifling soul of France. When France goes, I go. When Daladier sells France, he sells me. I am part of the bargain. When Flandin sends his telegrams to Hitler, he sends me. I could make fabulous sums in

Hollywood; I could lose myself in the swirl of New York. I should make conquests, gain fame — I cannot do it.'

'You know best,' I said sadly.

'Oh, Elliot, make me go!' She rose as she spoke, and her tears made it plain that she did mean what she said, but that it would be useless to try to persuade her.

'You Americans are alive. You have your share of the future. Flora will go on from day to day thinking mostly of others, *avec sa clarté aussi forte que sa timidité est pénible*. [With her clarity which is as strong as her shyness is painful.] Peanut will grow to be a man. I have the gift of prophecy today. He will be important to his friends, disdainful of ambition or glory. You, like Moses, will slip quietly out of this world at the age of one hundred and twenty, as deftly as you disappear from salons or cafés when conversation bores you.

'I love the screen. The screen loves me. It welcomes me and enfolds me. I love the public, and am loved a little in return. Only, when I think of what is ahead, I am afraid. In my profession, one is supplied with lines, sometimes well-written, often inspired. When Paris dies, I shall not know what to say. Please, Elliot, do not let me be banal.'

Hyacinthe's reference to Flandin's telegram touches on an incident that was typical of French politics in the fatal thirties. At the time of the Munich pact, Flandin, formerly Prime Minister and one of the outstanding Fascists of France, sent a telegram of congratulation to Hitler, doubtless having in mind that he should make himself solid with his future Führer.

Before the smoke of Hitler's seizure of Bohemia had cleared away, President Lebrun sent Marshal Pétain as Ambassador to Franco. Like so many under-sized men, Franco thought of little ways in which to make himself appear impressive. He kept the aged Pétain, already in his dotage, cooling his heels a week in Santander and then made him motor all the way to Burgos for a twenty-minute interview. That was indicative of the level to which France had descended; the France of the Bourbons and the Bastille, of Balzac and Zola, Voltaire and Rousseau, of Pasteur and Curie, Lucien Guitry and Debureau, Bernhardt and de Reszke. The list is so long, but no longer can be said to be endless. Franco's discourtesy was the harder to excuse in view of the fact that Pétain and his Cagoulards had been working for Franco all along.

It was about that time that von Ribbentrop came to Paris with a pact which bound Germany and France to keep the peace for ten years. He was received with open arms by his collaborator, Georges Bonnet. I walked with Pierre that morning around the Gare des Invalides, as near as we could get to the scene of von Ribbentrop's official welcome. I had thought, until that day, that in the course of my years as a newspaperman I had seen police precautions. I was very wrong. The place de la Concorde, the Quai d'Orsay, and all the streets leading in or out or around were packed with soldiers and police, shoulder to shoulder, and there were thousands of plain-clothes men to form a solid circle round the soldiers. The peace envoy's train had been shunted from the Gare de Lyon, where trains from Germany came in, to the Gare des Invalides, only a stone's throw from the Foreign Office where Daladier and Bonnet were waiting to sign once more on the dotted line.

Ribbentrop was kept at all times out of sight or reach of the Paris population. There was not a cheer or a hearty sound of any kind as his bullet-proof limousine rolled two hundred yards between the station and the grey stone building which had been decked with French and German flags, the tricolour and the swastika, so lovingly entwined.

I remembered a remark made years before by Henri Julliard. 'When they talk too much about peace, there's sure to be a war.'

34

'WOE TO THE WEAK'

The fall of Madrid was the signal for organized massacres throughout Spain that for sheer barbarity have not been surpassed in history. Alexander the Great had an entire city put to the sword, men, women and children, because the inhabitants had resisted his armies too bravely. That was an act of rage, on the impulse of the moment. Franco and his Phalanx went about their revenge coolly and methodically. The priests, their consciences salved by the promise that henceforward there should be no more secular schools in Spain and that Jesuit business monopolies should be restored, closed their eyes to the bloodshed, their ears to the cries of anguish, and their mouths to their co-religionists beyond the borders. In Barcelona, 80,000 Republicans were jailed, pending execution.

I have been told recently by refugees from Vienna who suffered under Hitler and, in escaping, had to pass through Spain that the impoverished Central Europeans shuddered at the sights of famine and ruin they saw as the train traversed the land of Franco. José, whose son's bicycle had felt the anti-republican disapproval of The Navet's concierge, was able to get news, and all of it was appalling. Not a line got into the newspapers through regular channels and no word has issued from Fascist Spain since. Within that wall of silence and censorship are horrors no mediæval dungeons ever witnessed.

Day after day, with her divine resignation, Madame Berthelot crossed the place Notre Dame to her job at the prefecture. At noon she ate her lunch *chez* Daniel, in a corner as far removed as possible from the noisy group of comrades, who could not relish their food without free-for-all arguments on the interpretation of Marxian paragraphs. Their brave comrades in Madrid were dying by hundreds and thousands, not being able to talk back to machine-guns. Milka warned her companions that their own hour was approaching and that they could expect no easier fate.

I joined Hortense the day that the abject *Paris Midi* came out with the headlines to the effect that Mussolini's speech of the evening before had taken a 'moderate tone.' With a mirthless smile, she handed the paper across to me and I read:

'If the democracies weep over the death of their dearest creature [the Spanish Republic] we have no reason to join them. Let's have no more talk about Latin cousinship. Relations between states are relations of force.

'The watchword is: More cannon, more ships, more planes, at any price, even if it should mean wiping out what is known as civil life.

'Woe to the weak.'

'I find that not moderate, but even a little strong,' she said. 'To wipe out civil life. — We are civil life, Monsieur, or rather, I am. You, as an American, see this carnival of unreason from a grandstand seat.'

'Not necessarily,' I said. 'We can't have civil life in America, all by ourselves.'

'I can form no idea of America,' she said. 'To us it is represented as a paradise with klaxons replacing harps and steel instead of streets of gold, with seraphim forbidden to teach evolution, and cherubs weighing seven pounds apiece, exactly, and fed on some cereal preparation that they relish in appropriate doses and eat in unison, as the violins bow together in an orchestra.'

Behind his counter, inhaling the fragrance of his peanut roaster, the smoke of which was blown his way by the breeze from the Seine, l'Oursin greeted passers-by and customers alike. In the summer season he had spread before him the delicacies of the coast of Normandy and Brittany, from the Pas de Calais, the Côte d'Or and Marseilles. He rose about three in the morning, sauntered over to the central markets, and selected his wares between pauses in the bistros. Prawns and langoustines; tiny pale shrimps and the black-tails as big as the diminishing crescent rolls; clams, periwinkle sand cockles when he could get them; razorfish, goose barnacles; baby sea snails to be picked out with a pin; huge *palourdes* and giant snails; the tender coquilles St. Jacques. L'Oursin took pride in his assortment, as old M. Corre had been proud of his dried beans and spices. Often l'Oursin lost money by having so many strange kinds of shellfish, but he made up for the financial loss in conversation. His life was a succession of conversations, and that was what meant most to him. At certain times they were acrimonious, but for the most part they were companionable and gay.

The period during which the husky chestnut man had championed the Popular Front, as against The Navet and the Cagoulards, had slipped away. Like a storm, the class hostility had gathered slowly in the rue de la Huchette, had burst into fury on the night the student had been stabbed and left dead on the pavement, and after spending itself had drifted away.

'*Commes les curés, il faut se taire quand on est dans le cirage,*' l'Oursin said to me, the day Mussolini had bombed the Albanians and taken over their small country as a gateway to Yugoslavia. The Duce had been so puffed up over his success in Abyssinia and his defiance and defeat of the French in Spain that he had brought out once again his dream of dominating his share of the Balkans.

A literal translation of l'Oursin's exact words would read like this: 'Like the priests, it's necessary to shut up when you're in the shoe-blacking', or 'When things are going against you, it's better to keep quiet as the priests do.'

In the summer of 1938, l'Oursin no longer roamed the street at night, bellowing threats to traitors and reactionaries. He had ceased worrying Alice by dragging André, the coalman, from bar to bar in search of opposition. The situation had taken such a turn that just then no one, not even the voluble Navet, was self-satisfied.

Concerning the dangers of popular government and social reform, the Right contingent had no further cause for worry. 'The haves' were firmly in control again. The Spanish refugees were not allowed to show themselves in Paris, but had been segregated into insanitary concentration camps, surrounded by barbed wire and African sentries who had been brutalized for just such purposes by Lyautey and the French High Command. What had been a brave anti-Fascist army had been starved and beaten into a resentful mob. Daladier was well along with his minor-league Kampf. He had repealed the forty-hour week, reduced the wages for overtime and removed the limit of hours. His backers were selling him the leavings of the arms and munitions not purchased by Hitler in Germany. His secret police were hounding the dissenters from Munich. The President of the Republic, the only man who could call an election and give the people a chance to vote Daladier out of office, was belching dutifully every time Daladier ate *choucroute garnie*. His finance Minister, Reynaud, had put over some of the neatest tax swindles ever suffered by a democratic population, decreasing the assessments of the upper brackets and penalizing the poor for working or trying to do business. Bonnet, his Minister of Foreign Affairs, was paving the way for French Fascism by coddling the dictators. His wife, the ravishing Odette who made up in looks and animation for her grotesque husband with his monstrous nose, was entertaining daily the female head of German espionage in Paris, one of the contacts of the notorious Otto Abetz, who organized the Franco-German youth movement and used it for fifth-column activities.

On July 29th, Daladier went the whole hog, and adjourned Parliament for two years, after having railroaded through the authority to govern France by decree, as Hitler governs Germany.

From the foregoing hints of what was happening in official France, against the rights of labour and Parliamentary government, it will readily be seen that the chestnut man was wise in holding his peace for the time. The Left, still technically by virtue of the will of the voters in control, had been reduced to impotence. Labour unions were split wide open. The representatives of the people had been sent home. My Liberal friends, crushed and disappointed, were accustomed to defeat. What awed the Right and frightened the rank and file of Fascist followers was the certainty of war. Their leaders had told them Hitler would behave, if appeased, that he did not want their land and goods but only 'living room'. Now, even the most stupid of the reactionaries had to face the fact that Hitler had hoodwinked Chamberlain and Daladier and that war was nearer each day.

On July 14th, I was again aboard the *Normandie*, bound for France. Just after I landed, Hyacinthe described the pageant the Government had staged to bolster up morale. With her gift for the exact phrase she said:

'The whole display was political, not military. Compared with the Russians or the Germans in a newsreel, our quick-stepping *chasseurs* and resplendent Spahis, with bands and trumpet corps that never can quite keep time, are *opéra bouffe*.'

In the early days of the summer it was Milka who was most hopeful, and because all our neighbours were so anxious to find something to cling to, all up and down the rue de la Huchette men and women who had looked askance at the Serbian 'Red' and had declared she should have been deported long ago, became respectful and asked her to explain. The hope of France, according to Milka, was the Russian army. After she had said this so convincingly and repeatedly that the idea seemed to belong to her alone, Daladier, in a speech, was quoted thus in all the papers:

'The participation of the U.S.S.R. in a mutual assistance pact is essentially desirable.'

It was generally accepted in our street after that that France was eager to sign up with Russia against Hitler. My friends were able to forget, for the moment, that Georges Bonnet was in their Foreign Office and that Chamberlain and his set still were doing business at the same old stand.

'Why Poland?' asked Maurice, the goldfish man. 'The old umbrella didn't care about the Chinese, the Africans, the Spaniards or the Czechs. Now he wants to guarantee Poland. Is that feasible? What can the British navy do so far away?'

'The Poles are the bitterest enemies of Russia, that's why,' said Milka. Ironically, about the time she had convinced all her neighbours that Russia would stand by, Milka herself had learned through her various channels of information that England would have none of it. In the first place, instead of sending an important or competent ambassador to Moscow, Chamberlain had dispatched a group of third-rate army and naval officers. Bonnet had followed suit, with a cynicism only he could achieve.

After having listened to the dangers that beset France and England which Stalin understood much better than Chamberlain or Daladier did, the Red leader pointed out that the Russian frontiers were vulnerable, too. His staff officers explained to the British and French mission what precautions were necessary, involving concessions by Finland, Esthonia, Latvia, etc. Would England and France undertake to guarantee the Baltic States against German infiltration or invasion, if Russia pledged herself to march against Hitler in case of further aggression in the West? That, for the Clivedens and Cagoulards, was a horse of another colour.

Long before the Stalin-Hitler pact was announced, Madame Mariette was sure the Franco-British negotiatons with Russia would come to nothing, and that view was accepted up and down our street. The newspapers of the extreme Left, *Ce Soir* and *L'Humanité*, kept up a daily bombardment against Bonnet and Daladier, insisting that a mutual assistance pact with Russia, with like obligations and guarantees on either side, be consummated.

'Whatever those people want is often right but never happens,' Mariette said sadly.

The plucky little woman, who had worked so hard and surmounted so many obstacles, knew that her hopes for a peaceful retirement on a little farm, where no one entered without knocking, were being shattered. Her husband, for whom she had fairly paid and who had learned to like her and respect her and never chiselled her money, had struck with the other railway workers in November, 1938, had lost his job, and instead of waiting to be forgiven by Daladier had got other work as an automobile mechanic in a garage. In case of a general mobilization, he had to report for duty on the third day. Mariette's steel-grey eyes were seldom warm and gay, but remained resentful and cold. The rich clients from across the place du Châtelet were received politely, and if they got drunk and left their money and papers behind, Mariette took care of them. But in her heart was burning a steady hatred for those who were profiting by France's downfall.

'If I had known that I would have to stay in this life for ever . . .' she said, the day that Chamberlain made his Albanian deal with Mussolini.

'I often wondered why you wanted to go to the country. It's so lonesome there,' said the naïve little Daisy.

'You'll go running to the country yourself, when the bombs begin to fall,' said Mireille.

Daisy opened her pale-blue eyes very wide.

'Tell me, Mireille,' asked the shapely little creature who did so well with the 'difficult' cases. 'Why isn't it better to have a big tall house over you, if those people are going to be *méchant* and drop things from the air?'

Daisy was a victim of the general débâcle, a little ornament of peace-time France, a candid girl who expected men to be amenable and honest in return. What she understood of the state of France and Europe, if it had been mascara, would not have sufficed for one of her long curved eyelashes, and still she was not ridiculous like Chamberlain. The bargain the sage of the umbrella had to swallow that day would have been too transparent for our little nymphomaniac friend of *Le Panier Fleuri*, who ranked low in the Binet scale and as high in the judgment book as Abou ben Adhem. Mussolini, swollen with arrogance like a pouter pigeon, told Chamberlain that if the British would contenance the theft of Albania, the Fascist troops, who under the non-intervention agreement were never in Spain, would be withdawn from that stricken country, not just then, but some time.

'That's nothing,' said Mireille, when the Albanian deal was under discussion. 'The French still have more *culot* [nerve or effrontery] than the big macaroni.' She handed over her local paper from Marseilles and pointed out an item. A very old woman had been arrested for selling beggar's licences for twenty francs apiece in the Cannebieère. The licences she had made herself on a hand printing press. When asked by detectives how she happened to be in that business, she said she had inherited it from her mother.

35
'A TIME TO SEW AND A TIME TO REAP'

On August 26th, the day three classes of French reservists were called into the army, the crisis that had been simmering at No. 19 rue de la Huchette, in the little draper's shop, came to a head. Tension had been mounting in the quarter, as war stalked nearer in the mists of the river and the shadows of the rue du Chat Qui Pêche. There was little hysteria, but an ominous quiet in which all events, large and small, restrained or violent, reverberated between the walls of the buildings like whisperings or shoutings in a well.

One heard screams of 'My son! My poor boy!' from Madame Luneville as the postman approached the door with a grey postcard in hand. That meant the summons to the colours, and Jacques, the young son, was still in the infantry. Point-blank the father had refused again and again to intercede with General de Castelnau. Increasingly bitter and frantic, the mother had threatened and raved. There was a crash of overturned furniture, followed by the voices of Jacques pleading with his mother to calm herself, the gruffer voices of Luneville the elder (45 years of age), and the postman who had laid the summons on the counter near the cashbox.

For a moment the quarrel subsided, and Madame Luneville, sobbing and praying, rushed upstairs. Luneville, sad-eyed, patient man, started picking up scattered goods and articles from the floor. Jacques helped him.

From above came the tearing sound of a window flung open, a whimper that rose to a scream. Across the street Maurice, the goldfish man, started pointing upward and supplicating ineffectively. As the Lunevilles, father and son, reached the pavement, Madame Luneville flung herself from the window and dropped like a plummet, but before anyone could shout or move again, her skirt caught on some kind of steel spike that had been embedded into the plaster wall between the floors. The material held and, upside down, shrieking in fear and agony, she was helplessly suspended.

The police, *Agents* Masson and Benoist, came running. There were calls for a ladder. Frémont appeared with a step-ladder which was too short by six feet. Luneville the elder rushed upstairs and tried to climb down where his wife was dangling, but could find no foothold. The two-voiced klaxon of the fire-department truck was heard in the boulevard, and the red waggon veered around the corner just as with a slow ripping sound the cloth of Madame Luneville's skirt gave way and she crashed to the pavement twenty feet below. She never moved. She was quite dead.

A summons to the army was a summons, and a death in the family was no excuse. When the body of Madame Luneville had been taken to the cot in the little back room, and the two priests, Fathers Panarioux and Desmonde, had followed, with faces grave and strained, Jacques picked up the fatal postcard. His jaw dropped, his face assumed an almost imbecile expression. Like a sleepwalker he turned to his father, who was sweating and trembling, and muttering something about whose fault it was that his wife was dead.

'*Mais, c'est pour toi, Papa,*' Jacques said.

That proved to be accurate. It was the father, not the son, who had been mobilized, in accordance with the policy of Daladier's Government to send middle-aged and experienced soldiers to the German frontier, so that they could rest quietly in the Maginot Line and would not be likely to fire off guns or high explosives that might provoke 'incidents' or otherwise annoy or anger Herr Hitler.

Intermittently that night the boulevard lights flashed on and off, as electricians who had not been mobilized tried to dim the street lamps. Methylene blue paint was daubed on the windows of the railway station and the corner cafés. The radio blared out recorded repetitions of Daladier's speech, stating that France, this time, would stand firm and honour her promises. Again, in bars and doorways, I heard bewildered men and women ask one another why it was so important to save the Poles when the Spaniards and Czechs had been abandoned. They knew they were in the war, which was to be declared almost any hour, but they would have liked to understand better the immediate necessity for action, after two decades of dilly-dallying.

About five in the morning, the residents of the eastern end of the street were aroused by a lusty thumping and indignant cackling like a Punch and Judy show. Madame Absalom, who slept fitfully at best, had opened one baleful eye just in time to catch a city worker in a white 'monkey suit,' or one-piece overalls and jumper, shovelling sand on her pavement from the back of a small truck. Mary the Greek, on the other narrow bed, sat up and blinked, exposing her dusky shoulders and one shapely breast, to the delight of the sand man and driver, who, in expressing their appreciation, caused Mary to giggle and L'Absalom to pound on the floor with her cane and lay about her as if the clutterers-up of the pavement were within striking distance.

'Don't get all nerved up, Grandmother,' said one of the men. 'We don't do this for fun. The sand must be taken in buckets to your roof, so if the Boches set the house on fire . . .'

What Madame Absalom suggested be lugged upstairs in buckets and dumped on the disturbers of the peace who should be at the front or else in jail can well be left unrecorded. The old woman's proposals, however, got a big laugh from *Agent* Benoist who sauntered into view, just as Mocha, the black dog from the Hôtel Normandie, made the first use of Madame Absalom's anti-incendiary sand pile. That threw the old woman into another tantrum. Mary by that time, had snuggled under the covers and gone to sleep again.

All up and down the side streets that morning, sand was distributed, and the early editions of the newspapers contained new decrees about wearing gas masks.

Most of the residents of the rue de la Huchette who were native-born Frenchmen or Frenchwomen had already obtained gas masks from the commissariat, and had been informed after the fact that they were to be taxed eighty francs apiece for the same. Father Panarioux who had spent the long night with Jacques Luneville at his dead mother's bedside, came out from the draper's shop at six, gas mask in a long cylindrical tin slung over his shoulder.

'Do you think they'll use gas, Father?' asked Mme. Lanier, as the weary priest trudged past.

'Probably not,' replied Father Panarioux. 'One seldom is prepared against the weapons actually employed either by the enemy or Satan, my daughter.'

'Just the same, eighty francs,' the laundress grumbled.

She closed her establishment, later in the day, and, dismissing the girls without waiting to finish the work already started, fled to the Seine-et-Oise in a taxi that had been commandeered by one of the army lieutenants who patronized her *clandestin*.

In the French Cabinet meeting, Reynaud found out that while he had been trying to arouse the sluggish Daladier sufficiently to effect mobilization, Georges Bonnet had 'secretly' telephoned Warsaw to make the Poles promise not to fight, even if Danzig was taken over by Hitler. The Poles, quite naturally, thought Bonnet was speaking with government authority.

Whether justly or not, all the Frenchmen, Right or Left in opinion, in the rue de la Huchette believed that the Soviet-Nazi pact was an all-clear signal from Stalin to Hitler to start war in Poland, and against France and England. Feeling was high against the Communists who, not having been informed of the amazing somersault on the part of their chief, suddenly began whooping it up for the Nazis and against what, even before it got officially started, was termed by the comrades 'an imperialist war'.

This gave Daladier the pretext he had long awaited. He had been determined to destroy the Communist Party in France, not because he cared whether Russian churches were open or closed, or were Greek Catholic or Roman Catholic. The Communists constituted the only opposition in the Chamber and the press to his dictatorship and his war against labour. So he sent the secret police to take over the two Communist papers, *Ce Soir* and *L'Humanité*, a few hours in advance of issuing a decree to make such action, shall we say, 'legal'. Milka, Pierre and (to a lesser degree) Pissy complained and got ready for martyrdom. The rest of the neighbours thought it served the Reds right. Even the gentle Hortense Berthelot was resigned to having the Communists silenced, since, as she expressed it, 'One could no longer be sure from day to day which side of the street they were parking on.'

In the prefecture, The Navet was busy with his superior, organizing what became known as 'passive defence.' This consisted of marking cellars suitable for air shelters, instructing concierges how to make them gasproof, issuing and enforcing rules about lights in shop or residence windows, and the appointment of deputies who were given to understand they had far-reaching authority to compel civilians to take the precautions prescribed. For the rue de la Huchette, The Navet nominated two deputies who were to patrol the quarter, and wear a band marked 'D.P.' on their sleeves. One was Panaché, the floor-walker, who had not been called into military service, the other was Gion, of the music shop.

The first victim was Madame Absalom, who threatened to throw her coffee mug at anyone who dared carry sand up her stairs toward the attic, and thereby furnish a W.C. for bugs and rats. At Panaché's request, she was fined eight francs for civil disobedience. In the confusion, however, the sand itself was left untouched, except by dogs, on the narrow pavement.

As the last week of 'peace' wore on, the tramp of soldiers' feet and the rumble of lorries, tanks and caissons was heard more frequently in the night. Troops were not much in evidence in the daytime, except in the neighbourhood garages which had been utilized as mobilization stations.

Since the Caveau had closed, Georges, the *garçon*, had worked smilingly in the kitchen *chez* Daniel. But as preparations multiplied and word got round that foreigners, anti-Fascist or Fascist without distinction, were to be sent to concentration camps, the amiable Serb decided it was time for him to get himself set for a long and comfortable war. Somewhere he got a French uniform and a set of papers, and on the night of August 29th, he put on khaki slyly, said goodbye to me and a few chosen friends and slipped out the back door, to escape the surveillance of M. Panaché. I was told in confidence by Daniel what Georges did that night. He had figured out that he would rather fight Italians than Germans, if he had to fight at all, and that he wanted to be attached to some unit that still used horses, so he would not be lonesome. Georges felt sure that eating and shelter would be better in the army than in the barbed-wire enclosures and prisons, and the freedom of circulation much more satisfactory. He sat in the avenue de la Motte-Piquet, near the place de l'École Militaire, about two hours, letting regiment after regiment pass by until he saw one that not only had horses but seemed to be headed south and not east. When the order to halt was given, at the corner, to let traffic pass in the busy *place*, Georges, looking to all intents and purposes like a regular French soldier, attached himself unofficially to the outfit of his choise by shuffling over and sitting on the back of a caisson. No one paid the slightest attention, and, moustaches waving up and down, Georges rode away. I have not been able to get further word of him, but I would place any bet within reason that my old friend and servitor is as well as can be expected to this very day.

36

OF AID AND COMFORT TO THE POLES

On the evening of September 2nd, the day before war was declared, a French friend of mine who ran a short-wave radio station which broadcast in French and English for the benefit of England and America telephoned me. We had always spoken English together, because, having lived so long in foreign lands, I preferred whenever possible to be mildly startled by foreign dialects of my own tongue than to run the risk of antagonizing foreigners by mis-using their language. A sharp voice of an operator interrupted:

'Speak French, if you please, or I shall cut you off.'

My friend told me that nearly all the men in his establishment had been mobilized and asked me if I would makeshift as a broadcaster until he could do better. Like Diogenes of old, I was ashamed to be idle in the midst of such feverish preparation for war; so I consented.

At 5 p.m., September 3rd, therefore, when the die was cast that spelled ruin and desolation for millions of my fellow-creatures all over the earth, I was cooped up in a small broadcasting room waiting my turn to read the most stuffy essay on Racine that it has ever been my misfortune to encounter. A lean French soprano of uncertain age and shop-worn features was mugging into the microphone and gesticulating as she sang: *'Parlez-moi d'amour.'*

As I followed her with my bit about Racine, I could imagine with what breathless interest the radio audience of New York and London was hanging on my words. I volunteered to write a daily description of Paris under stress of war, nothing censorable or informatory to the enemy, but local colour that would keep the customers awake. No one had time to answer yes or no. I heard a few brief bars of the Marseillaise only once that day, sung by a few departing French boys who were riding in a truck.

A few sharp reminders of that day persist. It was announced in the press that no gas masks were available for children under two years of age, *or* for foreigners. My own consulate could do nothing for me, so I got one from the Rumanian consulate, where fifty francs looked bigger than a gas attack to one of the young attachés. In one's third war, one begins to learn how to shift for oneself.

It was not that I expected Paris to be gassed, or believed, in case the Nazis did use gas, that the French gas masks would prove efficacious. The danger, or rather inconvenience, lay in another direction, namely, the new and overzealous 'passive defence' workers who might pick one up any moment if one did not have a gas mask in a can conspicuously slung over one's shoulder.

All up and down the narrow streets of the St. Michel quarter, and the wide streets of the Champ de Mars district where I had, and still have, I think, an apartment, concierges were working hard and arguing harder, trying to seal up their air-raid shelters and tape their windows, so that in case of explosions the danger from falling glass would be reduced. In the rue de la Huchette, the aged stamp collector, M. Dominique, contributed one of the humorous classics of the war. In the window of his little shop, before he closed it for ever, he placed a placard reading:

'Fermé à cause de la mobilisation annuelle.' It was announced that the markets which had made the night beautiful would henceforth be open only in the afternoon. Parisians were urged to leave the city. Street crossings were painted white so that pedestrians and stray drivers of vehicles could see them in the blackout.

After the stamp collector shut up shop, Luttenschlager, who had not sold an article of piety in a fortnight, followed suit. Closed shutters, like blinded eyes, appeared up and down the rue de la Huchette. Dorlan, the bookbinder, departed for the south of France. The Laniers had left in style several days before. In the Hôtel Normandie, the Jewish refugees stared out with frightened faces, trying to convince one another that Daladier and Bonnet would not treat them like enemies. Julien the barber was obliged to depart on the fourth day of mobilization, and Elaine did not relent. She promised him he would be horned like a mountain goat before his train had left the suburbs. Actually, he was not — not until several days later. The dry-goods shop, from which a small funeral cortège had passed, gave up and the stock was placed by Jacques in storage. The flower shop again was colourless and this time remained so. Young André, son of the coalman, drove away in a Renault truck, as did the husband of Mariette of *Le Panier Fleuri*. Dr. Clouet put on a uniform again and was assigned to a base hospital in Stenay. Dr. Roux, the dentist, moved his office to Nice, on the advice of Pierre Laval. The ageing Corres continued as usual in the Épicerie Danton. The publisher at No. 30 had never opened for business since Munich.

Having said good-bye to his son, who was a sergeant in the ordnance department, Henri Julliard in his lonely stucco home in Montmorency uncomplainingly died, and the yearly pumpkin he had trained to grow in the crotch of a pear tree rotted on the little platform. The tree died some months later.

I noticed that Bill Shirer, coming back to Paris with the German army for a little private Gethsemane and the public benefit in his own groping country, passed through the rue de la Huchette and stood a moment in front of No. 5, where he had been served and enlightened by Monsieur Henri in happier days. Jay Allen, having been released from the Nazi jail which was no prison to a man of Jay's guts and curiosity, spent some of the precious last minutes in Paris in the rue de la Huchette, and also paused at No. 5 and remembered, through dissolving shutters, what some of us had known there. Leland Stowe, that sterling American who reports men's spirit with gusto, no matter what luck they have, did not forget No. 5 or Monsieur Henri when he said good-bye to the town.

A circular was sent to me just the other day announcing an important new American newspaper in Chicago. On the list of talent was Wolfe Kaufmann, who taught the late Monsieur Henri to make potato cakes. Also I saw the name Rex Smith as editor. Likewise a chap named Pickering who ate the largest slice of a certain fish one night in our cellar of Robespierre, and helped Monsieur Henri lug in the roast goat that followed.

At the picture desk of the *New York Herald Tribune* sits a man named Ralph Franz, who found his splendid little wife at No. 5 rue de la Huchette. He is one of the old guard who has the same wife now, and they talk together about Monsieur Henri Julliard.

Waverly Root would not look blankly if one mentioned No. 5 rue de la Huchette, which never got into any tourist pamphlet, or guide book, or even *La Semaine à Paris*. Johnny White, of the new Chicago daily; half the boys on *Newsweek*; Kenneth Stewart of *PM*; Eugene Jolas; Robert N. Linscott, the late Sherwood Anderson who, I remember, was very wistful and envious because I could chat with the neighbours of the rue de la Huchette while he was helpless because of his lack of French. It was just the thing Sherwood loved to do and he felt the genuineness of the atmosphere and its relation to communities in America he had known. With their usual discernment, the people in the hotel sized up Anderson as a good fellow and significant man. Their judgment of foreigners whom I brought there was uncanny. Of the large number who were my guests or who came to call on me there at No. 5 the people of our book elected two as outstanding Americans without knowing a word they said or a thing they had done. The first was Sherwood and the second, our old friend Horace Liveright who, incidentally, took a passing shine to Elaine, the wife of Julien.

To continue with my list: Gertrude Stein and Alice B. Toklas, Virgil Geddes, Eva Gautier, Bravig Imbs, Edgar Calmer, and Robert M. Coates, who is now art editor of the *New Yorker*. Also, Jim Thurber, Dave Darrah, Hendrik Van Loon and E. E. Cummings, Jim Farrell, Helena Rubinstein; Whit Burnet and Martha Foley, editors of *Story* magazine; Bettina Bedwell, Dora Miller, Allen Updegraff, Louis Atlas, Jim Tully, Holger Cahill, who became national Director of Art; Archibald MacLeish, Librarian of Congress; Duke Ellington, Louis Armstrong, Josephine Baker, Paul Robeson, Morley Callaghan, Sonia Himmel, Catherine Huntingdon, Creighton Hill, Ernest Hemingway, Harold Stearns, and the late F. Scott Fitzgerald.

The painters got around too. Stuart Davis, Guy Pène du Bois, Buck Warchawsky, Joe Stella, Marsden Hartley, Ivan Opfer, Norman Jacobsen, Pop Hart, Mahonri Young, Howard Simon. And the musicians: Georges Antheil, Irving Schwerke, Edgar Varese, Carlos Salzado.

Paris under the blue light, with ghosts of regiments in dark streets and refugees in swarms in public places, and such patriots as Gion and Panaché (and thousands of others who were better men) roaming alleys to find fault with housekeepers and wayfarers alike, fascinated me and kept me from sleep. On the night of the first air alarm, I was near the rue de la Huchette and stepped into the shelter marked '92 persons' at No. 7. The first inhabitants to come, bewildered and shivering, into the cellar, were the aged Taitbouts, blinking like hoot owls and muttering to each other what probably was intelligible to someone. There were fourteen chairs, one of which was a stuffed easy-chair in bad repair.

'That is for the colonel,' Madame Tatibout said reproachfully, when M. Taitbout was about to sit on it. He muttered and shifted over. She remained standing, explaining to me that, when erect, one offered less of a target to a marksman in the sky. Father Panarioux entered with a punctilious '*Bonsoir, mesdames et messieurs.*'

Two pretty Catalan girls, both servants, appeared from somewhere, followed by one cop, Benoist, who could not stay, but promised to return later. The early days of the war meant grief and hardship to many of the French. What they brought to the young and good-looking, or the middle-aged and vigorous, members of the Paris police force and to abandoned cooks and chambermaids has survived a lot of slander through the centuries, but still goes on.

The din of sirens had died away before any new arrival was announced. Frémont, no longer having a family, a job, or a concierge's lodge of his own, had helped his neighbours rig up their cellars with an eye to comfort. He acted as a sort of doorman, as if no. 7 were a night-club, as indeed it was for a while. So when my old accordion teacher, instrument in hand, put in an appearance, Frémont welcomed him heartily, introduced him enthusiastically and then braved the dangers of the outdoors, evoking prayers from Madame Taitbout, in order to entice Pissy, who played the flute, from his own and proper dugout. Up and down the street boomed the voice of The Navet, who knew the 'raid' was being staged to test air defences and therefore was exceptionally brave.

There is always a big moment and we had it when the aged colonel, who was nearly ninety, was ushered in by his faithful Alsatian old maids. Colonel Montalban nodded politely to the priest, and then in a general way to the others, including the servant girls and me. He was neatly dressed in a World War I uniform, and could by no means take possession of the only easy-chair when there were women present. In fact, no one would take the largest chair that evening, and it remained unoccupied.

Moment No. 2 occurred when in came little Daisy of *Le Panier Fleuri*, eyes wide with wonder and apology. She had been off duty that evening, had visited a friend in another quarter and had been herded into No. 7 by Panaché, who would not permit her to join her co-workers in No. 17, a few steps farther up the street.

The Alsatian old maids glanced at the priest and at each other, not knowing whether a *fille publique* and an ex-colonel could sit in the same shelter. The colonel did not seem to mind. He was sleepy, but cocked his eye appreciatively at the frightened and embarrassed little Daisy and said, simply:

'Sit down, my daughter. It's cold outside.'

Elvira and Roberta not only smiled, but giggled. The accordion player struck up a tune, joined by Pissy. Somehow, a flute seems like a singularly inappropriate instrument for an air raid, since it has to be approached from the side with a grimace which makes a man look like an ant-eater. Then softly, from somewhere down in Elvira came a throaty Alsatian song, and instead of restraining her or discharging her without notice, the colonel roused himself and looked at her reproachfully.

'Why didn't you tell me you could sing?' he asked, crossly. (She had been in his service eighteen years.)

'Excuse me, Monsieur Colonel. We thought it would annoy you,' said Elvira and Roberta, practically in unison.

'On the contrary, I like music,' said the colonel.

From then on we had music, until five in the morning, when the air whistles and horns wailed in reverse and we all were released by Panaché.

As she departed for No. 17, little Daisy held out her hand politely and quite formally and said, with the utmost candour, to the colonel, who was just opening his eyes from an hour's nap: 'You are very kind, Monsieur. It is true that in time of war we should all approach closer to one another.'

Then she forgot herself, turned to the rest of us, and said, from force of habit: '*Au revoir, mes lapins.*' (Until the next time, my rabbits.)

Daladier, it seemed to me, fell far below the standard of eloquence set by little Daisy, just as Chamberlain had shown less understanding of Mussolini than did Mireille. Daladier's contribution to national defence and world humbug that day read as follows, as well as I can translate it:

'France commands today, and never have her orders been clearer or more imperious. Without hatred for people whoever they may be, with love for the victims. . . . France is conscious of her power.

'Every Frenchman is ready to do his duty, to give his life. . . . What would life be worth in an oppressed France?'

Across the rue des Deux Ponts from the Hôtel du Caveau, where the slums were, a street cleaner with no wife and five kids left his dependants in the local commissariat of police when he was forced to rejoin the army. This was made legal by decree. A loyal widow raised a terrific rumpus because no steps were taken to protect her husband's grave from air attack. The newspapers were so demoralized by Girardoux's literary censorship that in more than one instance they even got the date of the issue wrong, to the despair of future historians. Through all this, the members of the French Academy continued pottering with the official dictionary which fell so far behind the vocabulary of the ordinary taxi driver that it was useless except as a curiosity, and had been a joke for years. Duhamel, who had set himself up as an authority on America, made a touching address which said exactly nothing. That was possible with Academic French. According to the *Paris-Soir*, which smelled to heaven whether censored or uncensored and whether or not its editors are in France or America, German storm troops were taught to sing the 'International'.

Of course, the censorship pressed harder on the Left than on the Right, which was beginning to inhale the fragrance of clover.

In an air-raid shelter, an officious deputy of the passive defence arrested a man who had lost his gas mask to a neighbour during an air raid in a game of *beloîte*. The winner, as so often is the case, was not molested. There was no law to prevent one from having two gas masks, but a definite penalty attached to having none at all.

British troops, according to the censored papers, which not only had items deleted but other items supplied, were beginning to pour into France. One saw them rarely, but a few strayed into Paris and were described as follows by M. Girardoux's enthusiastic publicists:

'One sees again the English officers on the *grands boulevards*, a familiar sight in 1914, with their impeccable boots, bamboo swagger sticks under their arms. Officers of 1939 prefer the Rond-Point and Étoile to the Opéra and the Madeleine of the other war.'

The writer described three Britishers sitting on a *terrasse* in the Champs Elysées:

'. . . with their sportive allure, their red-brick complexions, their clear eyes and that aspect of the "gentleman" which all of them have . . . the three lieutenants smiled benignly on Paris over their three whisky-and-sodas, traditional like their elegance and *bon ton*.'

This is a fair sample of what my neighbours read, while wondering prayerfully what was happening in Poland and elsewhere. Madame Absalom, to whom newspapers had always been important, cut the air with her cane almost constantly and developed arm muscles in indirect proportion to the shrinkage of her neglected legs.

The municipal pawnship issued hurry calls to those who had pledges in Paris depositories, warning the clients that valuables would be transported to the country. Every experienced Frenchman knew that meant they would probably never be found again in any man's lifetime.

Pierre Vautier, in uniform, sought me out one day. Already Milka had been sent to a concentration camp, along with all the refugee Jews from the Hôtel Normandie, and Mary the Greek. Also the model, Nadia, who, because of de Malancourt's intervention, remained less than three days. Pierre was still secretive, but he wanted to make amends for having broken off our friendship after the Spanish adventure. I understood all too well. He had been hurt too badly by the colossal injustice of it all, as I had.

What Pierre had in mind I did not learn till later. Knowing as Aragon did, that all Reds would be used as decoys, Pierre offered his services in advance of being called and started sending affectionate notes to certain homosexual French officers who were rabidly anti-Left. These missives were so worded that any casual reader would have suspected they were in code. One by one, these pansy reactionaries began to disappear from their units, and, in many cases, nothing was heard of them until after the armistice, if at all. Pierre, knowing he was safe as long as the spy hunt continued, outdid himself in the use of his fertile imagination, which he had so long stifled with party dogma. I am sure his influence was salutary for his dying France.

37

'A TIME OF SNOW IN ALL ENDEAVOUR'

One clear autum morning in that most unreal phase of war where the enemy was busy in some distant land and all the news was bright and cheery from the office of M. Girardoux, and the sun, slanting from its autumn angle, gilded oblongs and slits so familiar in the rue de la Huchette, catching glints of goldfish in the windows, or chrysanthemum wallpaper, scarlet and white, of children too poor to be evacuated sitting in dark smocks on stone doorsteps, of rugs slung over railings to be beaten, of the signs of the shops, the customers and proprietors, vegetable carts (there still were green vegetables) and unreal realities patching indelible memories, I wondered, walking slowly up and down, staring at those housefronts, greeting and being greeted, being seen and not noticed, heard and not seen, existent and non-existent, in short, a ghost or pilgrim — I could not dislodge from my mind the question: 'How would these building fronts impress a man who had not been here before, a photographer, a traveller, a dweller in another quarter or country?'

Like a cold wind between me and the sun came the vision of another street, not a side street but the Grand Calle of Madrid, and how I had returned there breathless and shaking to see for myself what bombs and shells and inter-class hatred had done. From that street, except for broken windows and sandbags and not so many pedestrians and no song, the buildings looked about the same. Each one had been hit from above, or had been damaged in the upper stories, but from the street so little of the destruction was visible, so utterly nothing of the broken friendships, dispersed families, days gone by that ne'er return again, mistakes, achievements — life.

War, then, is a cancer, fatal before it shows, and sure of its victims before they feel the symptoms.

Two spots of colour, which is light, were the favourites of the sun in the rue de la Huchette: the window of Maurice, in *La Vie Silencieuse* where moved in deliberate constellations the exotic fishes, and the yarn shop of Madame Absalom. The former was of nature, the latter of man's artifice; hues from the mysterious, eternal, human answers in the form of dyes.

These two were among the last to be extinguished — one by chance, the other by design.

It was at the time that Russia was attacking Finland, a procedure that was played up in that Paris press as one of history's basest atrocities. This is not the time to try to discover what was behind it, what prompted the Finns, or the Soviet leaders, or what it meant to soldiers frozen stiff as ramrods before they could bleed to death at thirty below zero. In Paris it meant gravy for Daladier, who still had not been able to outlaw a political party among whose offences was a strong distaste for him. Of course, as Prime Minister and Minister of War and also Foreign Affairs, he did not make all the calls in little side streets. For that he called upon the Sûreté Générale. And the best and brightest and most discerning men of the famous Sûreté were sent after bigger game than we had in the rue de la Huchette.

Two Sûreté agents, in the big Red hunt of that period, came into our street by the western gate and made a perfunctory check-up in the Café St. Michel. They were told by Madame Trévise that the Communists had left her bar long before and were thick *chez* Daniel. In No. 32 the concierge who had punctured the Spanish child's bicycle, in the name of the true religion, assured the inspectors that if any Red had dared enter the doorway, the respectable Navet who worked in the prefecture would have reported the incident, and the venerable Judge Lenoir would have risen from his bed like Lazarus from the grave. The publisher's at No. 30 was closed. Next came *La Vie Silencieuse*.

In his goldfish shop, as usual, was Maurice. He had not sold a fish since Albania, or Austria, but, as I have mentioned earlier, his booklet chosen at random for the day, was entitled *The Communist Manifesto*, and the author was one Karl Marx. The book was bewildering to the candid-minded Maurice, since the text sounded fine, but he couldn't quite understand what it meant. With his usual politeness he greeted the callers, and gently rubbed his hands in anticipation of a sale. One of the detectives picked up the book, and in so doing disclosed his badge.

Now Maurice, although a man of simple tastes, was no fool. He had read a few papers, listened to Henri Julliard and Lucie Absalom and Father Panarioux in neighbourhood cafés, and was aware that official investigations led to trouble, in nine cases out of nine.

'Where did you get this?' asked Detective No. 1.

On the point of answering, Maurice suddenly recalled that the honest old woman who had sold him the book, without glancing at anything but the price, had been in business a long time and was having hard sledding.

'I don't remember,' said Maurice.

There followed an abusive dialogue, in which the abuse came from the detectives and was received with increasing calm by Maurice. These men were mistaken, he knew. He was not a Red. Finally, when asked how he could prove he was not a Red he nearly made a slip.

'Ask them. Ask the Communists themselves,' suggested he, then caught himself in time.

The detectives beamed. 'Ah, you know some Communists?'

'No, but surely you do. That's your *métier*.'

Three days later, after Maurice had been taken to prison and held incommunicado, *Agent* Masson went sadly to the shop, the door of which was still open. The fishes were dead and had begun to smell. The tenants of No. 32 were beginning to complain. The policeman took the tanks of dead fish and dying plants to the quai St. Michel and dumped the contents, then washed them out at a public spigot in front of L'Épicerie Danton, where bug-eyed old Corre, in smock, murmured and glanced across the street regretfully.

Father Panarioux and Father Desmonde, appealed to by a group of the neighbours, went patiently from office to office to give testimony for Maurice, but they never found anyone who had Maurice on his mind just when they called. Father Panarioux, almost as persistent as the Abbé Lugan, went firmly to The Navet and came out, very pleased, as The Navet, who seemed to be able to do anything in wartime, had promised to intercede for the goldfish man.

'*Penses-tu!*' (Imagine!) The Navet said to Jeanne, after the priest had departed. 'The *type* (meaning Maurice) 'spent all his time with those rowdies like the chestnut man. Of course, he'll land in jail. So will they, in time.'

And The Navet picked his teeth with a hairpin.

The same raid in our street struck a telling blow at Madame Absalom. The old woman had come to depend entirely on the loving care of Mary the Greek, who simply would not, in spite of a life of worry and privation, give up her beauty in Mediterranean style. The detectives found that Mary had no papers of more recent date than 1925 and took her in so that her status might be investigated.

No source of mine has diclosed to this day where she landed, after leaving the stadium outside of Paris for a camp in the south. I hope someone gives her Dubonnet, which is not good for her but makes her smile and sing, and that if anyone makes use of her shapely olive-tinted body he does it with gentleness and without contempt. Today her two boys in Detroit must be about 22 and 24 years old respectively, and if they read this book they may rest assured that, in so far as I know, their mother never did a fellow-creature any harm.

Milka had long been imprisoned in the Stadium; Pierre was in the service, as were Pissy and his son. The raid *chez* Daniel netted the investigators precisely nothing, but it frightened badly the good Madame Berthe, Monsieur Henri's sister-in-law. The restaurant remained open, and did as well as any, considering the new restrictions, the high prices and the lack of customers.

Being left alone, and still unwilling to get out of bed, Madame Absalom tried hiring a servant girl, but no girl would stay with her at night and sleep on a cot on the ground floor. So a close and mutually helpful relationship developed between the peppery old woman and the lonely Frémont, who had been taken back as postman soon after mobilization and now had some pay to spend but few companions with whom to spend it. From his wife in the country he heard nothing, although Yvonne wrote him faithfully once a week, urging him not to do two things he most enjoyed: namely, to drink and to play cards for money.

Frémont came to the yarn shop early every morning, built a fire, got Absalom's breakfast, fed it to her, brought her the papers and then went to work. At noon, a hearty meal was brought by Sara of the Hôtel Normandie. All evening Frémont would argue with the old woman, and to an outsider it might have appeared they were coming to blows. Actually, she never struck him with her cane and he never threw a bottle at her head. They fought about everything except the imbecility of French policitians and the prospects of winning the war. On these points they were as one: the French had no leader, civil or military; the Germans would surely take what they wanted, now that Poland had finished.

When the Stalin-Hitler peace proposals came forward, however, both Madame Absalom and Frémont were indignant and agreed that the war must go on.

One December evening, down came the snow, so rarely seen in Paris. It touched the rooftops of the rue de la Huchette, and from doorways and open windows, what few of the inhabitants were left looked upward in awe, caught large flakes in their hands, saw crystals melt on windows, woke the children, and in a cracked voice some woman sang: '*Noël, Noël.*' She was joined by the drunken voice of the chestnut man, who used the word '*merde*' all the way through, but did well with the tune. And then the fat horse-butcher Monge, and the lean Noël sang too, swaying drunkenly.

In the yarn shop, Frémont, singing off key, dragged the bed of Madame Absalom through the doorway and up to the front window, as she never in her life had seen the snow when it really lasted. And for a short time the footprints of l'Oursin, Monge, Noël and Frémont were discernible as they paced up and down, serenading her from the pavement. All the rest of the street was softly carpeted with white, with blue haze from the street lamps, until Mariettte, calling from the doorway of *Le Panier Fleuri*, invited the singers in for a glass of brandy — 'if you drunkards can hold another one,' she added, and dodged a snowball that went wide of its mark.

Even for the early mass at St. Séverin there was still some snow; so footprints of old men and women, and some small ones that still had not been evacuated, led the way to the working man's church. Father Panarioux said mass that morning and afterwards could not remember whether there were eleven or twelve to hear him, and after trying to imagine where some others were just then he started to pray, then changed his mind and asked the beadle not to sweep away the snow from the old church doorsteps.

Across the street, where the Bal St. Séverin used to be, old Germaine was wailing, having heard that day that Robert, the pimp, had died outside Forbach — shall we say for France? Anyway, he had worn the same kind of uniform as the worthier soldiers, had done what his officer told him and a little bit more, and had fallen facing the Siegfried Line, for which, the week before, the German High Command had ordered 100,000 rose bushes from Holland, to be planted in the spring.

Daladier's Christmas address had the following passage: 'It is our pride to conduct the war with method.'

The French losses, he said, were 1,136 on land, 256 on the sea and 42 in the air. In the other war, for the corresponding period, the losses were 450,000.

Whether the Prime Minister, so soon to resign so late, included our local pimp in his list, I cannot say, so perhaps the correct total should have been 1,137.

Way up on the fourth floor of No. 9, a child was born to the wife of the gas inspector who was one of the first French parents to benefit by the new law providing a bonus of 2,000 francs (£10) for the first child. For decades the French officials had known that France was slipping behind Italy and Germany in the birth rate, and at last something was being done about it.

Early in January, Madame Absalom had another visit from the officials. The only casualty was a bruise on the hand suffered by one of the government inspectors, but the visor of *Agent* Benoist's cap was cracked and the old woman's large coffee bowl was smashed. A short time before a decree had been issued requiring dealers in yarn to declare their stocks, since wool was badly needed for the soldiers in the Maginot Line.

Madame Absalom had heard about it from Frémont, who offered to take the inventory, but she would have none of it. When the inspectors came she simply grabbed up her cane and started swinging, sitting up in bed and calling them whatever came to her still active mind.

The matter was resolved by *Agent* Benoist, who had known L'Absalom many years. He winked at the inspectors, beckoned them into the Normandie bar and suggested that they make a fair guess as to how much wool the old lady had, since she was eccentric and very excitable. Not only did the inspectors comply in the case of Madame Absalom, but they stayed at the Normandie all day and guessed at the amount of wool in six other shops on their list, marking in the figures with Sara's calm help before staggering home.

Her newspaper brought to Madame Absalom the information that same evening that it had been decided to hold the Olympic Games the following August, notwithstanding the international situation.

38

A FEW ARE CHOSEN

The warm spring at last stirred the winter of inaction and discontent. Pétain was hobnobbing with Franco in Madrid and receiving such eulogistic press notices for home consumption that the big deal of the season escaped his eye. The little generalissimo arranged to purchase from England six million pounds' worth of war supplies, some of which could be obtained only in Egypt, for reshipment to Germany. The same device had worked well with American oil.

As ignominiously as he had risen to leadership, Daladier resigned as French Prime Minister, after receiving in the Chamber a vote of confidence 279 to 1. Three hundred of the deputies refused to vote at all. The dapper Reynaud, who spoke English after a fashion and had a neat way of turning phrases which, on analysis, proved to contain no meaning, took over the job. Reynaud's promise to the bewildered French was that he would 'pursue the war with energy.'

'Our only hope is that Germany might fail to attack. Is that possible?' asked Hortense Berthelot. There was little talk in those last days in the rue de la Huchette; so many of the talkers were away or dead or afraid to speak their minds. Daniel, the Serb, who had the only good restaurant left in the quarter, was not anxious to give credit to Noël, who was too proud to ask for it. In fact, since Daniel had got into trouble innocently enough with the Communist group headed by Milka, he had been increasingly careful not to encourage the old customers of the Caveau to patronize his modern place. Berthe, the sweet-faced sister-in-law of the late Henri, said nothing. She never crossed her husband.

Monge still sold a little horse-meat and the Satyr had found another job in a small hotel in Montparnasse when the luxury restaurant in the Bois had faded. These two could have eaten *chez* Daniel, but, knowing Noël could not afford it, they joined him at the Normandie, where now there was plenty of room.

As often as she dared, the patient Jewess, Sara, cooked special nourishing food and wrapped it warmly in clean napkins, and her husband Guy, who started so slowly and was coming up so fast, pushed a three-wheeled delivery cart out to the Stadium, where the refugees, their former clients, had huddled in coldest winter with thin shiny black clothes and one blanket apiece and for that reason were grateful for the warm spring sun. They had a way of sitting on benches, side by side, and not in groups but rows, as if they were in a synagogue waiting for services to begin. When they spoke, infrequently, two or three others nodded, and the rest starred silently ahead. They were dirty and had no water, bewildered and no one explained, and tired without sleep for nights and days until at last, once or twice in a fortnight, oblivion came and for hours they had the inestimable relief of non-obligation to exist at all. If the people in our street who were not Jewish were uncertain as to whether Hitler would attack, the refugees were not. They knew, and waited, coughing in the night and shivering in the sun and opening their eyes as slowly as they could, to prolong the sensation.

At No. 15, a situation had developed in the laundry that kept the neighbourhood in ferment for weeks. Edouard Lanier, the *gueule cassée*, had returned from the country and had left his wife behind. No one knew why. They had always been congenial and affectionate, and although Edouard had done no work of any kind since World War I, Madame Lanier had not complained. On the contrary, she had encouraged his idleness. There was a small room in the cellar of No. 15, at the back of the building, and in this Lanier lived all alone, washing infrequently, drinking red wine constantly and having no traffic with his neighbours. The front door of the establishment was locked and boarded, the cellar windows were covered with sandbags, the upper windows stained blue and criss-crossed with narrow strips of paper.

Clients of the legitimate laundry and the secret bordel pounded on the boards, but Lanier would not answer, or, if they persisted, he would shout for them to go away. He wept and roared sometimes about the other war, saying one was enough and that he shouldn't be called upon to fight another. No one had called him, but he objected just the same.

A few of the clients who had had laundry in the place when the Laniers had fled before Munich had retrieved their bundles on a day when Madame Lanier had put in an appearance. On that day Lanier had stayed in the cellar and refused to see her. She wept and pleaded and told the neighbours her husband was ill and that she didn't know what to do. But when all comers had been satisfied, there remained a lot of clothes, washed but not ironed, and so badly mixed up that Madame Lanier was not certain to whom they belonged.

Mireille, of *Le Panier Fleuri*, had been ill at the time, and Madame Durand, of the flower shop, did not venture back to Paris until later. When these women, so disparate in temperament, returned to the street, each one of them tried to get a word with Lanier, who would not listen to them. Mireille appealed to her friend, *Agent* Masson, who braved the disfigured veteran on one of his trips to André's wine shop. Lanier went into a rage and threatened to shoot, with his old service revolver, the first one who tried to enter his shop. He knew nothing about laundry. His wife had always taken care of that. Now she was gone.

Madame Durand tried to reason with Lanier herself and was called by him some names that more accurately might have been applied to Mireille.

When Mireille heard that Madame Durand had applied to the court and that Lanier had been served with a paper, she called on a lawyer friend and, on payment of fifty francs, preferred a similar charge. Lanier appeared in court and wept about World War I and the injustice of having two wars in one lifetime until the judge was quite impatient with the women who wanted a stricken patriot to bother about laundry. Nevertheless he sent a court officer with them to Lanier's place, and the *gueule cassée* was forced to unlock the main door.

Madame Durand, when she saw that her respectable laundry had been scrambled together with Mireille's sinful underclothes, refused to accept her linen unless Lanier would agree, in the presence of the officer, to have it laundered again at his expense. Mireille began to laugh, and as the infuriated florist turned on her, she picked up her dainties and hurried across the street to tell the other girls. The court officer could not terminate the affair until Madame Durand could be induced to go, since he had been instructed by the court to lock the premises and leave them as he found them.

Swaying and growling, eyes red with rage, Lanier lurched down to his cellar. In World War I he had used hand grenades, and having none handy, he lighted a small paraffin lamp and ascended the steep stairs. This he tossed between the laundry, the screaming Madame Durand and the officer, where it exploded, setting fire to the clothes and singeing off the eyebrows of his adversaries.

For the second time in twenty years, the fire brigade came to the rue de la Huchette and put out the small blaze. Seven days later, a squad of attendants lured Lanier from his cellar and took him in an ambulance to some kind of institution.

The story of Hitler's *Blitzkrieg* through Holland and Belgium, and the collapse of France, has not been told and never will, but the grand lines are familiar. When the break-through near Sedan occurred Étienne Corre had been stationed in a clump of trees with a machine-gun unit and didn't know, when the enemy approached, that his officers had started back for safety some hours before. He fired. The enemy fired. Some of the enemy died. He died. That was the end of the German, the English and the Italian he knew, and the hopes of being an important export broker.

Young Antoine Pissy, who had fought in Spain with officers and soldiers who would fight with rocks or their bare hands and die together, managed to avoid being caught by the Nazi troops, although they were all around him. He entered the Épicerie Danton, cap in hand, some days later, and told Monsieur Corre, and old Corre told Gabrielle, and they both told the young widow from Dijon.

There was the night when no one was left in the rue de la Huchette except Madame Absalom, Hortense Berthelot, Frémont, Monge, Mariette, Mireille and Daisy, Sara, Guy and Mocha, and Eugénie in the Café St. Michel. And detached from the others on the third floor of No. 32, Judge Lenoir, Madame Goujon and the screen star, Hyacinthe. In the afternoon, Elvira and Roberta borrowed the baby carriage from the gas inspector in No. 9 (the baby having died) and pushed away some of the valuables, including four decorations for valour in World War I, of Colonel Montalban. The colonel, dignified in uniform, in spite of his 88 years, walked down the street and away by the eastern gate in a military manner.

Hortense had been invited to take refuge with a relative of her dead husband near Orléans and had been on the point of doing so when she heard the cackle of Madame Absalom and decided to remain with her. Frémont sat with them, and, for once, was sober.

'How do you explain that, Mesdames?' he asked. 'I try to drink and can't.'

'Too late,' croaked L'Absalom, scowling at him shrewdly.

Sara, the Jewess, sat at her bar, all alone, while Guy was sweeping upstairs. No one passed on the pavement, until Monge came along.

'Hadn't you better go and get Noël?' Sara asked.

'No use. He won't come,' Monge said, and cursed under his breath. The lean taxidermist was sitting among his stuffed cats and dogs and tossing up and down in his hand a tin of cyanide of potassium. He wouldn't swallow the stuff, but he wouldn't put it down, either.

Sara looked at her worn hands and broken fingernails, and then at the dog-eared account book in which figures were scribbled on each page. Without rancour she picked up the ledger and tossed it with the dust rag on the shelf behind the bar.

Somehow The Navet got possession of a public bus, and into it he had loaded whatever he could carry, his unfaithful wife, Jeanne, his concierge, Gion and Bernice, Panaché, and the tailor, Saint-Aulaire. There was one other man, a stranger, who said he could drive, and having been tipped off that the Government was about to steal away to Tours, was as eager as The Navet was to travel that way. The bus, loaded beyond its normal capacity, got a start over the bulk of fleeing refugees, but progress was impeded because the frightened women asked the driver to stop now and then so that they could relieve themselves. After two such delays, The Navet, always in command, put an end to the practice.

'Mesdames! In the midst of a war one cannot stop every five minutes!' he said.

And back on the rue St. Séverin two dogs howled and howled, abandoned in an empty building.

39

BLACK RAIN

In future years will always be remembered the day of the black rain, when all those who could or would had fled, and the others were waiting. Some said it was because of oil from blown-up tanks and others believed it might be deadly gas sent by the Germans. A few thought and tens of thousands hoped it was the end of the world.

It was the end of the world in which Paris was supreme, in which France was alive, in which there was a breath of freedom. There was oil in the blackened air, and soot in the rain, and the wretched city was pressed upon by the lowering sky. Greasy buildings, empty. Dingy pavements, bare.

One of the first Nazi tank units to roar across the Île de la Cité must have been directed by someone who had misread a map, for the Panzers rumbled over the Pont St. Michel and instead of proceeding along the boulevard, so vast and utterly without motion, No. 1 tank turned into the rue de la Huchette and then, sharp right, to the rue Zacharie to get back to the Boul' Mich' again. The opening between Mariette's *Le Panier Fleuri* and the charred laundry of the Laniers was not wide enough for the turn, the old buildings being set at an angle, and the jocular driver at first was about to push off a corner of the bordel to make room.

Another German shouted something gay in German; so the tank spared Mariette's place, in which, wide-eyed, was cowering little Daisy with Mireille's arms around her. Instead, the Panzer crashed into the Lanier corner and broke down enough of it to pass along and out of sight, followed by four others which crunched over the unimportant ruins.

The news of the armistice terms found the chestnut man sitting on the parapet of the pont St. Michel. He had a few francs left and bought a paper as a man with a club foot lurched along with a few under his arm. The Café de la Gare had closed and the area in front, where l'Oursin had sold moist treasures of the sea, in shell pink and mauve and dark seaweed green, flat Portuguese oysters and others from the channel coast, was swept clean. Gone, too, was the sharp aroma of roasting chestnuts. The neighbouring news-stand in front of the Café St. Michel had blown down, and the first German troops quartered in the larger hotels along the quai, had gathered up the scattered papers. De Gaulle's appeal had spread, even in advance of its publication.

L'Oursin did not go drunkenly in search of his adversaries of the Right, since all of them were far away and about to be enthroned. (Practically the entire roster of the Cagoulards was in the new Vichy government.) Instead he walked, with his sailor's gait that swayed him from side to side, and found Frémont with Madame Absalom. At the corner of the rue de la Huchette, near the *place*, stood a pair of German sentries, one with phrase book in hand. Two more were in front of the Bureau de Police at the rue du Chat Qui

Pêche. The gruff old man and the lonely middle-aged man set out on foot in the general direction of the Norman coast, where l'Oursin said they could get jobs in a fishing boat. The Boche had already announced in *Paris-Soir*, which was taken over instantly by the invader, that producers of food, on land or off the coast, should get to work for all concerned as soon as possible.

'Why should you work for the Boche?' the old woman demanded. 'Can't you starve like the rest of us?'

L'Oursin winked and nodded to the grim old party who sat, ragged, in her untidy bed.

'To fish one must have petrol,' he said.

'What does that get you?' asked Absalom.

'One can sell the petrol for more than fish.'

'You want to get rich, you *salaud*? What kind of a son of *putain* comes here to my shop to torment respectable citizens of the . . .' Then she caught herself and frowned. 'The citizens of *merde!*' she added.

L'Oursin winked and slapped Frémont on the shoulder. 'With money one can get across to the English, and maybe now they'll fight,' he said.

All the spite left Absalom's wrinkled face. Chuckling and coughing she smiled.

'They're a thick-headed lot, but go ahead, *Mon vieux!*' she said.

And when Frémont hesitated at the door she growled:

'Don't you hang around. You're no good here. You're both a pair of boozefighters beyond help. Go on, little rabbits! Get your faces busted with the bloody English! Ha! Ho!' The rest was lost in coughing and gurgling which they heard a short way down the street.

Monsieur de Malancourt, a week before, had taken Nadia, who had spent three days in the dread Stadium, to his swell hotel on the Right Bank and before a priest, and then the only *mairie* he could find, he had married her once in church, kissed her hand, walked debonairly with her to the back door of the *mairie*, married her again in civil style, and kissed her on the cheek. He had gathered together as much money as he could, which filled a large part of his baggage, bought at a fabulous price the broken-down last year's auto from the Hôtel Ritz, and, stopping almost momentarily to give francs to those who needed them along the crowded highways where trooped the refugees, had proceeded on his one and only honeymoon. This took him through Vichy, where he had friends in high places he was willing to use just once more. There he signed over enough assets to Nadia to keep her almost anywhere any length of time.

At the Swiss border, as soon as her passport (a new one and as legally French as any document could be) was stamped and she was safely through the gate, de Malancourt held out his hand gallantly.

'I couldn't explain for fear of worrying you, my dear. I must remain behind — just a day or two. In Geneva, stop at the Grand Hotel,' he said.

Nadia made a touching Polish scene and meant it, but once across the border she couldn't get back without formalities. When her tears and sobs subsided a little, he held out his hands a little distance toward her and said:

'I've never commanded you!'
'No, *chéri*,' she said.
'This time I command. Please go!'

The weeping Nadia, as lovely at thirty-six as she had been at twenty-one, when de Malancourt had found her, was led, almost fainting, into the station. De Malancourt nodded to the chauffeur, tipped the attendants generously, and turned his head toward France, and his celebrated rear towards Vichy. The last heard of him, he was in Lyons, with no more francs to give away.

Soon the police were back on duty in the rue de la Huchette, but not for patrolling the neighbourhood in pairs, as in luckier days. Instead they tried to teach pedestrians and pushers of handcarts and children's carriages not to interrupt a German column when troops were marching down the boulevard.

The German command designated the Brasserie Dalmatienne as the suitable café for German officers in the quarter, and at meal times these busy directors of the occupation, for which the French paid more than they had for their own defence, convened *chez* Daniel. It was not the fault of the handsome Serb, now too old for the ring. Just what could he do?

The Navet and the tailor, Saint-Aulaire, were sworn in by a new agency from Vichy to carry on in Paris under the direction of Pierre Laval, and to his concierge The Navet said, when he returned to No. 32: 'You see now what those cowardly English have brought to us. At the most, they sent ten divisions, and all of them ran!'

The Nazi-controlled press contained editorials of that nature every day.

The Navet, outside his apartment, shows a rather self-satisfied air, and talks about the sufferings ahead and that France must work and pay for Bolshevik waste and English perfidy. In his bedroom, he still tries, with threats and cajoling, to make Jeanne name the man who dishonoured him, always referring to him in the singular. Madame Spook heard that Jeanne is denying herself what little sugar comes her way, in order to save it up until the quantity is impressive enough to denounce her husband to the Boche for hoarding. I shudder whenever I think of the individualist, Saint-Aulaire, in charge of a department of quantity production of convict and working clothes to be made from substitutes for cloth.

Of the able-bodied who were sent by the Germans to work in Germany — including André the coalman, Monge and Louis, the one-armed *garçon* — Guy, of the Hôtel Normandie, fares the hardest, not counting the dead l'Hibou. For when Sara was sent, for Jewishness and trying to feed other Jews in secret, to take a place on the bench beside her former clients in the Stadium, who had lost 'nearly half their pounds,' Guy ran amok and was clubbed into insensibility, while Mocha, protesting, was shot and his sleek black body tossed into the Seine. It must not be inferred that the visiting Germans, with wanton brutality, set upon this man and destroyed his ageing dog. Guy attacked them, in defiance of regulations, and was the partial cause of Maurice and some other hostages being threatened with death if their compatriots did not behave.

When informed that *Le Panier Fleuri* was to be taken over for the use of German non-coms., Mariette had what is known as a *crise de nerfs*, or nervous breakdown, and Mireille broke some regulations on her own account. She set fire to the joint, after warning Mado, Armandine and little Daisy, and, when arrested, was dragged away singing the Marseillaise. The fire engine came for the third time to the rue de la Huchette and put out the fire in time, and the first evening the non-coms. drank too much champagne and were warned by the officer of the day that any further disorder would be punished severely.

Of Hortense Berthelot there is little to say. The office in the prefecture in which she worked for years was discontinued; so she was sent upstairs to another one and still received patiently such citizens as were sent to her desk. She is yellow and thin, having eaten little else but chick peas and turnips in the course of last winter. Morning and evening she feeds what she can get to Madame Absalom, now seventy-eight years old and of very sound mind.

The Nazis made a fair haul in the rue de la Huchette, taking over the canned goods of l'Épicerie Danton, for which they paid in printing-press marks; the soap and cosmetics in Julien's barber shop; the wine from Alice, wife of André; the cotton goods of the Lunevilles; whatever was of metal in the paint shop; and the entire stock of dogs, cats and stuffing materials owned by the gaunt Noël. These were wanted for some weird *ersatz*. In each instance an inventory was made by a German, an estimate of value was made by another German, and a slip of paper was given to the owner or owners, which entitled them to call at an office where they could exchange it for a given number of marks, computed at twenty francs to the mark.

Noël, with the money he received, has been able to eat frugally about four months. He has volunteered to labour, no matter for whom, to take his mind from other things, but his gauntness makes him look unhealthier than he is, so no one will accept him.

When two German soldiers, both non-coms., came to the shop of Madame Absalom to take away her coloured yarns, she reached for her cane. One of the Germans, a blond young man from Hanover, having a grouchy grandmother of his own, was reluctant to carry out his orders. He prevailed on the other, a country boy from Westphalia, to ask Madame Absalom, in phrase-book French, if, in case they were lax in Nazi duties, she would hide the stuff away so they would not be shot at sunrise.

That brought about a change of mood in the indignant old woman.

'Oh, take the blasted stuff, *mes lapins*,' she said. 'We're all in the soup together, and you're younger. You'll suffer more than I do. Ha! He! Ho!'

Les Dernières Nouvelles, four months after the Nazis came, was about to go to press when the censor caught the following item which, since he held it to be discouraging and suggestive of discontent among the French, did not appear:

'Mlle. ——— ——— [the screen name of Hyacinthe Goujon] was found dead in her bedroom, and in adjoining chambers of her apartment, 32 rue de la Huchette, her mother, Anne Goujon, and her grandfather, formerly a judge, were also asphyxiated by the fumes of a charcoal brazier. The windows were tightly closed and the doors were sealed with old theatre programmes. The loss of Mlle. ―― ―― is a severe blow to the French cinema which has been showing an impressive recovery under government encouragement.'

It was two months later that a brief letter was delivered to me.

'My friend. I am afraid. I cannot convey to you the fear that is freezing like paralysis. You know how I wanted to live . . . I shall wait for a glimpse of the bats.

'I cannot be accused of self-destruction. It is not Hyacinthe who dies, but the life around her. . . .'